The Red Sox Be

The Red Sox Before the Babe

Boston's Early Days in the American League, 1901–1914

DONALD HUBBARD

Foreword by Peter Nash

McFarland & Company, Inc., Publishers
Jefferson, North Carolina, and London

LIBRARY OF CONGRESS CATALOGUING-IN-PUBLICATION DATA

Hubbard, Donald
    The Red Sox before the Babe : Boston's early days in the
American League, 1901–1914 / Donald Hubbard ; foreword by
Peter Nash.
        p.   cm.
    Includes bibliographical references and index.

    ISBN 978-0-7864-3911-9
    softcover : 50# alkaline paper ∞

    1. Boston Red Sox (Baseball team)—History—20th century.
I. Title.
GV875.B62.H83   2009
796.357'640974461—dc22   2009020612

British Library cataloguing data are available

On the cover: Long before the Cy Young Award, there was Cy
Young and his giant loving cup, presented to him on his own day,
August 13, 1908 (Boston Public Library, Print Department,
McGreevey Collection)

Manufactured in the United States of America

McFarland & Company, Inc., Publishers
    Box 611, Jefferson, North Carolina 28640
        www.mcfarlandpub.com

To Chick Stahl and
Donald Owen Hubbard,
Requiescat in pace

Acknowledgments

I would like to extend special thanks to the staffs of the National Baseball Hall of Fame, Harvard University and the Boston Public Library. Todd Haines and Jon Bomberger helped a lot in Chick Stahl's old town of Fort Wayne, Indiana. Peter Nash was very gracious in answering my questions about the Royal Rooters and tracking down artwork for me. Peter Golenbock is as terrific a person as he is a writer, and I thank him for patiently answering all of my questions and serving as a sounding board regarding the mysterious death of Chick Stahl. Richard A. Johnson continues to be a constant source of assistance and inspiration.

The *ESPN Baseball Encyclopedia, 4th Edition*, served as my statistical resource throughout.

Final and most heartfelt thanks and love go out to my Heavenly Triplets—Lori, Billy and Caroline.

Table of Contents

Foreword
by Peter Nash

Mortui vivos docent. Translated from Latin, this phrase means "the dead teach the living," and in Donald Hubbard's book about the first fourteen years of the Boston Red Sox, there are scores of characters and people of character associated with the franchise whose ghosts have been unleashed by Hubbard to teach a modern day army of animated Red Sox fans.

With his keen insight and thorough research he breathes new life into these long-forgotten characters from Boston's baseball past. Characters like Roxbury saloon-keeper and "king of the rooters" "Nuf Ced" McGreevy; suicidal player-manager Chick Stahl; Cy Young, the actual pitcher who won 511 games, not just the award named after him; and Bill Dinneen, one of the franchise's first world champion pitchers and the only player who still appears at Fenway today as the Dropkick Murphys' remake of the Sox fight song "Tessie" blares from the Fenway Park speakers.

These characters inhabited places like the Huntington Avenue Grounds, Fenway Park, McGreevy's Third Base Saloon, and even Boston's "Cradle of Liberty," Faneuil Hall. In their first fourteen years, the Boston Americans had five separate owners and ownership groups, but the one thing that remained constant was the dedication and loyalty of the Boston fans who had so easily abandoned their beloved National League "Beaneaters" for the new American League club that offered cheaper seats for the bleacherites. It was here that the American Leaguers took the lead (and some of the best players) from the champion Beaneaters, establishing their own identity as champions with the nickname "Red Sox"—given to them by their playboy-owner John I. Taylor in 1907.

At the turn of the century Boston was baseball's Mecca and Hubbard chronicles the lives and times of the heroes who puffed cigars and swigged whiskey in McGreevy's Third Base Saloon while rubbing elbows with the bookmakers and ward bosses who made up Mayor Honey Fitz's "Biggah, Bettah, Bah-ston." It is fitting that this revival of past glory comes at a time when the Red Sox franchise is basking in the glow of a new era of world championships. Hubbard, a fan himself, who snuck a transistor radio into CCD class to follow the Sox in the 1967 World Series, reflects the true continuum of devotion to the club by owners, players and rooters alike. He is one of the few people who have ventured to seek and find the site where Nuf Ced McGreevy held court in his first saloon and with this same passion he has presented a true people's history of the team.

This past year, along with my partner Ken Casey of the Dropkick Murphys, I recently resurrected McGreevy's Third Base Saloon on Boylston Street in the Back Bay. Through the support of the legion of Red Sox fans, the dead are once more revived and it is quite evident that the traditions begun in Roxbury at the turn of the century are alive and well in present day "Red Sox Nation." The dead do teach the living, but writers like Donald Hubbard can bring the dead to life as well. I hope you enjoy reading about this seminal period in this great nation's and this great sport's history. Nuf Ced.

Peter Nash • Cooperstown, New York

Peter Nash is the author of *Boston's Royal Rooters* and *Baseball Legends of Brooklyn's Green-Wood Cemetery*. He co-owns McGreevy's 3rd Base Saloon in Boston and founded the Baseball Fan Hall of Fame in Cooperstown, New York.

Preface

Having had fun writing the dual biographies of Hugh Duffy and Tommy McCarthy, the Heavenly Twins who starred on the great Beaneaters teams of the 1890s, I naturally did not want the party to end, so I plunged into the next chapter of this story, the founding of the other team in town, the American League's Boston Red Sox. Out of spite and perhaps the promise of financial reward—but primarily spite—the Heavenly Twins decided to help build the new franchise, making it the most popular team in the Hub.

Despite the popularity of the Red Sox today, few people know much about the origins of the team, other than that the original hard-core fans were called the Royal Rooters and owner Harry Frazee sold Babe Ruth to the Yankees, thereby shifting the balance of baseball supremacy from Boston to New York, at least until 2004. After the Babe leaves Beantown, the story seems to trail off until 1939, when a rookie named Ted Williams wakes up the echoes in Boston's Back Bay Fens.

The story of the Red Sox did not begin with Babe Ruth, of course. It began with Hall of Famers Jimmy Collins and Tris Speaker patrolling the field. And with Smoky Joe Wood, who won 34 games in a season, including a string of 16 straight. And Cy Young and Jesse Tannehill, both of whom pitched no-hitters. There were the Royal Rooters, too, those famous supporters having been won over from the crosstown Braves. Most important, perhaps, there were the great victories—including three pennants and the franchise's first two World Series championships. This formative period provided some of its most exciting and successful years. Then, and only then, came Babe Ruth.

Finally, a note on names. As this book was prepared for publication, questions arose, as they often do, regarding the spelling of Roxbury Royal Rooter and bartender Michael T. "Nuf Ced" McGreevy. Or is it McGreevey?

At least one census record has the surname down as McGreevey, and that spelling is the one used by the Boston Public Library for its "McGreevey Collection," made up of scrapbooks, photos, and other items donated by the tavern owner. The sign over the front of Nuf Ced's first saloon also had the *e* between the *v* and the *y*.

Nuf Ced himself spelled the name McGreevy, as does the author of my foreword, Peter Nash, a co-owner of McGreevys in downtown Boston.

For this book I used the spelling "McGreevy." Nuf Ced.

Prologue

Why was Cornelius McGillicuddy in Boston?

Arthur Soden, an owner of the Boston National League baseball team, pondered this question as he sat behind his desk at his Milk Street offices in downtown Boston one day in 1900.

McGillicuddy had several years earlier shortened his name to Connie Mack. He had shrewdly saved his money earned as a mediocre catcher for the Washington Nationals, and it looked now as if he intended to invest his stash. News had spread that he traveled back to Massachusetts to visit his family in the small village of East Brookfield, but no one believed it. East Brookfield sits about 60 miles west of Boston, and while no one saw Mack in his hometown very often, sightings of him in the state's capital kept popping up in the papers or along phone lines.

Rumors abounded that Mack had recently consorted with local baseball legends Tommy McCarthy and Hughey Duffy. Duffy was in the process of leaving the Boston National League club under acrimonious circumstances. McCarthy had received his walking papers from the team five years earlier and landed in Brooklyn of all places.

Soden had cause for concern. He and his partners, James Billings and William Conant, and their club, nicknamed the Beaneaters, had dominated major league baseball from the late 1880s until the turn of the century. Unfortunately, the triumvirate of owners had achieved greatness and wealth at the expense of their players, whom they compensated with miserly wages. Indeed, Soden had invented the Reserve Clause that for nearly eight decades thereafter bound a ballplayer to a club until the team decided to trade or release him.

Surreptitiously, Duffy had scheduled dinners with Mack to effectuate the formation of a rival local franchise in an anticipated new American League. The diminutive Duffy's feet tapped away on the old brick streets while trying to keep pace with the long, loping strides of the long-limbed Mack as they bustled from one beanery to another. Ambitiously, Duffy and McCarthy had scouted out land for the construction of a competing ball field. With competition came the threat to the Boston National League club that its penurious policies might cause an exodus of its talent from the established team to the new one.

Arthur Soden feared any challenges to his monopoly because it created uncertainty. He suspected that Mack did not mean well, but he did not know enough to stop him from formulating and advancing his plans, whatever they might entail. He knew he could not contact Duffy and McCarthy and ask them to let him in on the secret, or better yet, prevent any harm from befalling the Beaneaters; after all, they owed him no loyalty.

A recent attempt to form a revived American Association to rival the National League, spearheaded by Cap Anson, had foundered. Tommy McCarthy, who had rented land for a new Boston entry, had lost his shirt financially.

But this new American League was different and its founders had learned from the mistakes of others less fortunate. Unlike the still-born American Association, the American League representatives met in secret, meticulously crafting their enterprise, and had already begun to nibble away at their established competitors.

The new American League Bostons, of course, took hold and became one of the most revered major sports teams in the world, the Red Sox. And their owners kept nibbling away at the Beaneaters, later known as the Braves, stealing their finest ballplayers and their most rabid fans. Arthur Soden and his partners eventually despondently sold their interest, and although the Braves lingered for another fifty years, they never regained the devotion from the majority of the Hub fans.

In 1900, though, Arthur Soden knew nothing of the future but suspected the worst. His suspicions were not unfounded.

1

The Roxbury Rooters

At first Michael McGreevy just wanted his own joint. At the corner of Cabot and Linden Park streets in Boston's tough Roxbury District, he found the perfect spot to open his new saloon and thus become his own boss, escaping the drudgery of working as a clerk and taking orders from someone else. Today, there is nothing left to suggest that this plot of land at the edge of John O'Bryant High School once housed the cradle of Red Sox Nation.

A natural born entertainer, McGreevy did not cotton to sharing the spotlight with anyone else, and for a number of years in the mid–1890s he basked in his own glow. But with the rise of such talented fellow Irish Catholic stars as Hugh Duffy, Tommy McCarthy and Jimmy Collins of the local National League Boston Beaneaters team, McGreevy shrewdly calculated that his future prospects lie in befriending and embracing the legacy of these superstars.

McGreevy opened his pub in Roxbury on the widow O'Flynn's property. Running a saloon at that time in Roxbury was a daunting proposition. Alcohol fueled underlying resentments and latent mental illness, making the area unsafe for patrons and owners alike. But McGreevy's joint was different. It catered to athletes and their followers and housed gentlemen, most of them the sons of Irish immigrants who aspired to the better things in life.

Roxbury is still one of the roughest neighborhoods in Boston. It did not start out that way, but as one of the first six villages founded by the Massachusetts Bay Colony in 1630, a scant 10 years after the Pilgrims landed at Plymouth Rock. Apostle John Eliot scurried about trying to convert Indians, and in the midst of his other projects founded the Roxbury Latin School in 1645, the nation's oldest high school in continuous operation.

Primarily rural during its first two centuries of European settlement, Roxbury became a "streetcar suburb" of Boston, and was formally incorporated into the capital city in 1868. Thereafter it became increasingly industrialized and congested, particularly with poor German and Irish immigrants.

In *The Last Puritan*, a best-selling novel in 1937 (but probably set decades earlier) by George Santayana, two of the characters muse about the passing of a relative in Roxbury:

> "Going out?" his brother Peter inquired, noticing these unusual signs of restlessness and indecision.

I was thinking of it. It's a beautiful afternoon, and cousin Sarah Quincy's funeral is at three o'clock.

But it's in Roxbury.

I know: a considerable distance and an unsavoury neighbourhood. Cousin Sarah Quincy was in reduced circumstances. We can hardly blame her for dying in Roxbury if she was compelled to live there.

If Roxbury as a community did not get respect from the swells and ladies of Beacon Hill or the leafy suburbs, its mostly law-abiding citizens tried to carve out a piece of the American dream, and in doing so largely charted their way out of the district. While many of the Royal Rooters hailed from Roxbury, a considerable number had either left there or had never lived there at all. Once in town to see their favorite team, the fans had a short walk to McGreevy's, where everybody knew each other's name.

In the 1890s and early twentieth century, Roxbury was primarily Irish Catholic, as was almost all of Boston. Slowly, much of the neighborhood opened up to the great Eastern European Jewish migration; by the late 1950s and early 1960s, the area became almost overnight an African American enclave.

In McGreevy's time, Roxbury was at its most lawless period, resembling an outpost of the Wild West more than a district of the Athens of America, as proper Bostonians liked their City on a Hill to be known. And running a saloon proved an even dicier proposition, even for a savvy Roxbury kid like Mike McGreevy.

Several stark incidents of violence peppered this era of Roxbury barkeeping. For example, Alfred McCarthy walked into J.J. McNamara's on Shawmut Avenue and shot his friend David O'Neil behind the ear, before turning the gun on himself. No apparent motive preceded the murder-suicide, and baffled relatives could only theorize that a case of sunstroke confused McCarthy enough to kill his friend and neighbor.

Boxing legend "Young Kid" Carter (aka Patrick McKenna and James Jennings) walked into Garrity and Prendergast's establishment on Washington Street and approached a stranger named William McPherson. Preceding the Jimmy Cagney years of gangster films by several decades, Carter strolled up to McPherson and said, "I am going to get you, you dirty rat," and proceeded to fire three shots into McPherson for no reason.

It took almost no questioning by police for Carter to voluntarily squeal on himself. Apparently, the erstwhile pugilist had strangled to death a young woman named Mildred Donovan in nearby Lynn, the City of Sin, and had also killed two other people—one in the Midwest and one in Everett, Massachusetts. Carter was not executed for his crimes, but was adjudged insane and kept in a separate prison population, presumably for the remainder of his days.

Another time, Charles White patronized Daniel Crowley's joint, and after getting into a heated argument with the proprietor, was asked to leave. When White did not move fast enough, Crowley literally threw him out the door, left

The interior of Nuf Ced McGreevy's Third Base Saloon, so named because it was the last stop for the fans before going home. The bar has been revived today in Boston's Back Bay by Peter Nash and associates. Boston Public Library, Print Department, McGreevy Collection.

for dead. White contracted spinal meningitis due to the ordeal. The local police held Crowley and waited to see what happened to White to determine if they would charge Crowley for murder or for simple assault and battery.

Despite all of the violence, or perhaps because of it, purveyors of alcohol and breweries flourished in Roxbury. Five hundred guests attended the 1908 annual ball of the Roxbury Liquor Dealer's Protective Association, including Michael McGreevy, one of the evening's organizers. The ball took place at the Intercolonial Hall on Dudley Street, the center of Irish immigrant culture in Boston through the 1950s. Clearly, realistic dreams of money-making beckoned in the potent potables trade in the area, and as one of the most intelligent and outgoing tavern-keepers, McGreevy flourished.

Perceptive Mike McGreevy also knew that his business depended in large part on baseball. He eventually moved his saloon from the widow O'Flynn's building at the corner of Cabot and Linden Park streets to 940 Columbus Avenue, nearer the South End Grounds, home of the champion Boston Beaneaters. At the same time, he erected arguably America's first sports bar

(Hugh Duffy and Tommy McCarthy in Boston and John McGraw and Wilbert Robinson in Baltimore probably beat him to it) and adopted the persona of "Nuf Ced" McGreevy to complete the atmosphere.

Dubbed Nuf Ced due to his habit of ending arguments in his establishment by pounding his fist on the bar and shouting, "Enough said," he carefully culti-vated friendships with Hugh Duffy and Tommy McCarthy and his old friends from St. Francis De Sales parish in Roxbury, folks like him who aspired to more than a nasty, brutish and short life, who wanted their children to be known as "lace curtain Irish" rather than shantytown Irish. To accomplish this, McGreevy set himself up to become Boston's premier sports fan, a task he attacked with considerable vim and vigor, appreciating the already long and distinguished fan-dom in the city. But first he had to transcend Hi Hi Dixwell.

The first sketch of Americans playing baseball fittingly enough depicts some youngsters ranging along a diamond in the Boston Common under the golden dome of the State House on Beacon Hill in 1834. Although this charm-ing wood cut does not depict it, some interested bystanders most likely took in the game and thus constituted the first fans in the long and glorious history of Boston baseball.

While we do not know the identities of the first fans, or "cranks" as they were known in the nineteenth century, we do know the identity of the first unabashed fanatic, none other than General Arthur Dixwell. As described by baseball historian Fred Lieb, "[t]here was a rather noisy but kindly Boston fan of the period named Arthur Dixwell. He was a bit balmy, but everyone liked him, and baseball was his outlet. He would cup his hands and yell, 'Hi Hi,' to start rallies, and won the nickname of 'Hi Hi' Dixwell."

Dixwell, a trust fund baby, attended Boston Beaneaters games well into the 1890s, meticulously keeping score and lavishing gifts on the players. He even played an instrumental role in bringing Hall of Fame outfielder and catcher King Kelly from Chicago to Boston. An eccentric if ever there was one, Dixwell permitted a scraggly gray beard to increasingly dominate his visage while he broke with the Beaneaters' ownership for some reason or the other as the mil-lennium approached. Boston had temporarily lost its first superfan.

Nuf Ced rounded up a couple hundred of his closest friends from Rox-bury and more than filled the void. His band became known first as the Rox-bury Rooters, and later as the Royal Rooters. Many of his friends became very respectable gents, men who wore suits and ties and ate Sunday pot roast with the local priest on their way out of Roxbury and into the suburbs. Others like Charlie Lavis and the notorious Sport Sullivan, the latter who later helped fix the 1919 World Series, were angels of decidedly dirtier faces.

The earliest mention of royal rooters in the *Boston Globe* occurs in 1893. But rather than refer to any of McGreevy's friends, the reference is to small-case "royal rooters," welcoming back the Philadelphia Phillies for a series with the Boston Beaneaters.

The next mention of royal rooters occurred about four years later, at which time they fairly burst upon the scene. In 1897, the Boston Beaneaters, the lineal forebears of the current Atlanta Braves, challenged the three-time defending champion Baltimore Orioles. Although both teams had a series with other clubs at the very end of the season, their last series against each other essentially determined the pennant.

The Baltimore Orioles, led by Hall of Fame manager Ned Hanlon and joined by other future Cooperstown inductees John McGraw, Joe Kelley, Wee Willie Keeler and Hughie Jennings, had dominated baseball with talent and a mean and physically violent streak as wide as the Chesapeake Bay. Opposing them, the Boston Beaneaters, guided by taciturn manager Frank Selee, were captained by Hugh Duffy and led by such exemplars of the clean style of play as pitcher Kid Nichols, third baseman Jimmy Collins, and outfielders Chick Stahl, Sliding Billy Hamilton and Buck Freeman, a formidable constellation of stars in their own right.

It was Athens versus Sparta, with Boston playing the role of Athens with one major advantage—a train filled with Royal Rooters led by McGreevy. The Royal Rooters took over the Baltimore ballpark with horns and whistles and yells, negating in many ways the home-field advantage the Orioles normally might expect. Boston won two out of three games, and the legend of the Royal Rooters was cemented.

To suggest that McGreevy's group was the only supporters ignores the many thousands of fans who joined the approximately 200 Royal Rooters at their height. During the daytime games, particularly on weekdays, many of the Royal Rooters had jobs, and it was just as likely that bankers and lawyers attended the games.

Few generalizations regarding the fans can be made with the exception that males comprised almost all of the cranks of that era. Occasionally, magnates staged Ladies Days when all attendees supposedly exhibited their best behavior, but generally the games appealed to the menfolk.

Gamblers flooded each game to place bets or win friends and influence the players. Although most famous for helping fix the 1919 World Series, Sport Sullivan showed up often at games, as did more respectable one-time gamblers, such as Charlie Lavis. In terms of a threat to organized baseball, steroids in the 1980s and 1990s paled when juxtaposed to gambling in the early twentieth century. Gamblers often consorted with players and individual games, and series often carried the foul smell of corruption, making the sport itself little better at its worst points than professional wrestling.

A common misconception is that the Boston American fans came from a small group of largely Irish Catholics from the city's neighborhoods. In addition to the expansion of the fan base to all elements of the economy, the Americans almost from their inception encompassed an area stretching to the very borders of New England itself. Far away in Pownal, Vermont, a young laborer named Ambrose McConnell saved his money to see a game in Boston, a wish that only materialized years later when he started a game at the Huntington Grounds as a second baseman. The poor Beaneaters, and later Braves, duked it out unsuccessfully through their common existence with the modern Red Sox in the city's neighborhoods, while the American League franchise won the vast majority of the hearts and minds of New Englanders outside of metropolitan Boston.

The Royal Rooters existed for more than two decades, but their most famous episodes occurred in the 1912 World Series, when team owner Jimmy McAleer sold the seats normally reserved for them to third parties. At that point, the Rooters rioted, an event memorialized almost a century later in the Dropkick Murphys' remake of "Tessie." Eventually, Prohibition proved the death knell for the Royal Rooters because McGreevy either could not or at least felt he could not run a saloon illegally. By that time, the Red Sox no longer needed the Rooters anyway; they had developed a loyal fan base and no longer needed a large group of folks bringing in a brass band. Red Sox Nation was not a restricted group like the Rooters, as anyone who had a heart ripe for the breaking could join.

If the Royal Rooters eventually moved out of Roxbury, their descendants live today in the worldwide Red Sox Nation, a catholic group united by their love of the Olde Towne Team, sentimentalists all. They continue to live and die by the fortunes of their team, creating an intensity that not all baseball players can handle. Those who want to stay with the Red Sox thrive, drawing on the support echoing over several generations, and it all started on a small corner plot of land in Roxbury owned by the widow O'Flynn.

2

Hugh Duffy Loves and Leaves the Boston Americans

Hugh Duffy never thought Jimmy Collins would make much of a major league manager. As the captain of the great Boston Beaneater teams of the 1890s, Sir Hugh mixed pepper and praise to motivate a team compiled by manager Frank Selee, a much more retiring sort. In fact, few people placed much faith in Collins' leadership skills, because as others vocalized, he "is too quiet. He would not have spirit enough to say his soul was his own. He is not aggressive enough. He is not a leader. The boys could all [walk right] over him."

Nevertheless, the new Boston American League entry had to assemble a credible team very quickly, and Duffy must have sensed that the key to doing so rested in wresting Jimmy Collins from the established crosstown Beaneaters, also called the Nationals. While Duffy had served successfully as captain of the National League club for several years and had generated considerable respect and affection amongst his minions, his friends had largely long since left the team or retired. The younger Collins, meanwhile, maintained strong ties with players in their prime. Whether Collins might fail as a manager, which appeared virtually certain, meant little if the Boston Americans could not even field a squad of bona fide major league talent.

Born in the town of Niagara Falls, New York, on January 16, 1870, James Joseph Collins was baptized less than a week later at St. Mary of the Cataract Catholic Church. His father, Anthony Collins, walked a policeman's beat, as young Jimmy grew up in Buffalo, a city that he called home his entire life. A sharp student, Collins graduated from St. Joseph's College, and after graduation worked for the Lackawanna Railroad.

Collins also played baseball for the Buffalo Bisons in 1893 and 1894. After Collins hit .332 in his last year there, Frank Selee, a future Hall of Famer, bought his contract for $500, whereupon he rushed down to Boston as an outfielder for the 1895 season and foundered immediately. As an initial wash-out for the Beaneaters, Collins was loaned to the woeful Louisville franchise, where he matured quickly from a tentative fielder to a quick and aggressive one. Monitoring this transformation, Selee brought Collins back the next year, where he joined other future Hall of Fame legends Hugh Duffy,

Sliding Billy Hamilton and Kid Nichols, and helped secure two pennants for Boston.

With the possible exception of John McGraw, Jimmy Collins is considered the finest third baseman of the nineteenth century. His return to Manager Selee's favor coincided with an organizational youth movement. Team captain and long-time third baseman Billy Nash, who was on the verge of totally losing it, had been traded for Billy Hamilton, one of the most lopsided deals in history. To replace Nash, the Beaneaters needed Collins to thrive, which he did, in part by devising a way to negate the power of the Baltimore Orioles' secret weapon—the bunt.

The roughhouse Orioles (the lineal ancestors of the New York Yankees) in 1894 had supplanted the Beaneaters as the premier team in organized baseball, achieving this lofty place through a combination of talent, inside baseball and intimidation. Superstars Willie Keeler, Hughie Jennings, Joe Kelley and McGraw had become the most feared congregation in baseball, and one of their most successful plays was bunting their runners over, a tactic other teams had not solved. Jimmy Collins did by charging "in on bunt attempts and [throwing] barehanded to first base."

No less an authority than the O's John McGraw always considered Jimmy Collins his superior at the hot corner. Years later, McGraw, who had gained even greater fame as the manager of the New York Giants, had this to say about his old adversary:

> I select Jimmy [for the All-Time team] for his general excellence as a fielder, a hitter and a man. He was a great fellow on and off the field and a credit to baseball. Jimmy Collins was particularly adept at going for bunts. The art of bunting had just come into being when Collins began playing third base and he was one of the first to solve this style of play. I remember very well a game in which we had the opposing third baseman standing on his head trying to handle these tantalizing little jabs. Collins was playing the outfield. He was called in. In a few innings, it seemed, he had completely blocked our efforts.

In addition to his fielding, Collins hit .300 or better five times and even led all of major league baseball in home runs with 15 in 1898. A handsome man, Collins once received compliments years later by an early correspondent of the *Boston Post*, known by her byline, the "Post's Young Woman."

> Collins is a compactly built man of exquisite proportions. His face is lean, aquiline, with a strong muscular jaw and a determined mouth. His general color is a deep, rich tan, about the color of his hair. His manner is nervous, quick and decisive. At times, usually when it is least expected, he makes a move as sudden as greased lightning, and before you know what he is about, the whole thing is executed.

Like many ballplayers, Collins chafed at the cheapness of the Boston Triumvirate of owners, Arthur Soden, William Conant and James Billings, who colluded with other National League owners to pay a player a maximum salary of $2,400 a year. The Boston Americans ownership presented Collins with a package later revealed to consist of a $3,500 bonus for jumping teams, a $10,000 yearly salary and 10 percent of team profits over $25,000 a season.

After the 1901 books had closed, the total amount the club paid out to Collins ended up at $18,000, an enormous sum, that first year; for perspective, before the advent of the Players Association in the 1970s, many mediocre major league players still did not earn close to that amount in a season. Even had the parsimonious Triumvirs wanted to pay Collins more than the $2,400 maximum, they had no inclination or perhaps the financial wherewithal to remunerate their third sacker anything approaching that amount to retain his services.

Enter Cleveland magnate Charles Somers. Fortuitously for Collins, American League President Ban Johnson had enlisted the wealthy Somers to sponsor the new team, and Somers possessed sufficient capital to loosen the surly bonds that attached formerly dissatisfied Beaneaters to their old club.

Somers and his management team had specifically committed their team to a plan to not only survive, but to replace the Boston Nationals as the city's favorite team. The blueprint depended on many factors for its success. The new owners understood that the old South End Grounds had become a laughingstock in major league baseball. Beaneaters director James Billings had attempted two years earlier to move the team to a conceived new park on the Charles River Grounds, but had been overruled by his two partners, the tight-fisted Arthur Soden and William Conant.

Somers immediately committed his financial reserves to purchasing centrally located prime property from the Boston Elevated Railway Company and building a state-of-the-art facility on Huntington Avenue that shamed the traditional South End Grounds.

Secondly, the Boston Americans committed themselves to charging .25 cents for each customer to gain admission to their games, while the Boston Nationals had established a game charge of 50 cents for their potential customers. A discerning fan, or "crank," would have no difficulty in perceiving the difference in price and quality of accommodations after paying half as much to enter into a brand new facility instead of some dingy and overly cozy old ball field.

Of course, the novelty of paying a lower general admission for a nice park possessed a limited allure if the old ballpark still fielded a vastly superior product. As the third prong of his strategy, Somers declared a full-scale raid on the Boston Nationals' roster. He placed an early emphasis on obtaining Catholic players, particularly Irish ones, to establish an instant allegiance between the new franchise and its overwhelming, teeming Irish American population, led by the cadre of approximately 200 Royal Rooters. Parenthetically, Somers did not pit the Irish against the old-line Yankee populace either, as he courted superfan General Arthur "Hi Hi" Dixwell, the trust fund baby who had deserted the Boston Nationals over the past few seasons.

Someone had to break the ground for the new Huntington Street Grounds and that man, holding the spade, was superfan Arthur "Hi Hi" Dixwell. Dixwell drew this honor as an homage to the past, but the future lay with the Royal Rooters, represented here by Nuf Ced McGreevy, in the first row, fourth from the left. Boston Public Library, Print Department, McGreevy Collection.

But the destiny of the proposed Boston American League franchise rested on their obtaining (stealing actually) Jimmy Collins from the established Nationals. If the Boston Americans could entice Collins away, certainly he had the influence to persuade his best friend, star outfielder Chick Stahl, to come over, with perhaps others to follow.

James Billings recognized this as well, and in early March of 1901, on the same date that Charles Somers passed papers and purchased the Huntington Avenue Grounds, Billings announced that he had kept Collins in the fold. Throughout this time, Hugh Duffy and his brother-in-law, M. T. Moore, fanned out of the latter's law office and continued to recruit Collins, mesmerizing him with tales of wealth that awaited him if he only had the courage and foresight (and greed) to jump his contract with the Nationals and enlist with the new franchise.

On March 4, 1901, Hugh Duffy, Connie Mack and the prized third sacker met with Somers in Cleveland and emerged from their lengthy meeting to announce to the world the signing of new player-manager Jimmy Collins. The taciturn Collins uncharacteristically shouted, "I have signed to play with the Bostons, and shall have a team that will be first class in every particular. I know that the American League will make a complete success."

With the release of that information came the theft from the Boston Nationals by the Boston Americans Collins' best friend, star outfielder Charles

Sylvester "Chick" Stahl. Another rumored cross-town defection was pitcher Bill Dinneen, a friend of Collins and Stahl who won 20 games the previous year.

The signing of Dinneen may or may not have occurred, but on the very next day, first baseman Buck Freeman jumped from the Boston Nationals to the new club, as did St. Louis catcher Lou Criger. The signing of Freeman, who hit a then-unheard of 25 home runs in one season in 1899, augured well for the new franchise. But it was the less-heralded inking of Criger that potentially meant much more to the new team's fortunes due to his close friendship with his battery mate, pitcher Denton True "Cy" Young.

Criger and Young presented themselves almost as much of a matched set as Jimmy Collins and Chick Stahl, although the former duo had not played together that long. Cy Young had spent the majority of the 1890s throwing fastballs for the Cleveland club, run by Patsy Tebeau, the Billy Martin of his day. Criger won Cy's heart by devising ways to catch the fastball consistently, revealing little of the pain it caused him each time the ball struck his catcher's mitt.

Young garnered a reputation as a man who enjoyed to drink a lot, but he never allowed alcohol to make a fool of him, and he lived 88 years. A farmer from Ohio, he lived a simple life with his wife and liked to hunt and fish, but he burned with ambition every time he took the mound, constantly finding ways to improve his repertoire or use rule changes to his advantage. He came from the solid stock who unflinchingly fought for the Union cause in the Civil War. Had William Faulkner come from the North, he would have written approvingly of folks like Denton True Young and his family.

Never much of a hitter, Criger approximated the role of a skilled caddy to a great golfer. Almost always battling some illness or chronic injury, he never begged out of playing except when battling a nasty morphine addiction he had developed after receiving treatment for one of his many scrapes and bruises. He never learned to hit the baseball, but he specialized in defense, and his pitchers appreciated him enough to assure him of a 16-year major league career. Statistically, it is difficult to become too enthused about Criger, but the managers and pitchers who worked with him loved the guy.

Again, John McGraw picked Criger along with Ray Schalk as catchers for his all-time American League team.

> Lew (sic) Criger was a catcher of the old school and one of the classiest. He caught Cy Young, Bill Dineen (sic) and other stars for years. All of them pronounce him great. Criger was an everyday hard-working catcher that always could be depended upon. Though Lew was but a fair hitter he was very dependable in the pinches. His gentlemanly conduct, all around even temperament, made him most valuable to any organization. Lew Criger was a credit to the game.

A modern reader will have difficulty comprehending how many contemporaries honored the light-hitting Criger as one of the greatest catchers ever, but perhaps because of the poor equipment catchers used back then, his feats inspired awe. He possessed one truly exceptional skill—his pinpoint ability to throw out runners, both in the act of stealing a base and in leading off the bag. Every team in the turn of the century wanted Lou Criger, a statistician's nightmare, to be their starting catcher.

As hoped, with Criger came Young. Last-ditch efforts to return Young to St. Louis by their president, Frank DeHaas Robinson, proved ineffective. Somers permitted Cy to train on his own in Hot Springs (instead of the team's camp in Charlottesville) and lavished him with cash. Indignantly, Cy blasted his old boss for attempting to have him jump back from his new commitment to the Boston Americans, stating, "I'd never jump back from the Boston American League Club. Robinson or any other man hasn't got enough to make me jump my contract. I am getting more money in Boston than Robinson gave me, and after all, that's what I want."

Concurrent with the Young signing, the Bostons engaged in some wishful thinking that Cy's old pitching friend from Cleveland, Nig Cuppy, might regain his old form and become a winner again. Born George Joseph Koppe, this Indiana native won 114 games for Cleveland from 1892 through 1898, but had not won more than 11 games since 1896. Having played for the Boston Beaneaters the year before, he cast his lot with fellow cross-town defectors Collins, Stahl and Freeman and hoped for a return to his previous form in a new watered-down league.

Having aggressively raided the Boston Nationals' roster, Somers proposed a cessation of hostilities with the senior circuit leaders, prompting Arthur Conant to quip, "[n]ice thing to do, steal a club's players and then advise peace." The damage to the National League had occurred, and then some, but this did not prevent their owners from staging a bit of a counter-reformation of their own. Fighting fire with fire, Billings enticed contract jumper Bill Dinneen to renege on his deal with the Boston Americans and return to the Nationals, prompting Billings to tout the star pitcher as "the best man who wears a uniform." For their parts, Hugh Duffy and Jimmy Collins fumed, with Collins telling Dinneen that he "hoped his arm would drop off [with] the first ball he pitched."

As a consolation, another Nationals starter, right-hander Ted "Parson" Lewis, sent in the measurements for his new uniform to Manager Selee, but not a signed contract, and eventually he too joined his old friends on the Americans. Lewis, a Williams College man more suited for academia than professional sports, had nonetheless compiled a 78–47 career record, going 26–7 in 1898. His earned run average had increased a half-run in each of the past two years, but in an expansion league, he entertained reasonable expectations of a renaissance. If not, he planned to become a college professor.

Although Hugh Duffy had received an appointment to manage the new Milwaukee Brewers team, his efforts to fortify the Boston Americans did not cease. With Collins and Freeman ensconced at the corners of their proposed infield, the team lacked reliable middle infielders. Snooping about, Duffy procured two youngsters for the franchise, French-Canadian Fred Parent from Sanford, Maine, at shortstop and fiery Hobe Ferris, from Providence, Rhode Island, at second base. Sir Hugh fed the Bostons at his own Milwaukee Brewers' expense, as Ferris and Parent starred for their club in the early twentieth century.

The *Post's* Young Woman described Parent as "a dapper little man, wiry, quick and almost effeminate. He has a naturally mincing walk, steps daintily and appears self-conscious.... By nature Mr. Parent was designed for a society leader-by accident, good gift and nimble feet, he became a baseball player." Far less genteel, Ferris' "distinguishing points were the vicious cuts he gave that little slippery ball and his essentially masculine 'curse words,' I guess that's what they were, from the expression of his face. Also, I heard a couple."

The exertions that Hugh Duffy undertook to bring a quality American League team to Boston did not escape the notice of the *Sporting Life*, which later gushed, "Too much credit can not be bestowed upon Hughey Duffy for his work in getting that team together, for it was largely through the co-operation of Duffy that Boston got one of the best ball clubs ever put together ..." a sentiment shared by the *Boston Globe's* Tim Murnane, one of the greatest sportswriters in the city's history. Decades later, Duffy returned to the Red Sox to manage, coach and instruct them over the course of the last thirty-something years of his life, becoming a template for Johnny Pesky to emulate later. But for now, Duffy headed west to manage Milwaukee, leaving behind the aggregation that he helped create—Jimmy Collins' team. While Duffy stocked the Boston club with stars and promising rookies, his own Milwaukee squad suffered in comparison.

Saying their farewells to their old Beaneater captain Duffy, Collins and Chick Stahl remained in Boston, and as the roster filled out, their new teammates assembled and met each other and headed south for spring training. En route to Charlottesville to train, the Boston Americans awkwardly bumped into the Boston Beaneaters, who had coincidentally hopped on the same train. Uneasiness aside, Collins and Duffy had formed a nice club with the following players initially in the fold that spring: Pitchers Cy Young, Win Kellum, Nig Cuppy, Fred Mitchell and a bunch of young arms named McKenna, Kane, Connor, Parker and Katell; catchers Ossee Schreckengost, Lou Criger and Larry McLean; infielders Freeman, Ferris, Parent and Collins; and outfielders J. Jones, Chick Stahl, Tommy Dowd and Charlie Hemphill.

A character, Ossee Schreckengost later roomed with another famous eccentric with the Athletics named Rube Waddell, their eccentricities often fueled by excessive alcohol consumption. While not as technically sound a receiver as Lou Criger or as well respected as a teammate, Schreckengost could hit. To fit his name in box scores in the newspapers, he has come down to history also known as Schreck.

One of the game's original space-shots, Schreck once got his team kicked

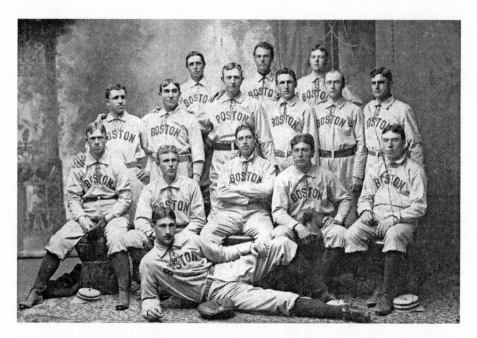

Team photograph of the first Boston Americans club. Strong but silent manager Jimmy Collins sits in the front row, armed crossed. Very tall and difficult to control, reserve catcher Larry McLean is lying down in front. Boston Public Library, Print Department, McGreevy Collection.

out of dinner by nailing his steak to the wall. He also put it into his contract that roommate Rube Waddell could not eat crackers in bed. In an early game in 1901, while behind the plate, Schreck did not go after an easy pop-up because he heard a fan yell out, "You can't get it." After the ball dropped, the same fan yelled, "You're easy."

Larry McLean was a big (6'5") good-looking guy from nearby Cambridge who couldn't catch or hit in the nine-game stint he had with the local team. Born John Bannerman in Nova Scotia, he later went on to have a good career in the National League, primarily with Cincinnati and New York.

And yet he gained more fame in the manner of how he died, shot to death in a Roxbury bar on March 24, 1921. In 1921, Prohibition had taken effect, but this did little to deter McLean and his buddy, Jack McCarthy, a former major leaguer. McLean's biggest career impediment was his lack of self-control, as "[h]is disregard for baseball discipline retarded his progress as a big leaguer." After 1913, no one could stand him on their team, and Big Larry began to increasingly punish his body by dint of his alcoholism, drifting "about and gradually [becoming] conspicuous among the habitués of the underworld."

In an attempt to circumvent the Prohibition laws, an extraordinary compound of ethyl alcohol called "Jamaica Ginger" flooded the market and McLean and McCarthy both became addicted to it. They spent much of their time rolling into speakeasies and making asses of themselves; only two weeks earlier, McLean had been arrested for drunkenness. By March 24, their reputations had preceded them as bartender James J. Connor put up with their abuse until he finally asked them to leave.

Brave, drunk and stupid, McLean and McCarthy tried to leap over the bar to assault Connor, who rapidly yanked a revolver out of a drawer and shot McLean in the heart and McCarthy in the stomach. The stalwart McLean did not go softly into the night as he "staggered to the side door and stumbled to the Northampton St. sidewalk, falling at the feet of Miss Mary A. Lyons and Miss Ruth Williams, district nurses, who were waiting for a street car. He was dead."

The police booked Connor for murder, but most of the witnesses corroborated his story, even though they were all inebriated themselves. Connor received a slap on the wrist and receded from baseball history forever. McCarthy survived, due in large part to his mother and brother each valiantly donating a pint of blood to save his life. He fled the city as poor McLean was laid to rest.

Yet if McLean had wasted his life, he certainly did not want for a role model in Manager Collins. Despite the concerns many had about his ability to run a club, the taciturn third baseman commanded respect from his players, many of them rookies who needed nurturing, while assuaging long-time veterans who might have chafed under the tutelage of a holler guy. A players' manager, Collins' popularity was grounded in respecting people who, like him, jumped leagues and did not like to be told what to do. He was one of them, and in the absence of a controlling owner, Collins became the face of the franchise.

Sportswriter Jacob Morse attributed Collins' early success to the fact that the manager was "quiet, yet determined, when he says a thing he means it, does not yell at his men, the men play together and would 'go though fire and water for their captain and the team was unified in their approach to the game." Collins and Duffy had seen to it that they had assembled (mostly) a group of positive players, undoubtedly recalling how a talent like Cy Young was wasted in Cleveland by the mismanagement of drunk and out of control Captain Patsy Tebeau.

Collins needed all available karma because his club had to play its first ten games on the road, and they split their wins and losses on their series away from home. This all changed on May 8, 1901, with the opening of their ballpark at the Huntington Grounds.

The grounds do not exist today, having been taken over by building at Northeastern University, where many of the old memories are lovingly preserved. A critical reminder of the former glory at this locale is a statue of Cy Young situated at the old pitcher's mound. Nevertheless, more than a hundred years after the ballpark's opening, Huntington Avenue and the nearby train tracks provide a glimpse, however imperfect, of what it must have been like to walk to a game there.

The players did not march to the park as customary, as they had just alighted from their train from Washington at Back Bay Station. Having no time to stop for even a snack, the new club played its first home game on "empty stomachs." A cadet band played tunes for the spectators, all 11,500 of them, a fine crowd for the era, as peanut vendors sailed their bags over the heads of patrons to their eventual customers. Two "tally-ho" coaches drove in from center field, one of them containing Tommy McCarthy, Boston's only native son to ever make the Baseball Hall of Fame, and one of Duffy and Mack's conspirators in bringing American League baseball to the Hub. The crowd waved small American flags handed out for the occasion.

As a public relations ploy, General "Hi Hi" Dixwell threw out the first ball, marking his return to rooting at the expense of the cross-town National League Beaneaters. It was a nice touch for a nice man, but the future belonged to the Royal Rooters, who like "Hi Hi" had shifted their allegiance to the new club. Indeed, after Opening Day, his name almost completely disappears from the sports pages, except for brief mentions, whereas in the nineteenth century he exerted an omnipresence over the local sporting scene.

Since the inception of the Boston American League entrant, millions of men have attended games at the Huntington Street Grounds, and later Fenway Park, and no one noted the identity of the first man to enter the stadium as a fan; his identity has long been lost to history. But the identity of the first female rooter is definitely known, as the management made certain that Mrs. Charles Somers, the wife of the club owner, became the very first female to attend a home game.

Cy Young started for Boston and won, supported by 21 hits and 12 runs from his offense, as his team steamrolled Connie Mack and his star second baseman, Napoleon Lajoie. Auspicious start aside, not even the great Young could carry the club, and it began to play poor ball, sinking to fifth place by the middle of May. Relief came to the team in July with a number of games against Hugh Duffy's Milwaukee Brewers, a team Collins' men swept in a four-game series, which brought Boston into fourth place behind Chicago, Detroit and Washington. In the last game on June 11, Collins gave his old captain "a loving cup and diamonds," a token of appreciation for all Duffy had done for him and the city of Boston.

Collins received a gift days later when rookie George Winter of Pennsylvania and Gettysburg College started a game against Detroit and allowed them only five hits at the Huntington Grounds on the way to starting his career with eight consecutive wins. Nig Cuppy had nothing left and Parson Lewis did not seem to have his heart in baseball any longer, but the arrival of Winter helped to energize the Boston team, which narrowly trailed Chicago and Detroit in the standings.

Four days later, Winter pitched his team into second place in the pennant race, defeating Chicago, marking Boston's fourth straight victory over the "White Socks." Venting their frustration after a controversial balk call went against them, the Chicago players "gathered howling about the umpire, but it was of no avail, and [Chicago pitcher] Callahan was sent out of the game for using language not on the score card." Winter did not lose a game until mid–July, when he lost to the Philadelphia Athletics and future Hall of Fame pitcher Ed Plank, a college friend of Winter.

Winter certainly jump-started the team with his victory over the White Socks. The next day, Cy Young's pitching and timely hitting by Buck Freeman and Freddy Parent helped vault the team into first place, and the Bostons proceeded to win twenty and lose only five games for the entire month of June. The club slowed down a bit thereafter, but still played over .500 ball for July and August. Chicago went on a bit of a surge to regain the lead, but Boston invariably clawed back to ratchet up the race as the summer wore on.

On August 23 against Cleveland, Cy Young gave up one run in a game at the Huntington Avenue Grounds to gain the 5–1 win. Batting third and fourth, respectively, Jimmy Collins and Buck Freeman accounted for six of the eight team hits and all of the RBIs. The team also played host to English athletes from Oxford and Cambridge, who were awed by the catching and throwing skills of the players and experienced jolly good cheer from inspecting the bats after the game.

After the win against Cleveland, Boston stood a half-game below Chicago in the standings. Boston was poised to capture the top spot, but unfortunately embarked on a 5–12–1 spree until they were able to regain their footing against Washington in a home-and-away series, commencing on September 11. Around that time, weightier matters diverted the hearts and minds of good Americans, of which Bostonians are some of the oldest and the proudest.

On September 6, 1901, an anarchist shot the president of the United States while attending the Pan-American Exposition in Buffalo, New York. Even baseball fanatics had their attention diverted as the president experienced a recuperation period that actually worsened his condition; McKinley died on September 14, a victim almost as much of the treatment of his medical team as the ultimately fatal shot fired by assassin Leon Czolgosz. Before he died, McKinley beckoned for his wife, and their "farewell was long and unutterably sad."

The day after the anarchist shot the president, Boston traveled to Chicago and was swept in a four-game series. In the first game, on September 7, a confident Jim Callahan won, 4–1, defeating Parson Lewis, who in contrast "look[ed] like stage money." The next day, Chicago prevailed again, this time by a score of 4–3 as Cy Young threw too good a pitch to Dummy Hoy, who drilled it hard enough to knock in the tying and winning runs. As Tim Murnane related, "The crowd rushed on to the field and carried the Chicago men to the club house on their shoulders. With one exception everybody admitted that it was the greatest game they ever saw. A Boston man claimed it was a poor game."

On September 9, Chicago all but sealed the deal by defeating Boston in a double-header by maddening 4–3 and 6–4 margins. In a template for future disasters, in the first game Boston pitted Fred Mitchell against Jim Callahan, a pitcher who thoroughly outclassed him. Collins yanked Mitchell in the second inning and his reliever, Parson Lewis, pitched well thereafter, but Collins made two crucial errors to seal the White Socks' win. In the second game, Chicago scored five runs in the first inning off George Winter. They countered with pitcher Clark Griffith, and again, superior pitching trumped inferior pitching. As the Boston Americans left for Washington, the sweep had placed them six games behind in the loss column.

On September 19, the *Boston Globe* proclaimed "NO HOPE NOW" after Chicago won a double-header in Baltimore and Boston had its game stopped on account of rain. Parson Lewis started for Boston and was swamped in the brief time he threw, with the *Globe* editorializing that "[t]his start once more emphasized the fact that the American team should have been strengthened in the box (i.e., pitcher's mound) long ago if the championship was to be played for to a finish." Commenting upon all of the young players that Owner Somers had furnished him during the season, Collins deadpanned, "I have had all I want of youngsters this season." On September 19, Collins' team did not play in order to honor the recent passing of President McKinley.

There would be no pennant for the Boston Americans in their inaugural season.

Essentially, Boston did not win the first American League pennant because Chicago received a bit more from its (almost) over-the-hill pitchers. In their last few years in a very small but highly competitive National League, Clark Griffith, Jimmy Callahan and Roy Patterson had hardly thrived, but with the influx of sub-par talent and the accumulation of marginal talent with the expansion of roster spots in major league rosters, the Chicago starting pitchers statistically improved upon their performances.

It did not hurt the Windy City that its entrant had three solid outfielders in Sam Mertes, Fielder Jones and Dummy Hoy; Boston had only stalwart Chick Stahl in center field, saddled down with woefully weak showings by Dowd and Hemphill. Still, the Boston Americans had made some strong acquisitions in young players like Hobe Ferris and Freddy Parent, who promised to man the middle of the infield much longer than their Chicago counterparts.

In what would become a tiresome and dreadful abuse of power, American League President Ben Johnson ensured Chicago's Clark Griffith's transfer to the New York franchise, an obsession that not only hurt the White Socks team, but haunted the Boston Americans in the years to come.

Finagling aside, Boston did not win the pennant because the team had been unable to hold Bill Dinneen to his commitment to jump from the Beaneaters to the new American League club. Going back home to Buffalo for the winter, captain Jimmy Collins already began to formulate a way to bring Dinneen to his club and keep him there.

3

'02 and Out

In the bleak midwinter of 1902, just after the cleanup from New Year's Eve parties had concluded, Jimmy Collins traversed New York, from Buffalo to Syracuse, to meet with Big Bill Dinneen. The previous year, Dinneen had pledged his troth to the Boston Americans, only to return to the nearby Beaneaters. In the off-season, he subsequently met with his lawyer, who assured him that he might go safely where his heart and his financial prospects beckoned. At the old Globe Hotel, it took Manager Collins only ten minutes to wrap up formalities and sign Dinneen, the talented right-hander.

Unlike the end of the previous century, when a team might win a championship largely due to one dominant starting pitcher, teams in the early 1900s relied on at least three and as many as five front-line talents. Fortunately for his new mates, Big Bill had finally established a home with the sons of Jimmy Collins at the Huntington Grounds by gaining control of his pitches. The big right-hander would win more than twenty games in each of the next three seasons for the Boston Americans.

Across the border in Massachusetts, Cy Young had starred in 1901, and the fans' fingers were crossed in hopes that his magic might remain with him another year. Thanks to departing pitcher Ted Lewis, Cy had obtained an offer to coach the Harvard baseball team and accepted it. Young informed the club's owners, whoever they were, that he intended to arrive to spring training a bit late due to his other obligation. If anyone objected to the arrangement, Cy never knew about it.

Collins was optimistic that the remainder of his staff might round off nicely, a pitching corps that included returning phenom George Winter and other promising hurlers, such as Fred Mitchell, Bert Husting and a young left-hander, Otto "Pep" Deininger. Husting pitched very well in spots with a poor Milwaukee club during the previous year under manager Hugh Duffy, who probably recommended him to Boston now that the Brewers had moved to St. Louis without him. Boston also signed another swift throwing southpaw, David Williams, "even though Collins is credited with having said that he did not know anything about the man."

While the addition of an ace pitcher upgraded the club, some enduring improvements also came in the field, where Boston had strengthened itself considerably. Promising Patrick Henry Dougherty, nicknamed "Patsy," jumped from Cincinnati to join Chick Stahl in the outfield. Hailing from New York state, Dougherty brought with him a most unruly mop of hair, which looked like steel wool or a Brillo pad parted in the middle when he took his hat off. In 1901, poor Chick's cohorts in the outfield had been the inconsistent Charlie Hemphill (his career seemed to alternate yearly between very good or very poor batting campaigns) and Buttermilk Tommy Dowd, who never played another major league game. Boston also had brought aboard an experienced outfielder named Charlie Hickman, but Patsy Dougherty threatened Hickman's presumed starting status almost immediately.

To complete the rebuilding, the club traded good-hitting but flaky catcher Ossee Schreckengost to Cleveland for switch-hitting first baseman Candy Lachance. Born George Joseph Lachance in Putnam, Connecticut, Candy batted adequately, but his presence at first base permitted his new team to move Buck Freeman to the outfield. Plus, he looked like a true baseballist. By the late

Patsy Dougherty, after he changed Sox. Boston strengthened itself dramatically by adding this young and speedy star to its roster, and the fans loved him. He reciprocated these feelings. Library of Congress.

1890s, most men had forsaken the bushy mustaches, beards and mutton chop sideburns for the clean-shaven look. Not Candy, who wore a thick, black 'stache that would have made the late King Kelly beam.

With Chick Stahl, Patsy Dougherty and Buck Freeman patrolling the nether regions, the Boston Americans possessed one of the better hitting trios in the majors at that time. The team had begun to cast away its vestiges of an expansion team, seeking to truly field a champion. Joining Lachance in the infield were returning favorites Hobe Ferris at second, Freddy Parent at shortstop, and Jimmy Collins at third base.

With the departure of Schreckengost, Lou Criger nailed down the starting catching job. To help Criger out, the team procured the services of John Warner, who jumped from his contract with the New York Nationals. Warner fortunately did not share any of the many eccentricities of "Schreck" while spelling Criger, who always seemed on the verge of physical collapse. Allegedly, Warner was not fond of Catholics, an intolerance that Jimmy Collins did not take long to discover.

In addition, the club had nifty new uniforms. Instead of a generic Boston printed on their chests, the players now had two large, vaguely English–style letters in capitals: B A. They also wore, at least on the road, solid blue hats. In symbolic as well as tangible ways, they continued to abandon any hint of similarity between their club and the Boston Beaneaters.

The issue of who actually owned the Boston Americans dogged the team the entire campaign, and undoubtedly added to the stress of Manager Collins, the face of the franchise. *Sporting News* correspondent Peter "Hi Hi" Kelley opined on the season's Opening Day that "neither Somers nor Killilea is the owner." "Hi Hi" erred in rendering this judgment, but certainly Charles Somers had very little fettle for owning a team in Boston, a city he neither resided in nor possessed any devotion for, while Killilea began to buy more shares of the club.

During the season, Collins often did not know how deals involving his players had occurred until after the new arrivals showed up at the Huntington Grounds and the departing Bostons cleaned their modest changing space. It is equally unclear who finalized the transactions. For those fans who remember the convoluted ownership squabbles involving the Boston Red Sox after the death of Thomas Yawkey, such internecine bickering did not begin in 1983, but rather had its origin from the outset of the club.

The chaotic management of the Boston Americans resembled an even crazier early-season, three-game series in Baltimore against the Orioles. Fiery John McGraw managed the team, which was a reflection of the man himself and the style of play embraced by McGraw's mentor, Ned Hanlon, the instigator of the fine Baltimore teams of the middle-to-late 1890s. The city suffered from a paucity of entertainment options that week as only a circus competed with the American League contests and most potential patrons "eschewed the red lemonade and the equestrienne in pink tights..." for the real three-ring spectacle at the ballpark.

The teams had split their first two contests, with Chick Stahl leading Boston to victory in the first game with a bold steal of home. In the rubber match, both McGraw and his fans smelled blood on May Day, which emanated not from their opposition, but from an unfortunate Baltimore policeman. Fast forwarding, Big Bill Dinneen had slightly out-pitched his rival so that his team led, 6–3, in the ninth inning. With two strikes on him, McGraw lined a pitch over first base that he and the fans judged fair but the umpire, a chap named Sheridan, called foul.

On the next pitch, Dinneen drilled McGraw in the rear with a fastball. Instead of awarding McGraw with first base for being hit by a pitch, Sheridan ruled that McGraw had not done enough to avoid the throw, compelling McGraw to bat again. Disagreeing with this decision, McGraw let Sheridan have it, as "he was moved to make remarks as to and about Sheridan that blistered the paint off the press stand." Not fond of his tormentor and liking him less with each insult, Sheridan ejected McGraw, causing some fans to cajole the remaining Baltimore players to attack the poor umpire. Baltimore did manage to score a scratch run, but the fans did not feel the least bit assuaged and nearly rioted. Twelve policemen escorted Sheridan off the field, whereupon one fan threw a brick that opened up a gash on the face of poor Officer Smith. It was in many ways the typical ending of a Baltimore-Boston contest at the turn of the century.

The Baltimore Orioles might rough-house the Bostons, but they posed no threat to Collins' designs on the pennant. The Philadelphia Athletics did. Connie Mack helped create the Boston Americans, and in 1902, he helped submarine their bid to win the league pennant with a little finagling of AL President Ban Johnson. By way of explanation, the structure of the American League in its formative period only faintly resembled the system later established in professional baseball in the twentieth century with its relatively weak commissioner and clubs spending millions of dollars for free agents.

In 1902, President Ban Johnson reigned over the American League, and his interpretation of what best suited the interests of the whole, or at least folks he favored, held complete sway. Johnson wanted his friends to succeed, but more importantly he wanted the league to take root. When he perceived the precarious state of the Philadelphia franchise, he took action to ensure Mack's team did not founder.

Traditionally, the funneling of pitchers from the pitching-strapped Bostons to Philadelphia has been cited as an example of how Johnson exerted the weight of his office to force teams to sacrifice their chances of winning the pennant for the greater good of the corporate whole. The first suspect transaction occurred when Philly purchased Bert Husting from Boston, whereafter he went 14–5 for his new team.

According to historian Fred Lieb, Connie Mack was "so badly off for pitchers that at a special meeting of the league called by Ban Johnson, Somers let Connie have three of his secondary pitchers—Bert Hustings (sic)[and two others]." Parenthetically, what prompted Philly to lose some of its players had its origins in the National League Phillies trying through the courts to block their cross-town competitors from obtaining contract jumpers.

In the lower court, this tactic proved successful, but the Pennsylvania Supreme Court ruled against the American League. To circumvent this ruling, some of the Philadelphia players, the most notable being future Hall of Fame second baseman Nap Lajoie, simply did not play for the Philadelphia American team. Lajoie joined the Cleveland team, the National League did not succeed in breaking up the league, and Mack needed some new players.

That Johnson prevailed upon the dubious Boston ownership may have occurred, and Husting's stellar record after his sale lends credence to conspiracy theorists who believe that Johnson deliberately tipped the scales to ensure a Philly dynasty. There are some problems with this belief, not the least of which is that in his last start for Boston, on April 25, Husting was tagged for

15 runs and proved "easy pickings" for the opposing Washington team, a "slaughter" witnessed by Ban Johnson in person. If Johnson meant to punish Boston, he might have insisted the team keep Husting in its lineup after the spectacle he saw. More likely, Ban Johnson facilitated Philadelphia's rise by allowing the team to add future Hall of Fame hurler Rube Waddell and promising rookie Danny Murphy to its roster, thereby developing into a threat to win the championship. Johnson clearly did not feel that in sacrificing Husting to Philly, Boston was losing much.

Boston also had convinced itself of the incomparable qualities of a Beloit College pitcher named Merle "Doc" Adkins, heralded as "the best box artist the middle west has turned out in many years." A few months shy of his thirtieth birthday and weighing in at well over 200 pounds, Doc did not resemble the typical freckled-face rookie of his day or any other day, but this affected little his reputation as a mound messiah. Why worry about losing Husting with Adkins coming in to resurrect the fortunes of Boston? Meanwhile, at this time the true star, proven veteran Cy Young, pitched a masterpiece in a ballgame that lasted only 66 minutes.

That is about how long the pitching career of another budding flame-thrower lasted. Young lefty Otto "Pep" Deininger received his first and only major league start on May 30, at home against Detroit. Born in Wasseralfingen, Germany, he immigrated with his family to Boston, where he resided close to the Huntington Avenue Grounds in the city's Roxbury District. At that game his friends came out to cheer a clearly nervous Deininger, who coughed up five runs in five innings before being relieved by Fred Mitchell. In his only other major league appearance, more than a month earlier, he came out "wilder than a catbird," while getting hammered on that occasion as well.

By the end of the month, the club released him, but Pep endured in the minor leagues and even helped the Harvard baseball team. While his dreams of a career playing for his hometown team did not materialize, he lurked in the minors for years. Deininger reinvented himself as an outfielder and a pretty good hitter, returning to the majors for a cup of coffee in 1908 and a much longer stay in 1909 with the Phillies, for whom he batted a respectable .260. The center of gravity for producing baseball talent had begun to shift from East Coast cities to the South and California. And although no one appreciated it at the time, Pep would be one of the few Boston boys, joining others such as Hal Janvrin, Bobby Guindon, Tony Conigliaro and Manny DelCarmen, to play for the American League club. He continued to reside in Boston for another forty-eight years until his death in 1950.

A much sadder case involved George Prentiss, whom Collins had hoped to make a mainstay on his staff. Prentiss had struggled to a 2–2 record with a 5.67 ERA until he obtained his release and caught on briefly with Baltimore. In early September of that season he died, a shock to many of his ex-teammates, because "[m]ost of them did not know he was sick."

While green pitching prospects continued to struggle at the Huntington Grounds, phenom Patsy Dougherty hit his way into the outfield starting lineup, replacing Charlie Hickman, who soon secured his release. Dougherty ran swiftly, hit baseballs often, and stole bases, and his Irish background certainly did not hurt him in the estimation of the Boston fans or manager Jimmy Collins. Exasperated by his team's lackluster performance, either Collins or one of the team owners conducted a purge, shuttling off pitcher Fred Mitchell to Connie Mack, sending David Williams to Scranton to see if his arm might improve, releasing Pep Deininger outright due to immaturity, and releasing Hickman upon the emergence of Dougherty. The changes did little to elevate the team, which won only one more game than it lost in June.

That's not to say the doldrums did not often prove quite exciting. In a more serious replay of the previous month's attack on the umpire in Baltimore, in a June 22, 1902, game against Detroit, a poor arbiter named Johnstone inflamed the crowd, which assaulted him with fists and "light missiles" after a 7–5 Boston win. An estimated 200–300 rowdies tried to take a swing at him, and he only escaped serious injury because the Boston and Detroit players formed a protective cordon around him while escorting him to the dressing room. The stirring win did not motivate the moribund Bostons, who proceeded to lose two out of the next three games against Washington.

Collins correctly perceived that his strong and silent approach to managing had its limits, so on June 24 in game against Washington, he employed a time-honored tactic to ignite his team. He got himself suspended.

It was not hard to do. Frustrated at his team's mediocre fielding and hitting, he lost control after a close call at third base went against him in the fourth inning, culminating in his ejection. Umpire "Parisian Bob" Caruthers, a former major league pitcher, accused Jimmy Collins of four-flushing, while the manager claimed he only argued two outrageous calls. Ban Johnson liked to suspend people almost as much as he enjoyed building a winner in Philadelphia, so any protestations fell on deaf ears.

Interestingly enough, following the ejection, Kid Gleason came in from center field to replace Collins at third base while pitcher Bill Dinneen played center field on one of his days off. The team almost won the game due to the nifty relief pitching of Doc Adkins, who held off the opponents in relief with only "two [hits] being negotiated off the fat boy's benders." Incidentally, the Boston scribes did not let up on the rookie, as little more than a week later, one advised "Collins should run about 30 pounds off Fatty Adkins."

No one was getting fat except Doc Adkins as the Boston Americans staggered into town for a Fourth of July double-header in Baltimore. Long before the team became the Red Sox and reeled off memorable and often violent series against the Yankees, the Boston Americans got most of their thrills against the Orioles, and this holiday proved no exception. As *Boston Globe* legend Tim Murnane described it, "There was a Fourth of July air about the playing that brought out a gun chorus several times during the progress of the contest. Bing, bing, bang, bang, went the shots from the revolvers, until one thought himself in Kansas City, where the cowboys go to relax a little."

In the first game, Winter held off the O's in a wobbly ninth inning for a 5–3 victory, notable mainly for Freddy Parent's fine hitting and fielding and judicious manufacturing of a key run in the sixth inning. The afternoon game proved the far more memorable as Cy Young pitched for twelve innings to guide his team to an epic 5–4 victory.

Some questionable fielding by generally reliable Patsy Dougherty and Lou Criger kept Baltimore in the hunt, and the Orioles nearly won the match when Kip Selbach tripled with two out in the 11th. Determined not to earn one of his ultimately 511 major league victories by guile, Young recorded the third out of the inning by punching out Jimmy Williams.

In the twelfth inning, Baltimore did finally touch up Cy for a run. (Do not adjust your set, this was 1902 when the home team often batted first in an inning.) In the bottom of the twelfth, Kid Gleason, batting for Young, flied to right. Atoning for his previous fielding miscue, Patsy Dougherty singled to center and Jimmy Collins walked. Clutch-hitting Chick Stahl then came to bat and stroked a beauty to right field, scoring Patsy, with Collins scampering to third when he alertly noticed the right fielder fumbling the ball. Buck Freeman, who had batted futilely in five previous at-bats, powered the ball to left-center, and the O's fielder "dropped the ball at full reach, concluding the contest, as Collins jogged home with the winning run."

As so often occurred in 1902, rather than capitalizing on such stirring victories and building momentum for coming contests, Collins' squad thereafter went on a 3–9 swoon over the next dozen games. The Bostons won only against powerful Philly while inexcusably losing four of those games against a woefully mediocre Cleveland congregation, proving that all too often this Boston American team could not win the little ones.

Reeling from their fourth straight loss to Cleveland, a 14–4 blowout, the Hub's cranks went apoplectic. Tim Murnane jotted down some of the comments that he claimed emanated from clergymen and such estimable fans as future Hall of Famer George Wright: "Such ballplaying." "Schoolboy work!" "Doesn't Collins know how to make these fellows play ball?" "Why, they look frightened!" "Can't the club hire pitchers with good arms?" Everything, it turns out, except "Yankees suck!"

In an usually harsh critique of both the game and the recent fortunes of the team in macrocosm, Murnane criticized the club's penury at not landing quality players, Collins' managing, and the folly of trotting out a sore-armed pitcher like Long Tom Hughes from Baltimore, whose every pitch caused him extreme physical agony. Even the utility player Gleason, subbing for star outfield Chick Stahl, came in for a lambasting. This followed a philippic Murnane delivered a couple days earlier when he chastised Bill Dinneen, maintaining, "William Dinneen's poor luck is caused considerably by his lack of control of himself when a level head is required." Boston has never been a haven for the faint-of-heart ballplayers, and in a slump, even the thick-skinned suffer. At this point of the season, Boston stood in fourth place, behind league-leading Chicago, followed by St. Louis and Philadelphia.

And then a streak of a different stripe began, and playing in Boston became sweet once again.

July 19—Cy Young shuts out leader Chicago as Buck Freeman hits a home run and Patsy Dougherty slugs home his team's other run with a triple;

July 21—Bill Dinneen pitches a strong game and everyone in the Boston order with the exception of Chick Stahl gets one hit;

July 22—Cy Young completes the sweep of Chicago, with Patsy Dougherty banging out three of his team's seven hits;

July 23—Bill Dinneen emerges from having pitched two days earlier to win the first game of the series against St. Louis by a score of 3–2. He pitches all 13 innings as slick-fielding Hobe Ferris scooped every ball in his direction. To ease the wear on their pitchers, the Bostons acquire Tully Sparks;

July 24—Cy Young returns from short rest to survive a rally in the ninth to win a 4–3 game, made possible also by some clutch hitting by Jimmy Collins and fine fielding by keystone combination Freddy Parent and Hobe Ferris;

July 25—On Ladies Day, Tully Sparks wins his debut with Boston as Chick Stahl thrills the crowd and presumably causes his legion of female admirers to swoon with his acrobatic catch in the outfield;

July 26—Opening a series against Detroit, Bill Dinneen continues his recent mastery over opposing batters while Candy LaChance legs out two hits and receives rare kudos for his work at first base;

July 28—Cy Young wins his 22nd game of the season with the assistance of Candy Lachance and Chick Stahl, each of whom connect for three hits in support.

With the streak at eight wins, Boston vaulted two spots in the league standings, hovering behind only last year's champion Chicago team by a thin .01 percent. The Bostons finally lose on July 29 by a score of 6–5, behind the pitching of sore-armed Hughes and newcomer Sparks.

The recent surge in the team's fortunes did not escape the notice of the larger world of baseball and the eyes of former Boston Beaneater manager Frank Selee in particular. With the Chicago Nationals, Selee assembled a team that will establish "the Cubs" as the predominant team in baseball, and during a working vacation he decided to visit his former charges Jimmy Collins and Chick Stahl in Boston (figuring if he could get Collins, he could get Stahl) in a bid to lure the stars away from their team. The move proved unsuccessful, and even makes Collins crack a bit of a smile. Selee earned his reputation as a keen judge of talent and an easy man to play for, but Collins was calling the shots. Perhaps Collins also had not forgotten playing on some Selee-led teams that were not altogether hospitable for Catholic players like himself. The offer was politely declined.

In their *Red Sox Century*, Glenn Stout and Richard A. Johnson correctly identify the Ides of September, when Boston faced a double-header against league-leader Philadelphia as the key day of the season. Anticipating success, sixteen thousand cranks ventured out to the Huntington Grounds for the festivities, a huge outpouring of support for that era.

As was their custom, the hazy team ownership did not plan for such large crowds and thousands of adventurous fans took the liberty of upgrading from their 25-cent bleacher seats to the pavilion. Between the two games, the fans roamed the field and were within a few feet of first and third base and encroached on the outfielders' domain. As a result, "the whole thing was turned into a joke." The *Boston Post* less charitably characterized the episode, claiming that "the crowd scattered about the diamond like a swarm of locusts...."

Dinneen lost the first game to Eddie Plank, which was no disgrace since Plank won 20 games that year and 326 over his career. And yet the game did not hinge on losing to the better man that day. Hobe Ferris embarrassingly let in four of the six runs against his team by his inept fielding after he originally arrived to work late. One run came in when he threw way off the mark to catcher Lou Criger,

Scrappy second baseman Hobe Ferris complemented the other side of the Boston Americans' keystone combo, providing grit where Freddy Parent exemplified a more gentlemanly approach to the game. Parent kept a respectful distance from his mate, who later kicked a teammate in the face. Boston Public Library, Print Department, McGreevy Collection.

while he later booted a ground ball hit to him and threw to the wrong base. Ferris did not begin to rein in his errors until he had also interfered with a throw, as his team lost the first game, 6–4.

The second game pitted future Hall of Famers Cy Young against Rube Waddell. The usually stalwart Young coughed it up badly in the fifth inning when six runs crossed the plate for Philadelphia, while Waddell allowed only two runs for the entire conflict. Despite the rout, heroic Chick Stahl ran into the crowd and made a brilliant catch and then pegged a throw to an ailing Jimmy Collins to double up the A's, but to no avail. Had the Bostons won both games, they would have been one game behind Philadelphia; by losing both, they now stood five games back. The umpire mercifully called off the slaughter in the eighth inning to let Connie Mack's men catch a train home.

Gallingly, while Ban Johnson fed Philly with Boston's pitchers, George Winter, expected to build upon his impressive 16–12 rookie mark, regressed as he suffered from some type of whispered physical malady and struggled to a 11–9 record, a trend that increasingly marred his ensuing efforts.

Sadness blended with sweetness that September when Boston finally signed a promising young left-hander named Nick Altrock, who through the 1904–1906 seasons won 19, 23 and 20 games, respectively. Altrock did not do much for his new club in 1902, but he proceeded to embark on one of the most colorful careers in baseball history. Quite possibly, at this stage of his life Altrock drank too much, which when combined with his cock-eyed disposition produced a synergistic reaction that seemed to irritate the staid Jimmy Collins. Collins did not mind drinkers—no one outdrank Cy Young, for example—but he did expect his players to take a sober approach to their duties on the field, a task the naturally outgoing and clownish Altrock could only suppress temporarily at best.

The Philadelphia Americans, thanks to the infusion of pitchers from the Hub, won the American League race, followed by St. Louis (the previous year's Milwaukee Brewers), with Boston in third. The usual post-mortems came in with one paper squaring the blame on LaChance and Ferris. The *Sporting News* seconded this emotion, suggesting that "... Lachance and Ferris are now very unpopular in this proper and staid city."

The *Sporting Life* attributed Boston's fall to (1) "lack of teamwork," (2) "the idleness of pitcher Winters," and (3) "the occasional disability of such players as Stahl." A week later they supplemented this analysis by also citing the injuries to Collins and Dougherty being key, along with Long Tom Hughes being "practically useless" until the final games of the year.

The sportswriters definitely took a glass half-empty approach to the 1902 Boston Americans campaign. Cy Young posted a circuit-leading 32–11 record while also pacing all pitchers in games started, games pitched, innings pitched and complete games. Bill Dinneen proved the model of consistency with a 21–21 record, but he had also pitched 60 more innings than the previous season and needed a rest. George Winter did not pitch at all at the end of the year, but did pitch in luck earlier, while Long Tom Hughes pitched effectively in a few contests at the end.

Patsy Dougherty batted .342 in the league while Jimmy Collins batted .322 and Chick Stahl .323. These three stars had led the club in batting, although all of them had been sidelined with injuries or had played hurt through long stretches of the year. Buck Freeman led the league in runs batted in and ensconced himself in the top five in hits, doubles, triples and home runs. Whereas the team had made several moves in the field in the off-season before the 1902 campaign, with the exception of procuring a couple of utility players, the team returned the same players for the 1903 season.

With one qualification. Although few off-seasons moves occurred, Big Bill Dinneen went home to Syracuse, and sometime before spring training of 1903, he matured and emerged as a superstar.

4

Jimmy Collins
Cracks a Smile

A swell of optimism greeted the Boston Americans' chances in 1903, an odd sentiment perhaps for a team that finished in third place the year before and had made no changes in its starting infielders, outfielders or catchers. While historian Bill Nowlin has convincingly proven that before the adoption of the Red Sox moniker by the team in 1907, the Boston Americans had no nickname, a fan in April of 1903 suggested that they be called the "Standpats" due to their apparent off-season unwillingness to unload their starting fielders.

This complaint is not entirely fair. Attempts were made to unload first baseman Candy Lachance, replacing him with Wid Conroy, a light-hitting chap who during the course of his career played every position in the field except pitcher and catcher. And the Bostons did entertain an offer for Hobe Ferris in exchange for a generic player named Williams, but they did not close on that deal either.

The team enjoyed training in Macon. The town prided itself on its many theatrical shows and even brought a circus to town. More importantly, a five lane bowling alley beckoned the healthy young baseballists, as it was "extensively patronized by the ladies...." By way of a brief digression, a favorite part of our national pastime is attempting to read between the lines concerning the social lives and proclivities of dead ball era players.

Certainly, some players who had contracted a sexually transmitted disease and thus became disabled often had scribes describe their condition as suffering from malaria. George Winter seemed to suffer from malaria for long spells. Although the term often popped up, it is impossible today to determine in most cases the true nature of a player's malady. Maybe Winter did carry malaria.

On a deeper note, a temptation exists in the absence of hard facts to suppose that virtually every ballplayer at the turn of the last century spent all of his free time at whorehouses; the proof simply does not appear to support this assumption. Baseball players were celebrities in the early 1900s just as they are today, and to suggest that they invariably cavorted with prostitutes presupposes that they did not have a number of women seeking their company more as camp followers. In crass terms, why would a ballplayer have to pay for sex when ample opportunities existed for free gratification?

Of much more importance to the team, ownership had finally coalesced around Milwaukee lawyer Henry Killilea. Cleveland's Charles Somers had made an American League franchise possible at the Huntington Grounds, but he had too many ties to other clubs. The Boston Americans needed an owner dedicated to the advancement of that club alone. It helped too that Killilea and Collins got along well together, and Killilea did not limit his skipper monetarily to procure talent.

Killilea also assigned an energetic business manager named Joseph Smart to improve the physical plant at the Huntington Grounds. Smart went right to work, hiring local artisans to install new right-field fences, a new grandstand ticket office, a new bleacher entrance, and a coat of paint to the park

Traditionally, Boston's American League rooters have expressed their devotion for their club quite often in manifestations resembling religious fervor. In further blurring the distinction between church and club, on March 22, Captain Collins led a half-dozen of his charges into a High Mass at the "cathedral" in Macon, Georgia, a group that likely included Chick Stahl, Freddy Parent, Buck Freeman, Candy Lachance, Duke Farrell and Bill Dinneen. On that

Safely ensconced with the Boston Americans, Big Bill Dinneen plotted out a path to even greater success than he had already achieved with the Boston Beaneaters, and he achieved all of his goals in the next three years. Library of Congress.

same date, a much more important baseball development occurred, little noted at the time, in which the team owner let Collins determine whether to keep bench player Harry Gleason or pawn him off to Chicago.

What the move indicated is that like Somers, Killilea had decided to act as an absentee magnate, permitting a trusted baseball man like Collins to make the personnel decisions, a role the manager relished. With a later owner who thought he knew it all, Collins chafed under the arrangement. But as the de facto CEO of the franchise, he flourished as he went about building the finest ball club in the world. As for Killilea, he hardly merited a passing infrequent reference in the press for the duration of the regular campaign while he went about tending to his flourishing Milwaukee law practice and other concerns. Sadly for Harry Gleason, Killilea probably had no inkling of who he was.

Eschewing seismic shifts in personnel, the team nevertheless did bring in as a reserve catcher the legendary Charley Farrell, a popular local figure who once played for the pennant-winning Boston Beaneaters in 1891. A native of the town of Marlboro in central Massachusetts, he early in his career earned the nickname "the Duke of Marlborough." Like Candy Lachance, he sported a now-unfashionable mustache, and came into camp at Macon, Georgia, "with his expansive front and his wider smile...." In a week, Manager Collins and his training regimen trimmed fourteen pounds off the popular rotund receiver, with the Duke vowing to walk off at least another sixteen pounds.

In other utility news, the club kept Harry Gleason in limbo while it tried out John O'Brien and George Stone as infield/outfield backups. In fact, O'Brien, Stone and a player from Baltimore named Jones auditioned in spring training along with Candy Lachance for the first baseman's position, indicating Collins' dissatisfaction with Buck Freeman's fielding there the previous season and a determination to make this position a priority. Catcher Warner jumped to New York, and no one missed his surliness.

Having scarcely tinkered with the fielders and hitters, the Bostons' management continued to rely on pitchers Cy Young, Bill Dinneen and George Winter. Winter had nearly wasted away toward the end of the previous season, spending months in the hospital and at one point weighing 80 pounds. Yet he had shaken his malady and promised to come back strong in the new year.

Weakened Winter may have concerned some, but Long Tom Hughes had worked out his sore arm. In the spring exhibitions, Hughes had shown that he had made a remarkable recovery, and that Baltimore (which during the off-season had moved to New York) had made a mistake in giving up on him.

The pitchers all had their signature moments in 1903. Long Tom Hughes surprised many by becoming one of the finest pitchers in organized ball that year, the more so because supposedly his arm had died. It had become known too that he was a bit of a flake and somewhat hard to control, even for someone so even-tempered as Jimmy Collins.

Until Collins met future owner John I. Taylor, no one aggravated him so thoroughly as Long Tom Hughes. At 6'1", Tom Hughes was only "long" by the standards of the day, but he did possess a pirate's personality. With his talent, he should have left a legacy as one of the greatest pitchers to emerge from the first decades of the twentieth century; instead Tom Hughes almost always let his team down.

He was the type of fellow who early in his career probably calculated the amount of salary he might make if he stayed in training and dedicated himself to his profession and then how much he might make if he did not care at all, and decided that making a sustained effort at maintaining excellence was for suckers. For instance, in the middle of July 1908, the *Sporting Life* reported that Long Tom had married Annie Gantz, "one of Washington's exceedingly attractive ladies," a surprise to no one who knew the swashbuckling ballplayer and his love for attractive women.

What should have bothered everyone on his team, management and players included, is the fact that he staged a wedding in the middle of the season
and took some time off, a serious *faux pas* both then and a hundred years later.
Players always got married in the off-season, devoting their whole energies and
passions supposedly to the tasks at hand during the baseball campaign before
turning to personal matters during their hiatus.

A great story about Long Tom has him in the grill room of a Chicago
hotel in 1911, being heckled by a fellow patron, Edward Johnson, "a Chicago
artist." Johnson was giving Hughes a hard time about a recent poor outing on
the mound, in no way painting pretty pictures. Since dueling was no longer in
vogue, Long Tom challenged his tormentor to go outside and settle the matter like a man.

Johnson accepted the offer while popping off, "You're on…. If you can't
fight any better than you pitch, I'll win easily."

A referee was mutually agreed upon, Charles King, and the pugilists went
outside to an alley where they took off their "hats, coats and neckwear" and
started pummeling each other. Being idiots, Long Tom and Johnson "took a
severe drubbing and were bleeding freely when arrested" by the local police.

Johnson and the referee King spent the night in jail, but Hughes got off
with paying a $50 bail bond and then skipped bail, thereby extricating him-
self from another jam and letting the other guys suffer. This type of activity is
what Manager Jimmy Collins had to put up with in 1903.

Compared to his brother, Edward, who also pitched briefly for Boston,
Long Tom was a choirboy. Back in Chicago, Edward Hughes, a policeman who
may have been off-duty, one day chanced upon a huge ruckus involving Henry
McIntyre. McIntyre had just murdered four people and barricaded himself in
his home on Irving Street, as a cordon of policemen gathered around not
knowing what to do. Someone even suggested blasting the home with dyna-
mite.

Edward Hughes sized up the situation and calmly walked toward McIntyre's house, while his fellow policemen protested that he re-chart his course
of action. He did not listen, opening the door to the McIntyre manse and walking inside, at which time the multiple murderer fired his gun at the policeman
and missed. Not wishing to be an ungrateful guest, Hughes returned the favor
and then some, plugging McIntyre with two rounds from his service revolver.
Henry McIntyre died before Edward Hughes left the house to tell his fellow
policemen what had happened.

Coming from this type of fearless background, Long Tom Hughes scoffed
at the rules that restrained other ballplayers and, in part, contributed to their
successes, both with their bosses and in furtherance of personal and team baseball goals. His considerable talent kept him in the major leagues for thirteen
years, during which he lost more than 20 games on three occasions, settling
for a 132–174 lifetime record. We will never know if Long Tom had the poten-

tial to be the finest pitcher in the major leagues at the dawn of the twentieth century, but he had the most style by far.

Hughes got off to a perplexing start in the big leagues. Pitching for the Cubs in 1901, he won only ten and lost twenty-three games, but he also struck out 225 batters, which ranked third in the National League and remains one of the finest totals ever for a rookie. Hughes jumped to Baltimore the next year, and the Boston Americans purchased him in the middle of 1902 for the same reason they took chances on broken-down hurlers for years afterwards: the off chance they might catch lightning in a bottle.

In 1903, they achieved their goal. Hughes thrived in Boston, striking out fewer batters while allowing less opposing runners to score as his teammates supported him enough to win. One of his most significant victories occurred the day that he and Cy Young each shut out St. Louis in a double-header on June 28. He had already shut out St. Louis earlier in the month, in a game where Lou Criger caught runners "napping" off first and third bases and also threw out a runner stealing second. This time, more than 20,000 hostile fans spilled onto the field, with ropes restraining the cranks and hits landing in their area going as ground-rule doubles.

But if Hughes largely disappointed everyone, in 1903, he won nearly three out of every four decisions, dominating the American League with scant effort. That year, he could be Long Tom, get the girl, drink all night and still step onto the mound and make grown men shake their head in disgust.

Jimmy Collins might not have liked it or approved of the way his ace trained, but he tolerated the behavior so long as the victories kept coming.

If Hughes exemplified the dark, black Irish Catholic persona, Big Bill Dinneen personified the more sunny side of the coin. His name suggested something quite different, for his parents had named him after labor agitator Big Bill Haywood, one of the founders of the Wobblies Union (formally the Industrial Workers of the World), a man who probably murdered the former governor of Idaho and later moved to Russia, where he was lionized by the Communist leadership.

Standing 6'1", Dinneen loomed over many of his teammates and opponents, but rather than engaging in fisticuffs at the slightest provocation, a contemporary described him at this time as "a likeable Irishman, full of wit and enjoys a joke better than anything." Other than the physical stature, he bore little resemblance to Big Bill Haywood. He had a knack for making money in various capitalistic endeavors, and ten days after his career ended in 1909, he donned the umpire's gear and became one of the ultimate authorities in American society for the next few decades.

Before he became an arbiter, Dinneen had plagued the men in blue, one day arguing every single call against him even in the case of accurate calls, by legendary ump Tim Hurst. Hurst marched to the mound and told Dinneen that he knew Big Bill had a date and wanted to be thrown out, so Hurst told him he would not eject the pitcher under any circumstances. Hardly mollified, Dinneen loudly protested every ball that Hurst called thereafter.

Dinneen reportedly decided to retire as an umpire decades later after see-

ing the miserable state of major league pitching for too long. In one game, he grew so disgusted at the limp offerings of a Yankee hurler that he turned to catcher Bill Dickey and remarked, "I think I could go out there and do better myself, even at 60!" The story is apocryphal, as Dinneen umped for another three years until illness forced his retirement. Nevertheless, when he exited, he had earned the respect of all in organized ball for his fairness and even temper.

A third pitcher, Norwood Gibson, a product of the University of Notre Dame, possessed the matinee idol physical perfection admired by women and envied by men. Gibson had pitched and matriculated at Notre Dame for five years, earning a few non-amateur dollars at the "summer resorts throughout New York." Upon graduation he spent some time pitching for Indianapolis, and seems to have played on the Cincinnati club for a brief period before catching on with a minor league team in Kansas City.

Long Tom Hughes, with the Washington club, late in his largely disappointing career. His brother Ed played with the Boston Americans briefly and once calmly walked into the barricaded home of a four-time murderer and shot him dead. Library of Congress.

At one point he came under the tutelage of former Boston Beaneater pitching great and future Hall of Famer Kid Nichols. The *Herald* reported that "his work with Nichols was very fast," which may infer that the Kid taught young Norwood a new pitch, perhaps the spitter. In any event, he became a highly coveted player by 1902, and perhaps on the recommendation of Chick Stahl, who was familiar with nearby Notre Dame (he even coached there at one time), the Boston Americans snapped him up.

By early 1905, around the time the spitball he employed began ruining his arm, he still stood out, as one reporter remembered:

> Collins and Gibson are the beauties of the team, without doubt and they can play ball, too. Next to Collins, in point of physical fitness and in favor with the crowd is Gibson the pitcher. Brown as an Indian, as are the others, fond of picturesque poses and moving like oiled machinery when he does move, that is Gibson.

The club's improvements to the grounds almost matched the beauty of their young pitcher, which proved fortuitous since the team hosted an all-time attendance record of 27,658 patrons at its opening double-header against the previous year's champions, the Philadelphia Athletics. Perhaps reflecting a new-found confidence in his young starter, Collins opened with Bill Dinneen on the mound and was rewarded with a 9–4 victory in the morning game. Before the 1903 season, major league baseball introduced the two-strike rule for the first two foul balls, and Dinneen amongst his peers seems to have benefited the most by this new edict because it dramatically reduced his pitch count.

In the afternoon contest, Cy Young did not fare so well, getting hammered, 10–7. Fortunately for his team, it proved a momentary lapse in his abilities and otherwise did not herald a diminution in his considerable skills. The old farmer still had a lot to give. Owing to the perception of Lou Criger's tenderness and to the appreciation of the offense that their new acquisition could bring to the plate, Duke Farrell started both games at catcher.

Farrell, already a popular player, threw out five potential Athletic base stealers, and he also belted out three hits. In the second game, the Royal Rooters stopped play to present the Duke with a diamond ring, and to show his appreciation, the affable catcher rapped out another hit. He seemed a perfect fit.

Unfortunately, despite a great start (hitting over .500), the Duke of Marlborough was injured on April 27 while sliding into second base in a game against Washington, causing his removal from the lineup. Walking on crutches, the injured star bemoaned his fate at a ballgame he attended as a spectator, musing, "I never was so well satisfied with a berth, and never so disappointed, as I was anxious to play with Jimmy Collins right here among my best friends."

Caught virtually unprepared, the club had to order backup Lou Criger, who had suffered from some malady since spring training, out of his street clothes and into a uniform as the crowd patiently waited for action to resume. Jacob Morse solemnly proclaimed that in the case of Farrell, "It is a loss they cannot possibly replace," a sentiment seconded by Tim Murnane. Lacking a viable alternative, Jimmy Collins called upon Lou Criger to take over the catching chores as a full-time starter.

Everyone underestimated Lou Criger, a fellow who resembled a skinny version of Wally Cleaver from the television program, *Leave it to Beaver*. He also had the misfortune of being one of the few hypochondriacs in history whose every worry and fear proved to be justified, with positive tests backing up every lament. The more he labored under physical disability and discomfort, the better he seemed to perform, a trend borne out by his performance in 1903.

A contemporary named Louis Heibroner remembered how Criger, a natural fighter, ran his hands through his hair when upset, and when all of his hairs stood up, he began throwing punches at people. He was almost always out to prove his thin frame belied a wiry toughness: "Many players tackled Criger because he looked like a weakling. Criger would fight any six men on earth in those days, and if someone didn't pull them apart too soon, Lou would lick all six by sheer perseverance."

In the end, Criger took control of the position, so much so that by June 15, the *Globe* ran a picture of him with the simple comment, "A Great Back Stop." Had Criger not risen to the occasion, it is difficult to see how the Bostons could have achieved the level of success they did in '03, particularly with generally unreliable pitchers like Hughes, or youngsters like Gibson and Winter, all of whom needed a strong backstop when their turn came up in the rotation. Criger filled the breech.

To buttress the catching corps, the Boston Americans signed "Broadway Aleck" Smith, who despite his nifty nickname had never proven himself ready for primetime. The club also outbid the Chicago Cubs and Frank Selee for University of Illinois star Garland "Jake" Stahl, no relation to Chick Stahl and, ultimately, no major league catcher either.

Deficiencies as a receiver did not deter Jake Stahl from becoming one of the most prominent figures in the early history of the franchise, but for years Boston either seemed intent at getting rid of him or wanting him back after they hastily disposed of his services. League interference through the person of Ban Johnson may have played a role in the outwardly mixed emotions the team had for the player, but for years the club yanked around this estimable athlete and gentleman.

Hailing from Elkhart, Illinois, Garland "Jake" Stahl has often been listed mistakenly as an Elkhart, Indiana, native and has at times been referred to as one of Chick Stahl's brothers. While Chick Stahl came from a large family of more than twenty siblings, Jake Stahl was one of the few people from the era and general area who was not one of them. Unlike Chick, Jake Stahl went to college at the University of Illinois, where he starred not only in baseball, but also for the Illini's varsity football team as a left guard. Befitting his status as an interior lineman, Jake was large for the turn of the century at 6'2" and approaching 200 pounds in weight. Long-time athletic department head George Huff always complimented Stahl as the best baseball player Illinois ever produced.

At Illinois, Jake did not stand out as a "colorful [person but was] well liked on campus. He was a somewhat retiring member of Sigma Chi...." At school, Jake fell in love with a classmate named Jean Mahan, whose name has been spelled about a half-dozen different ways, and whose father was a president of a prosperous Chicago bank. They wed in her father's vacation home in Pasadena, California, and Jake intermittently returned to banking. He graduated from Illinois in 1903 and pursued the trade of the ballplayer, with the fallback of a lucrative banking position there at all times.

Having reinforced the catching corps, the Bostons saw Chick Stahl become injured in mid–May, under mysterious circumstances, after batting 4-for-5 in a game against Cleveland. The next day he could not play, replaced by sub Jack

O'Brien, who stunk, upon which the club dropped from third to fourth in the league standings. On May 28, Stahl left the team to attend his father's funeral, with no hint concerning when he might return to the lineup, due to a "sore stomach." The loss of the star center fielder could have proved fatal, and yet in contrast to the previous year's squad, the 1903 edition seemed to handle adversity as a challenge to overcome rather than an excuse for non-perform-ance.

The Bostons completed an eleven-game winning streak by the first week of June and after the tenth game, Joe Smart felt so giddy about the team's per-formance that he ordered Jimmy Collins to buy each player a new set of shoes. Everyone pitched in during this skein, most notably Buck Freeman, who socked three timely homers to help sweep New York, and Captain Collins, who raised his average in one week by nearly 60 points.

Young Norwood Gibson exemplified the advantages of a deep pitching staff in late June when he and his teammates stood poised behind the reign-ing champion Athletics in the standings. On June 20, Gibby started in lieu of Cy Young, who had not rejoined the team after attending his mother's funeral. The young Fighting Irish hurler pitched all ten innings to hold off Napoleon Lajoie's squad, causing an uncharacteristically ebullient Jimmy Collins to exclaim, "I've killed the hoodoo [i.e., curse].... I believe that we will be at the top of the heap within a week." Collins prophesied correctly, for a week later Gibson started against St. Louis and shut them out, after which Boston led Philly by two games in the win column and three in the loss column.

An early August home-and-away series against Philadelphia emphasized the dominance that Collins' men had over their nearest competition when time came for a showdown. Collins could not take credit for the victory in the first game at Philly on August 5, because in the first inning the umpire ejected him from the game for arguing after being thrown out at second base. Serv-ing as a useless accelerant on the bench, Long Tom Hughes also got tossed for using offensive language while screaming at the umpire. No matter, Big Bill Dinneen pitched a shutout to take the first game. Afterward, the sharpest gam-blers began to place the big money on the Athletics, a harbinger of the likely outcome of the next contest.

The next day, the savvy gamblers won as Chief Bender turned the tables on Cy Young by a 4–3 score, to pull the Athletics within three games of league-leader Boston in the loss column. Collins and some of his men put up an unholy kick as the umpire called the game, but it did not change the decision or the ultimate outcome.

Unchastened after being tossed from the first game of the series, Long Tom Hughes defeated Ed Plank as Freddy Parent, Patsy Dougherty and Collins hit everything in sight to lead the team to a win in the rubber match, 11–3. McGeehan relieved Plank, but the offerings of the A's reliever, described as emanating from a "peculiar 'spiral' delivery," did nothing to cool the Bostons' bats as the slaughter continued. In derogation of team spirit and togetherness, eccentric A's pitcher Rube Waddell disappeared for the entire contest.

Both teams then boarded the same 8:05 P.M. train from Philadelphia to Boston to play three games at the Huntington Grounds. Once in the Hub, 14,000 rooters wearing bowler and boater hats cheered on their team to an easy victory as the Bostons scored eight runs in the second inning to win going away, 11–6.

Rube Waddell again vanished, and after he was found, he sat on the Bostons side of the field as a spectator. With Ed Plank pitching, Connie Mack predicted an A's victory to Ban Johnson, but Cy Young avenged his loss in Philadelphia and led his men to a 7–2 rout. Ban Johnson magnanimously expressed his positive feeling for Boston capturing the league flag.

Like a dog hunched with its tail between its legs, Waddell returned to his team but lost, 5–1, as Boston trotted out Hughes, a pitcher only slightly less crazy than Rube, to win the final game of the homestand. Mack's men now stood seven games out of first place in the loss column as the *Globe* noted matter of factly, "It looks like one more pennant for Boston." Hughes rose to the occasion despite not having his fastball, relying instead on his wonderful slow curves to pull himself through and cast the Athletics well behind his team in the race.

Having disposed of the Athletics, the Boston Americans coasted to the pennant. Cy Young led the circuit with twenty-eight wins and also outstripped the competition in innings pitched and winning percentage. Big Bill Dinneen and Long Tom Hughes followed with 21 and 20 wins, respectively. Norwood Gibson spitballed his way to 13 victories, with hard-luck George Winter whittling out a 9–8 mark.

All-world left fielder Patsy Dougherty batted .331 and scored more runs and made more hits than anyone. Buck Freeman led the league in home runs and runs batted in, and Chick Stahl batted .274 in limited duty due to injuries. Captain Jimmy Collins hit .296 and Parent batted .304. Candy Lachance and Hobe Ferris failed to hit much, but Ferris always excelled in the field. Having Lachance at first base instead of Buck Freeman as expected resulted in marked improvement defensively.

Holding it all together was catcher Lou Criger, who had been supplanted as the starter by the popular Duke Farrell, but by necessity stepped up to reliably guide the pitching staff and keep opposing base-runners honest. He did not hit either, but his defense made him the most coveted catcher in baseball that year. With the season winding down, the Bostons relished their quest to the pennant, with the possibility of a surprise after that.

The two leagues had spent 1901–1902 trying to extinguish each other, but with peace came shared financial opportunity. Certainly Killilea could not care less about previous hard feelings and did not even seem that engaged with the actual ownership of a ball club. For the first time ever it appeared that a World

Series was a real possibility, mainly because of the ecumenical impulses of Pittsburgh owner Barney Dreyfuss, who consciously decided not to take the league wars of 1901–02 personally, a sentiment shared by Killilea, to the extent he cared little about the issue one way or another.

Dreyfuss also owned a juggernaut in the National League, with the Pirates having won the last three pennants. Although the club had suffered in the league wars with stars like Jesse Tannehill and Jack Chesbro ignoring their contracts, management shrewdly restocked their club, so much so that the Pirates looked upon Boston as a relatively easy mark. With only positive reasons for instituting a post-season tournament, and few if any negatives, the leagues temporarily made peace and a post-season tournament was arranged between the perennial National League powerhouse Pirates against the upstart Boston Americans.

5

Tessie Wins a World Series for Boston

Before the first World Series in 1903, what at the time passed for organized baseball had staged various post-season tournaments, the most notable of which was the Temple Cup, which pitted the top two teams in the National League in mortal combat. The Temple Cup never took root. Many observers believed it cheapened the accomplishments of the team that won the regular season pennant, and there was an almost total lack of interest exhibited by its participants. The fans were not thrilled about the concept either, and after 1897, the Temple Cup disappeared forever.

At the conclusion of the 1903 season, there was little reason to believe that a World Series would prove even as enduring at the Temple Cup, and indeed, no 1904 Series was held. Still, an uneasy peace between the leagues had reigned in 1903, and Pittsburgh's remarkable owner, Barney Dreyfuss, expressed enough charity and faith in his fellow magnates to make the first games a reality.

Unlike the revolving-door ownership of the Boston Americans at the turn of the century, the Pirates enjoyed stable ownership from 1900 through February 5, 1931, when Dreyfuss passed. Elected to the Baseball Hall of Fame in 2007, much too late, this generous spirit loved his team and made it a permanent Pittsburgh institution.

Less generous, Boston owner Killilea tried to pay his players a relative pittance, but since their contracts expired at the end of September, they threatened a strike and also discussed striking out on an exhibition series of their own. Killilea blinked—he could do little else—but he engendered much ill will from his players during the negotiations.

With the labor issues settled, the Pirates fielded a most impressive squad, having won three straight National League pennants. Any discussion of the team in this era begins, but does not end, with its all-time shortstop, Honus Wagner. He was born John Peter Wagner in what is now Carnegie, Pennsylvania, in 1874. Photographs taken of Wagner during his playing days somehow portray him as a short and squat ballplayer when in fact he stood at a then very tall 5'11" with a weight hovering around 200 pounds—more a Cal Ripken type of body than a Luis Aparicio model.

Too much focus has also been placed on Wagner's batting statistics without emphasizing what a terrific athlete and quick fielder he was. Having stated that, the man did win eight batting titles, retiring with a .328 batting average. His 723 steals rank 10th all-time almost a century after he stopped playing.

While Wagner fell off the wagon later in life, as a young man he abstained from alcohol and tobacco. His aversion to the latter temptation reached such a degree that he demanded a tobacco company to cease and desist using his image on one of its baseball cards, making his rare surviving card one of the most valuable commodities in sports collecting history. A devout Catholic, Wagner died in Carnegie, Pennsylvania, after living a very full 81 years.

If Wagner exemplified the class of Pittsburgh, player-manager Fred Clarke demonstrated its sass. Elected to the baseball Hall of Fame in 1945, he, like Wagner, had a brother who also played briefly in the major leagues. The resemblances ceased there, as the smaller Clarke liked to boast and trash-talk all of the time. He fielded his outfield position well, could draw a walk, stole a bunch of bases and more often than not hit over .300. Dreyfuss, to his credit, perceived that Clarke's braggadocio sheltered his players from outside pressures and his leadership qualities outweighed his obnoxiousness.

Clarke rounded out his starting outfield with Ginger Beaumont and Jimmy Sebring. Joining Wagner in the infield were first baseman Kitty Bransfield (a native of Worcester in central Massachusetts), second baseman Claude Ritchey and third baseman Tommy Leach. Exemplifying the truism that almost every turn-of-the-century baseballist had a weird nickname, Ed "Yaller" Phelps caught. Pitcher Sammy Leever also had another nickname, "the Deacon," but it did not catch on that well because the true ace of the staff was Deacon Phillippe, one of the greatest Pirate pitchers of all-time. Had he played a bit more major league ball, Phillippe would have been a certain Hall of Famer.

Although Dreyfuss had promoted this post-season series, the team that had dominated the National League had succumbed to physical injury and mental illness, respectively, to two of its best pitchers, Sammy Leever and Ed Doheny. Nicknamed "the Goshen Schoolmaster," Leever had developed a bawky arm by season's end after posting a 25–7 record. Magnate Dreyfuss attributed Leever's sore arm to his failure to wear a sweater during a cold game against the Boston National League team late in the regular season.

Doheny's wounds were more deep-seated and intractable. On July 26, 1903, while the team was in Cincinnati, he became convinced detectives were following him and left the team to return home to Andover, Massachusetts. He briefly returned to his team, but by early September, he became a complete nervous wreck. On October 11, he utilized a nearby cast-iron stove leg to repeatedly strike on the head his psychiatric nurse, a gentleman named Oberlin Howarth. Howarth sustained a serious gash to his head, while the court committed Doheny to an insane asylum in Danvers, Massachusetts, leaving his wife, his young son and his brother (a Catholic priest) to wonder why it all went so wrong.

Despite this unfortunate episode, the games continued and the Pirates took a train to Boston for the commencement of the Series. The day before the first game, some of the Pirates sat around their hotel during the day, choosing only to venture into Beantown for an evening at the theatre. Led by Honus Wagner, many of his confederates defied the bunker mentality of their other teammates as they traveled across the Charles River to see a football game in which local collegians from Harvard defeated Bowdoin, 29–0.

While the Pirates gallivanted around Greater Boston, Jimmy Collins kept his men on the field practicing before the opening match. Perhaps he wanted to keep his players away from local gambling buddies, a group that had insinuated themselves ever deeper into the fabric of the game. Told that Collins tabbed him as Boston's starting pitcher, Cy Young deadpanned, "All right… I will try to be there." For his part, Fred Clarke proclaimed, "We are sure to win and I can't see the result any other way."

Undeterred by Clarke's guarantee, the fans came early and en masse to the game that day. The Roxbury Rooters carted in a gigantic ball and bat to mark their area behind first base. Perhaps in an attempt to draw more attention to themselves, they also waved tiny American flags while making noise with all types of obnoxious instruments.

Gambling did not provide a subtext in the first World Series game—it was the main story. Days before, such notorious gambling kingpins as Sport Sullivan and Charles Lavis made their rounds, gathering up suckers who chose to bet with these well-financed sharpies. Sullivan, of course, gained later infamy as one of the main conspirators behind the eight Chicago White Sox players throwing the 1919 World Series. But even at the turn of the century, Sport had more than a sporting interest in the National Pastime.

Lavis always found himself in trouble of one sort or another, and always scrambled out of it due to his fealty to the Boston Catholic Archdiocese and his friendship with local baseball legends and politicians. One of the principal Royal Rooters, Lavis found his sanctuary in church and his thrills in gambling parlors, a habit dating back to at least 1885.

In addition to Sullivan and Lavis, a number of lesser lights populated the Vendome Hotel, searching for pigeons from Pittsburgh willing to bet on their own team. A mysterious dapper gentleman scurried around the lobby of the Vendome looking for Pirate fans to bet with, allowing that he had $10,000 to gamble with. That description fit J.J. McNamara, who rubbed elbows with "Hubey" Curley, a Roxbury gambler who had $6,000 with which to wager. Stout and Johnson have concluded that this game was probably fixed so that Boston would lose.

The contest started off innocently enough with the first two Pirate batters flying out, once to Chick Stahl in center field and once to the catcher

Criger. Tommy Leach came to bat and with two strikes "tapped one of Young's straight ones past Freeman for three bases." Wagner singled home Leach, and when Wagner then attempted to steal second, it proved a simple task "as Criger was a bit slow and Ferris was very much surprised," giving Wagner the base without a fight.

The funny business persisted. Kitty Bransfield sent an easy grounder to Hobe Ferris, and "after evading several stabs, the ball rolled up Hobe's sleeve." Safe at first, Bransfield galloped to second base for a steal. "Criger, instead of whipping the ball in his usual fierce style, hesitated and then threw high out, into center field..." as Wagner trotted home and Bransfield reached third base. Next up, Claude Ritchey drew a walk, and when he attempted to steal second, Criger threw the ball to third base. Sebring then came to bat and singled home both Bransfield and Ritchey. The Pirate catcher struck out, which should have retired his team for the inning, but Criger let the ball go and Phelps ran to first base. The ninth man up in this farce, pitcher Deacon Phillippe, finally struck out.

One of the problems was that even when "money went begging" at 10–7 or even 10–6 odds in favor of Boston, few Pittsburghers or other speculators felt like laying down bets, a fact that quickly changed once the game began. After the first inning, gamblers picked up on the change of fortunes "and the odds quickly changed after the first inning." Clearly, "the too evident anxiety of the locals in the early stages of the contest literally threw away whatever chance the Bostons had to win."

Not that Hobe Ferris' play improved that much, as he muffed another ball directed at him in the fourth inning. But almost magically Cy Young settled down, and after the fourth, coughed up only one more run. Boston staged mini-rallies in the seventh and ninth, perhaps for appearances sake or to reflect the shift in the odds involving the gamblers in the stands, but to no avail as the team lost the first game, 7–3.

The thousands of dejected fans staggered as the game ended, and "when the curtain fell and the Boston team walked moodily from the field, poor Cy Young was the picture of disappointment and chagrin." The papers savaged the Boston Americans much worse than their opposition on the diamond did, as one rag noted that "Dougherty was completely at sea," while Manager Collins was "not seen at his best" and Lachance and Ferris "were almost as puppets...." One competing paper more charitably chronicled the shortcomings of starter Cy Young, commenting that "it's not often that Uncle Cyrus fails to land the money, even if he is a bit fat."

The *Boston Globe* insisted that "[b]oth teams played ball, without any attempt at funny business," a defensive and curious comment to make. Others did not share this certitude, as the *Boston Post* observed that "many around town last evening asked if Boston lost on purpose." The Pittsburgh papers did not subscribe to the conjecture that the game had been fixed, because their writers and subscribers believed in the superiority of the National League and their team in particular. Still, the *Pittsburgh Times* did leave the door a tad ajar by observing, "Ferris was manifestly nervous, but why Lou Criger should have become inoculated with the same disease is inexplicable."

In retrospect, the questions of those fans seem rhetorical. Ferris and Criger, in particular, two players not on the field for their hitting prowess, participated in plays that more accurately appear to not have been errors, but calculated attempts to hand Pittsburgh the first game. These men could not hit even if toiling on the level, and kept themselves in the majors by their sterling defensive credentials; to believe they made such hideously overstated errors strains credulity. It appears that more likely than not, the first World Series game ever was fixed.

As Lou Criger's file at the National Baseball Hall of Fame Library reveals, in a "secret affidavit" to Ban Johnson prepared much later, the Boston catcher admitted he had been approached and offered $12,000 to help throw the 1903 World Series. Criger did not own up to actually taking affirmative steps to effectuate the fix, but his confession, made many years after he retired, lends credence to the suspicions that at least in the first game of the first Series, Criger took a fall.

As if to perpetuate the city's misery, Charles E. Grant, a gent known primarily as being the last surviving grandchild of one of the participants of the Boston Tea Party, died. All in all, it was not a good day for Boston.

Pirates 7, Boston 3; Pittsburgh Leads Series, 1–0

With the hint of scandal attached to the first game, on October 2, the Boston Americans turned the tables on Pittsburgh behind the shutout pitching of Big Bill Dinneen. Unlike the day before, the skies were overcast and only about 10,000 fans attended, although about 50 Royal Rooters seated themselves behind first base, while one daring fan outside the park a quarter-mile away sat on top of his house to cheer for the home team. The defection of several thousand fans did not prove a hindrance as the crowd that did appear exercised their voices to a pitch louder than "horns, megaphones, whistles and clappers."

Patsy Dougherty created more noise by hitting the first pitch in Boston's half of the first inning to right field for a home run. Striding to the plate with "grim determination in his eye," Patsy walloped the first offering of the Pirates' weakened Sam Leever and "[t]he ball did not roll to the ropes (separating the fans standing in the outfield from the remaining field in play), but Dougherty, by the grandest sprinting and a desperate slide at the plate, scored a home run." The crowd erupted, "with everyone on his feet, cheering like mad" with each stride their hero took.

After Collins flied out, Chick Stahl hit a sharp drive to center field for a double, and with the fans still clapping and screaming, scored on Buck Freeman's hit to the same area of the outfield as Boston established a 2–0 lead in the first inning, a lead it never relinquished.

Clarke pulled Leever after just one inning, inserting as his replacement right-hander Bucky Veil, another Pennsylvania native. Veil compiled a modest 5–3 record in 1903, his rookie season, and walked almost twice as many batters as he struck out. But with a lame Leever and Ed Doheny still under psychiatric care, Clarke had little choice but to place his trust with the rookie. With the assistance of a fine double play combination of Honus Wagner and Claude Ritchey behind him, the Pirates' reliever calmed the situation, and with the exception of one *faux pas* later in the game, managed to pitch quite well, giving his team every chance of narrowing the deficit as the game progressed.

Undoubtedly, Dougherty heard the rumors of suspicious performances by his team the day before, or at best, insults concerning his team's inept efforts, and he had every reason to want to squelch such talk. Most of the gamblers who lost heavily the day before took heart since it looked like they might even their losses with a hometown victory. Later, in the sixth inning, Dougherty came up "smiting," as one fan yelled out to him, "Put up your bat, are you posing?" Patsy lifted Veil's pitch out of the park, this time hitting it just over the left-field fence, marking only the second time a batter had ever pushed a ball out in that section of the Huntington Grounds.

Boston's bettors made up for their losses from the day before as Pittsburgh owner Dreyfuss allegedly took a beating by betting on his boys. The eventual 3–0 victory did not begin to tell the story of Boston's dominance as its hitters rapped out eight hits to the Pirates' three. Poor Veil pitched in only four and two-thirds innings for the rest of his career after the 1903 World Series. For his part, Big Bill Dinneen hurled a shutout, and for the Boston faithful, life made sense once again.

Boston 3, Pirates 0; Series Tied, 1–1

The next day nearly 19,000 fans paid to attend the third game of the Series, with scalpers gouging their customers with prices as staggering as 75 cents a ticket! Meanwhile, thousands of other stalwarts climbed over the fences to view the action. Not only did the attendance set a record at the fairly new Huntington Grounds, but it rivaled only an 1884 ballgame for the largest gate in the city's history. Among the attendees who actually recalled baseball in Boston almost twenty years earlier was Hall of Famer and retired local legend George Wright, who may have been at the '84 contest.

Not all patrons and gate crashers acted as dignified as Wright. More than an hour before game time, the team halted further ticket sales, but by that time anarchy reigned. The crowd overflowed from the stands and went past any restraining ropes in the outfield. They leaked right onto the diamond, as fans mingled with their idols.

The *Boston Morning Journal* reported that "the police were particularly helpless...." Desperate times required a temporary return of chivalry, as "[a] number of ladies were caught in the crush, but big Jake Stahl played the gallant and conducted them to safety." Not to be outdone in the knightly deportment department, Chick Stahl heard the screams of two women crushed in the bleachers and he and one of the Pirates "distinguished themselves by wedging their way through the crowd and rescuing the helpless women." While the fairer sex awaited rescue, "A little fellow on crutches moved about in the dense throng and seemed to bear a charmed life."

At least a hundred police along with the grounds staff tried repeatedly to push the crowd back. The policemen pulled out their clubs and temporarily pushed back a section of the crowd, only to see their efforts wasted as the fans returned to the diamond once the crisis passed. Punches were thrown. Finally, Officer Louis Brown emerged from a clubhouse with a long rubber hose that his cohorts used as both a rope and a club to disperse the masses, who finally relented and returned to a reasonable distance from the diamond.

As the police restored control, the fans still encroached on much of the outfield territory, a detriment to the Bostons' starter that day, Long Tom Hughes, whose "curved pitching style generally results in high flies...." So many fans crowded into the outfield that the game itself was played almost entirely on the infield. The Pirates took little time to take advantage of Hughes and his surprisingly ineffective pitches.

Large games magnify the strengths and weaknesses of professionals, and likewise can dramatically alter the perceptions that fans or management might have for a player. Hughes punctuated this point. Collins sensed immediately that Long Tom Hughes did not possess the willingness to bear down and control the opposition, so he called upon Cy Young to relieve. Hughes' personality did not cause him many problems when he won, but in defeat, Collins saw latent faults in this pitcher not readily apparent in the regular season, and he never allowed Long Tom Hughes to pitch for his team again.

This development shocked Young, who had been assisting the team with ticket sales and was not even dressed in his uniform. As Young hastily prepared to enter the game, Collins had no choice but to permit Hughes to continue throwing the ball to the Pirate batters, a feat he performed with increasing incompetence. He gave up a run in the second and walked Beaumont in the third, when Fred Clarke drove a double into the fans to score Beaumount.

The crowds ensured victory for Pittsburgh as the Pirate batters lofted lazy fly balls, normally certain outs, into the ranks of the Boston rooters and beyond the reach of the Boston fielders. Chick Stahl and Patsy Dougherty stood helpless as they saw routine catches enveloped by the crowd. Problem

Boston American fans took over the Huntington Grounds during the 1903 World Series. The fans' zealotry and encroachment on the field of play probably cost their club at least one game in the Series. Boston Public Library, Print Department, McGreevy Collection.

was, Deacon Phillippe, pitching for Pittsburgh, faced the same obstacles and prospered.

Finally, the great Cy Young emerged from the dressing room to quell the rally, and like Bucky Veil did the day before, kept his team in the game. By the end of the third, though, Boston trailed, 3–0. Deacon Phillippe needed no more support as the Pirates cruised to a 4–2 victory and a lead in the Series again.

Pirates 4, Boston 2; Pittsburgh Leads Series, 2–1

Having seen Boston largely squander its home-field advantage in the first three games at the Huntington Grounds to fall behind two games to one, a determined gaggle of Royal Rooters prepared to leave by train with the team for Game Four in Pittsburgh. In previous games, their vivacity had not had as much of an effect, with gamblers splitting loyalties in the first game and an avalanche of fans drowning out everything and anybody in the third game. But now things had to change.

Initially, though, the Rooters did not tip the balance enough for their idols to win on the road. The grass was wet and slippery on October 6, as Pittsburgh won again, this time at their home park, by a 5–4 margin over Boston and Bill Dinneen, to take a 3–1 advantage in the Series.

The Royal Rooters' Nuf Ced McGreevy jumped on top of his team's dugout in the fifth inning to lead the band and the team on to rally. "It was the Boston rooter's first real chance to unbottle their enthusiasm, and they cut loose in royal style, Mike McGreevy doing a dance on the roof over the Boston players' bench, amid a megaphone pandemonium." The hoopla proved of no avail in the end as Boston only eked out one run that inning.

In the seventh, Phillippe, Beaumont and Honus Wagner all singled and Tommy Leach cleared the bases with a triple to guide the Pirates to a 5–1 lead. Boston answered in the ninth off a very tired Phillippe with three runs, one run too little, as Pittsburgh now led the Series three games to one. An ecstatic Iron City crowd circled Phillippe, carried him over to the clubhouse and did not let him be until he shook everyone's hand, a task that took him a half-hour to fully accomplish.

Pirates 5, Boston 4; Pittsburgh Leads Series, 3–1

Boston roared back in Game 5 with an 11–2 pasting of Pirates pitchers Brickyard Kennedy and Thompson. Cy Young started and scattered six hits as his own men answered with fourteen hits of their own. An under-the-weather Jimmy Collins displayed his contempt for Long Tom Hughes by prohibiting his pitcher from suiting up for the game. Back in the Hub, a special wire to Miah Murray's poolroom kept the folks at home with up-to-the-minute action.

As Barnes noted for the *Journal:*

> The Boston rooters also had their inning today, and they were really a feature of the game. They never lost their sand, were always in evidence, with their cheers and their singing, and their gameness was often applauded before everything came their way in the sixth inning. They made a hit with the spectators by singing "Tessie" to brass band accompaniment before the game began, and were a part of the attraction in the day's sport, only second to the players on the field. They created quite a hit by placing a pickanniny in the foreground holding a horseshoe for luck.

Parenthetically, the version of "Tessie" sung in 1903 resembled little the rousing and tuneful remake by the Dropkick Murphys 101 years later. The original was the aural equivalent of fingernails across the blackboard, and with playful lyrics substituted to poke fun at the Pirates' starters, it irritated opponents, a fact that the Pirates themselves acknowledged.

Ah, the sixth inning. Kennedy had pitched shutout ball until then, but his fielders choked. Big mouth Clarke dropped Chick Stahl's fly ball and after Freeman singled, Parent hit a ball right at Leach, who "threw like a flash" to Wagner, covering third, who dropped it to load the bases. At this point the Royal Rooters were out of their minds, making massive amounts of offensive noise.

Unnerved, Kennedy threw his pitches high to Candy Lachance, who walked to first, scoring Stahl.

Hobe Ferris then hit an easy grounder to Honus Wagner, who again lost his head by trying "to make a clever play with a backhand toss to third, but as Leach was not there the ball rolled toward the crowd and Freeman and Parent scored." The rout was on, a task made even more amazing as Cy Young tripled off his adversary, setting off the Rooters again into apoplexy.

Strangely, Clarke kept Kennedy in during the seventh, at which point Boston scored another four runs. Thompson mercifully relieved in the eighth and only surrendered a run in the next two innings, but the humiliation was by then complete. Leaving Exposition Park, parade marshals McGreevy, Charles Lavis, Hubey Curley and Jack Keenan led the Rooters through the streets of Pittsburgh with their booming German brass band in military formation, as "[e]very man had has badge on and carried red, white and blue canes, also red, white and blue parasols." Fred Clarke and Barney Dreyfuss did not appreciate it yet, but despite their team still leading the Series by three games to two, they had just been mathematically eliminated.

Boston 11, Pirates 2; Pittsburgh Leads Series, 3–2

Sore-armed Sam Leever went back to pitch the sixth game of the World Series, and like his teammate Kennedy the day before, pitched well in spots and not so well at other times. In the third, Boston drew first blood when with two outs, Big Bill Dinneen swatted a grounder to Wagner that the big shortstop blocked, but did not stop from becoming a base hit. That brought up the top of Boston's order, and in succession, Dougherty, Collins, Stahl and Freeman reached base. Predictably, the Royal Rooters went insane again, and until Freddy Parent grounded out to end the frame, three runs crossed the plate.

Undaunted by the Rooters, Pittsburgh's fans devised some tricks of their own. When Boston took the field, the fans tore up newspapers and programs, and when a still wind passed over the park, they released the confetti to the confusion of the Bostons, who vainly searched for the baseball in the midst of the apparent October snowstorm.

Boston scored a couple of runs in the fifth and an insurance score in the seventh to the immense satisfaction of Boston hurler George Winter, who was watching the game in the stands in his street clothes, having bet $100 on the contest. Hobe Ferris, the club's resident red ass, rode the umpire so hard at one point that he complained to Collins, who turned to Ferris and "threatened Hobe with a spanking and the latter subsided, as he knew what Jimmy would do if he started in."

In the seventh, the Pirates staged a rally of their own, "as the crowd was shouting like an army of madmen...." With one out and two on, Ginger Beau-

Big Bill Dinneen fought authority and authority always won, which explains in part
why the Boston hurler became an umpire ten days after retiring as an active player.
A hatless Big Bill (center, foreground) and a Pittsburgh policeman exchange sharp
words during the World Series, while the Royal Rooters caused all sorts of trouble
above the Boston dugout. To the left of Dinneen, peacemaker Chick Stahl just wanted
to play baseball. Boston Public Library, Print Department, McGreevy Collection.

mont hit a sharp one over the pitcher's mound, a shot Dinneen futilely stabbed
at with both outstretched arms, plating Sebring and Phelps. Fred Clarke rapped
another hit to left-center field, causing the Pittsburgh faithful to start "slap-
ping one another on the backs, jumping up and down, and such yelling was
enough to put any twirler up in the air."

A cooler man than Jimmy Collins never donned a Boston Americans
uniform, and from third base he strode out to Dinneen to marshal his
confidence. Believing in trusting in God but locking the door to his car,
Collins had Cy Young warming up. Big Bill did provoke the Pirates' Leach
to hit a fly that Chick Stahl easily snared, but Leach tagged from third for
the third Pirate run. The situation worsened as Clarke stole third and Dinneen walked Wagner and Bransfield to load the bases. Pittsburgh had in this
inning scored three runs off Boston's starter, and with two outs and the bases
loaded, pinch-hitter Claude Ritchey came up to bat to break the game open
for Pittsburgh.

As Fred O'Connell called it:

Imagine Harvard having the ball on Yale's one-yard line on the third down at Soldiers Field, with 11,000 wildly excited people cheering like mad.... In that few brief moments 1,000 Pittsburgers rose from a slough of despond into a state of almost drunken ecstasy, and 100 royal rooters from Boston watched with death-like silence their team's apparently safe lead of six runs dwindle to three, with three Pittsburg men on bases and Claude Ritchey, one of the best "pinch" hitters in the game, at the bat.

Big Bill Dinneen had a long career in baseball, becoming an umpire once his playing days ended. While he won more than twenty ballgames on four occasions, he ultimately retired with a losing record, enduring some hard luck at the end of his career. But on October 8, 1903, not Cy Young, nor Mel Parnell, nor Roger Clemens, nor Pedro Martinez could have acted any more resolute than Big Bill, who reared back and let sail. Ritchey got a slice of it, the ball seeming to float harmlessly into foul grounds as both Jimmy Collins and Freddy Parent converged around it, but neither Boston fielder could pull it down as "they were disconcerted by the wild scramble of a number of boys." This home court advantage might have deterred a lesser foe, but Dinneen's next pitch to Ritchey caused him to hit the ball fair, right to Parent, who promptly dispatched with the threat.

Frighteningly, the Pirates threatened again in the ninth, and had this been more modern times, George Winter would have been warming up in relief rather than hedging his bets in the grandstand. No problem, with Fred Clarke on first, Fred Parent either caught or fielded the ball and doubled up Ginger Beaumont at second. Candy Lachance did not know if Parent had trapped the ball or not, so the Boston infielders repeatedly tagged out the Pirate runners just to make sure.

At the conclusion, "[o]ne mad howl went up in Section J. Billy Dinneen (sic) was carried around the diamond on the shoulders of his friends and that Boston will win the series is not being considered now except in the form of an absolute certainty." Because the Royal Rooters had allegedly stiffed a local band out of an exclusive contract, Mike McGreevy was arrested and the case promptly went to trial.

With the Series tied and the last game in Pittsburgh scheduled for the next day, a Friday, Fred Clarke and Barney Dreyfuss went scheming to postpone the game until Saturday to give Deacon Phillippe one more day of rest and get more fans into the park for the weekend game.

Collins, of course, went ballistic when he heard the news, storming over to meet with the Pirates' management to alter their decision, which was clearly a move to permit Phillippe, their only hope on the mound, more rest. Clarke contended to Collins that "[i]t is too cold for a ball game," to which the Bostons' skipper retorted in disbelief, "The weather is as fair for one team as it is for the other, and we would like to go on with the game and have it over." But Pittsburgh had the last say as the home club and the cancellation remained in effect as Collins cooled his heels and Deacon Phillippe nursed his arm.

Boston 6, Pirates 3; Series Tied, 3–3

For Game Seven, Pittsburgh steeled for a reversal of fortune, with the city's large employers granting half holidays to its workers and seeing throngs from all over western Pennsylvania and West Virginia in to root for the Pirates. To counteract the Royal Rooters and their band, Pittsburgh fans hired the Italian band that McGreevy fired, and the two competed during the game with a Battle of the Brass Bands, playing patriotic and popular songs of the day.

It did little good, as a relatively well-rested Cy Young squared off against Phillippe, with Boston prevailing, 7–3, on October 10. Young pitched steadily while the Boston hitters bled Phillippe for one or two runs per inning throughout until they had thoroughly demoralized their opponents. Sensing something special, the Royal Rooters cheered mightily for Phillippe while the locals returned the honors to old Cy. After the game, the Pittsburgh fans kept the cheers up for the Boston Americans as they boarded their bus for the ride to the train back east for the eighth, and if necessary, ninth games of the Series.

The Royal Rooters accompanied the Boston Americans, and on another area of the train, the Pittsburgh Pirates made their headquarters. Hundreds of fans greeted the Bostons at South Station on the afternoon of October 11, cheering Collins and carrying Cy Young around on their shoulders. The Pirates wisely alighted earlier at the Huntington Street terminal, thereby missing out on this spontaneous pep rally.

Invigorating as the greeting at the train station was, Collins rattled off clichés of seemingly good sportsmanship while his counterpart, Fred Clarke, continued with his misplaced braggadocio.

Clarke was about the only Pirate spouting off, as almost as an omen, October 11 was the day that former pitcher Ed Doheny went berserk for the last time in public, assaulting his nurse and easing his way into permanent institutionalization. As one Pittsburgh paper screamed in its headlines, "ED DOHENY IS NOW RAVING IN MADHOUSE!" The event punctuated the obvious: with Leever hurt, Pittsburgh had only Phillippe.

The Boston Royal Rooters agreed, as they had taunted Brickyard Kennedy back in Pittsburgh with the tune of "Tessie" and the following words they substituted for the real lyrics:

> Kennedy you seem to pitch so badly,
> Take a back seat and sit down
> Kennedy you are a dead one,
> And you ought to leave the town,
> Pittsburg needs a few good pitchers,

Such as Boston's pennant lifters,
Phillippi you are the only, only, only one.

Boston 7, Pirates 3; Boston Leads Series, 4–3

For the eighth game Clarke trotted out Phillippe as expected, but it was the Boston hurler, Big Bill Dinneen, who worried his manager much more. The Boston ace "pitched most of the game with the index finger raw as a piece of meat," so Collins had Cy Young warming up again for most of the game with reserve catcher Duke Farrell in case Big Bill faltered. He need not have worried as Dinneen's combination of speed and curves in a very dark and overcast Huntington Grounds completely mesmerized Clarke's crew.

Phillippe typically pitched like a champion but his teammates did not earn a run with which he could work, while an unlikely Boston batsman, Hobe Ferris, knocked in all three of his team's runs to pace the victory. Thoroughly sick of hearing the Royal Rooters, the *Pittsburgh Times* commented that the Boston fans "rendered 'Tessie' on innumerable occasions."

In Boston, fans fanned out to the local saloons to celebrate their world championship, with seemingly everyone permitting him or herself to get royally drunk, with one notable exception. Nuf Ced McGreevy poured drinks but did not imbibe. Boston's most famous bartender was ever a teetotaler.

Boston 3, Pirates 0; Boston Wins Series, 5–3

A nine-game series proved too long, and a happy but exhausted Boston team almost immediately dispersed back to their winter homes. Pittsburgh only had one healthy pitcher as Boston kept wheeling out like a drill press their incomparable duo of Young and Dinneen. Collins all but banished Long Tom Hughes from the team, warmed up Norwood Gibson only briefly, and had George Winter in street clothes for at least one game, and yet he always had one more ace to play than Clarke.

Each team only had one Hall of Famer in the field. Collins hit .250 and fielded well while managing his team effectively, while shortstop Honus Wagner fielded poorly and hit barely above the Mendoza line. His counterpart, Freddy Parent, hit over a hundred points better and fielded his position with aplomb and skill, a fact that Parent proudly remembered more than six decades later.

To the end the Pirates management believed in their team as the finest in the world, attributing their demise to the fact that they had, as Clarke put it, "only one pitcher." Dreyfuss echoed the theory, citing Doheny having "went wrong" and Leever being incapacitated; if only he had worn that damn sweater in the end-of-the-season game against the Boston Nationals!

As it had done throughout the Series, the *Pittsburgh Times* again squelched rumors that the games had been fixed. Perhaps they were not, but gambling had so corrupted the sport that every error or strikeout in a clutch situation cast a pall over each contest. It seems shocking today that it took another sixteen years for the whole horrible business to reach critical mass in the 1919 World Series, where sharpies like Sport Sullivan continued to operate behind the scenes.

6

John I. Taylor
Owns Boston

During the off-season following the first World Series, Boston's Henry Killilea, or more properly American League President Ban Johnson, began casting about for a new owner for the team. A local baseball fanatic, former United States Representative John Fitzgerald, immediately indicated an interest and the financial wherewithal to buy the club.

Of course, Fitzgerald, nicknamed "Honey Fitz," is known nowadays as the grandfather of President John F. Kennedy, but at the turn of the century he had established a reputation as an ambitious Boston politician, or "pol," meriting attention and a bit of watching-out-for from potential opponents. Fitzgerald had hosted the Royal Rooters when they came down to Baltimore to cheer on the old Boston Beaneaters in 1897, and he had maintained warm friendships and alliances with many of them.

Owning a team obviously might furnish him with potential advantages, and not just restricted to financial ones. As a beloved team owner of a successful club, Fitzgerald might reach a larger audience and earn the love and respect of local and loyal rooters. Most importantly, he had access to $140,000, or just about as much money as Killilea desired for the sale to occur. It seemed only a matter of time before papers passed and the sale to Fitzgerald became reality.

Meanwhile, Jimmy Collins realized his long-time managerial ambition of having a front-line left-handed starter when the team traded Long Tom Hughes to their New York Highlander rivals for the much-shorter Kentuckian, Jesse Tannehill. At first the trade stunned many as Tannehill had rung up a 15–15 record the previous season with an ERA much higher than that which Hughes compiled. Still, Tannehill had won more than 20 games on four previous occasions with Pittsburgh in the National League, so hope reigned supreme at the Huntington Grounds that the diminutive hurler might replicate his feat.

The news followed quickly on the heels that American League President Ban Johnson intended to improve the New York franchise, a seeming low priority since the two leagues had declared peace a year earlier and taken steps to heal old wounds and address claims to players by individual franchises. One never truly reconciled with Ban Johnson, though. What transpired in future years resembled more of a Cold War between the leagues, which in large part mandated that the American League's New York team, the Highlanders, prosper in the backyard of the established National League club, now managed by the prickly John McGraw.

In essence, Ban Johnson forced the trade upon Boston because he perceived Long Tom Hughes to have much more potential to win big in 1904 and beyond. Killilea, as his puppet, quite willingly complied with Johnson's wishes to improve the New York club at the expense of the Boston franchise, just as he had done with Connie Mack's Athletics with Boston's pitchers in 1902. That Hughes' career had reached its pinnacle in 1903, while Tannehill stood poised to become the unofficial comeback player of the year, soon became apparent and encouraged Johnson to further calibrate the balance of power between the two franchises once the season commenced.

The trade smelled bad, but during the Boston Americans' home opener on April 18, 1904, the fans cheered mightily as the team raised two banners representing American League and World Series supremacy, and Henry Killilea closed the deal to sell the team not to Honey Fitz, but to *Boston Globe* scion John I. Taylor.

The news elicited an explosive reaction from Fitzgerald, who swiftly denounced the maneuverings. A maverick, Honey Fitz might have concerned Johnson, who did not relish independent underlings, but more likely, Johnson could not resist having the son of the *Boston Globe's* General Charles Taylor run the local nine. Reading the handwriting on the wall days earlier, Fitzgerald foresaw subservience to New York without his stewardship of the team, noting, "Boston has been rather slow, I think, in allowing outsiders to step in and reap harvests from enterprises of all kinds in this locality, and it is about time to stop it.... New York interests control our steam and street railways and other quasi-public utilities. The time will soon come when we shall apply for a guardian to take us in charge."

As a team owner, John I. Taylor proved a disaster. He had been given the advertising chair at the *Globe* for something to do, but while he enjoyed sports, he enjoyed drinking a lot more. Stout and Johnson quote Freddy Parent, who recalled more than six decades later, that Taylor was "drunk half the time." Like General "Hi Hi" Dixwell, Taylor was a spoiled son of a wealthy and prominent White Anglo-Saxon Protestant family in a Boston teeming with poor Irish-Catholic immigrants and their equally destitute children. But the backgrounds meant little, because in truth, John Taylor would have been a screwup no matter what was his race, creed, breeding or educational background.

But the fans of Boston did not know much about Taylor at the time and they were not in a mood to have anything spoil their party as they reveled in the previous year's success while anticipating greater laurels ahead. For the first time the club had local ownership, Ban Johnson had a bigger stooge than

Somers or Killilea, and there was nothing the *Boston Globe* intended to do about it except back the new club owner to the hilt.

On Opening Day, though, the fans with the exception of General Dixwell (whose doctor prohibited him from going out in the inclement weather) did not let the "cold wintry blasts" spoil their fun. The defending champions marched onto the field with near-perfect precision, while local politician Big Mike Sullivan gave Massachusetts Lieutenant Governor Guild last-minute instructions on how to properly grip and throw the opening pitch. Jerome Kelley struck a mighty gong to signify the start of play while alert Boston plainclothes detectives arrested notorious national pickpockets John Long and a suspect known as McLaughlin.

April has been called the cruelest month, but for Boston fans, it proved a bonanza as their Americans bolted out to a 10–2 record by dispatching the good (Philadelphia), the bad (Washington) and the ugly (the New York Highlanders under obnoxious manager Clark Griffith).

Cy Young continued to quietly display his expected excellence during the month of May. On the fifth, the Bostons faced the formidable Philadelphia Athletics and their star pitcher, Rube Waddell, with Collins tabbing Young as his starter. Waddell talked a lot of early twentieth century trash before the game, while his opponent approached his task much more privately.

While Waddell pitched a decent game by holding Boston to three runs, Cy Young fared much better, keeping the A's hitless through nine and two-thirds innings, at which point Connie Mack decided to let Waddell hit for himself rather than insert a pinch-hitter. Having flapped his gums all week, Rube certainly did not want to look like a rube, so he took a fierce cut off one of Cy's servings and drove it deep into center field.

Helplessly, Cy Young stood on the mound as he charted the flight of the ball. He did not need to worry because ever-dependable Chick Stahl got under it and cradled the ball in his glove for the third out of the inning and the completion of a perfect game by his teammate.

The Huntington Grounds bellowed, with the sound of a thunderous "roar as if a hundred cannons had belched forth." Middle-aged men jumped onto the field to shake Young's hand, and one of the silver-templed throng even pressed a yellow bank note into the pitcher's palm. Long after Young had retreated to the dressing room, a line of people formed around the pitcher's mound so that each fan might walk up to the top and stand where the great Cy Young had just made history.

The club's rooters, royal and not so regal, ran amok, but "It was not only the fans that acted like maniacs just let loose, but some of the Boston players forgot themselves for the time being and did a little waving of arms and jumping around." Big Bill Dinneen and reserve outfielder John O'Neill in particular "had their faces wreathed in smiles and all the other players were adorned with a broad grin of approval...."

In the dressing room, the usually modest Young held court, clutching the baseball that Chick Stahl had so recently caught, pledging that he would never surrender it, even if someone offered $100. He praised his fielders, certainly Patsy Dougherty and Stahl, who had made some difficult catches to preserve perfection, with Dougherty going right up to the left-field fence to snare a potential home run. Yet this day Young savored, "happy as a child," talking about how his fastball had a bit more bite than usual and his curves danced all over. In the opponent's clubhouse, Rube Waddell anointed Cy Young the best pitcher in the world.

As always, Young got by mainly through the employment of overwhelming speed to his delivery. One of Lou Criger's sons recalled decades later that his father, when catching Young, "used to put a thick steak in his catcher's mitt between his hand and catcher's mitt and after nine innings it was pounded into a shapeless mess." Bill Carrigan, a catcher who caught Cy as he passed his fortieth, birthday attributed the legendary hurler's success to his being "very fast, his control was next to perfect and he had a 'rubber' arm." Carrigan also maintained that the gentle Young never embarrassed a catcher by shaking off a pitch, but just stared ahead until the catcher altered the sign. Whatever he did, and virtually whenever he did it, it worked.

The next day, one of the newspapers claimed at that time that only two other pitchers had ever thrown a perfect game—John Montgomery Ward and a fellow named "Richardson." It is believed today that Ward and John Lee Richmond pitched perfect games within a week of each other in June 1880, and that since Young's masterpiece, only fourteen have followed in the major leagues.

As impressive as the perfect game proved to be, less than a week thereafter Young added to his legend by outlasting Detroit Tigers pitcher Twilight Ed Killian in a fifteen-inning game won by Boston, 1–0. Appreciating a fine performance by the opposition, the Boston rooters applauded Killian when he batted in the later innings.

Young had done everything within his power to win the game for himself, fielding his position "superbly" and banging out three hits, including a double, but his teammates simply failed to support him when they came to bat. Until, of course, the fifteenth inning. With one out and John O'Neill at second base and Duke Farrell parked at first, Patsy Dougherty came up to the plate, gripping his bat with fire in his eyes, having been made a fool all day by Killian.

"Hit it out," yelled the fans as Killian peered down at his prey. As Killian reared to throw, O'Neill broke for third base, and the Tiger pitcher let the ball go with all of his remaining strength. Dougherty sat on the ball and drilled it to left field, scoring O'Neill "[a]mid the frantic howls and cheers" cascading in the friendly Huntington Grounds. Young thanked Patsy Dougherty while he rounded first base and trotted toward the dressing room, as the Boston

Americans opened up what proved to be a sweep of Detroit. Oh, did the Irish in Boston love their Patsy Dougherty!

With matters proceeding so swimmingly, only Ban Johnson could muddy the waters. Cryptically, Johnson and former team owner Henry Killilea ventured into town in mid–June. The normally loquacious Johnson had no comment concerning why he had come to visit, and he and Killilea crept off as furtively as they came.

On June 17, 1904, team treasurer Carl Green laid a bombshell on the loyal rooters by announcing a trade with the New York Highlanders; Boston received utility infielder Bob Unglaub and cash for star outfielder Patsy Dougherty. The worst type of pandemonium gripped the Hub faithful immediately and a firestorm of criticism of this transaction erupted in its aftermath.

The ultimate indignity, having one's name misspelled on his baseball card, was one of the many slights suffered by poor Bob Unglaub during his career. His name was not Unclane, but there definitely was something unclean about his trade to Boston for Patsy Dougherty. Library of Congress.

On paper, the trade made absolutely no sense. Dougherty, a fan favorite, had batted .331 and .342 during the previous two years, notching third and fourth, respectively, in the final order of batting leaders in the American League. He stole fifty-five bases and ran well from first to third. He played in considerable pain in 1902, demonstrating the opposite of what a few had wrongly accused him of—namely indifference.

Unglaub never starred in baseball, and even his name makes him sound like the kind of guy in which no one wanted his baseball card. As of June 17, he had batted only 19 times for 4 hits and a measly .211 average in his major league career. No one considered him much of a prospect, and even the Boston Americans conceded they picked him up solely as a utility player.

The move stunned Dougherty, who went on record to proclaim, "I'm good and sore and I won't stand it.... I got a dirty deal and I am the most surprised man involved. I am now out of a job." Upset that he had lost his position with the champions, he threatened not to report to New York without receiving some of the money Boston reportedly received as part of the trade consideration.

Continuing to articulate his hurt, Patsy let fly:

I can't understand why the management should be bent on breaking up a pennant winning team. My relations with Collins and all the members of the team have been most pleasant. I must have been playing good ball, else they would have sent me to the bench. These circumstances make it all the more surprising, and to be candid I do not know what to think. I am inclined to think that someone higher in authority than the president of the club is back of the deal, but who I do not know. If I did I might be able to figure it out. They have sold me for a sick man. Unglaub who was given in exchange as a sort of bonus, has been sick in the hospital all season, and they tell me it is likely he will not be able to play this season. He is now is a New York hospital under treatment.

Endeavoring to control his emotions, Dougherty tried to pen a letter to his wife but found he could not. His friends gathered around to console him and convince him he had to report to New York. The trade outraged virtually everyone. National League Commissioner Harry Pulliam, smarting over the transfer of the American League Baltimore franchise to New York, protested that Ban Johnson had deliberately meddled in the struggle for New Yorkers' affections by forcing a trade from Boston to prop up and, indeed, greatly improve the Highlanders.

Speaking from his perch on the *Sporting Life*, Jacob Morse panned the decision, "It is beginning to look as if the New York Americans had more of a chance to land a pennant then they had a few weeks ago.... Of course the team was pretty well worked up over the Dougherty deal."

The *Boston Herald* chimed in with, "The move was made to help out New York and the excuse that it was done to strengthen Boston is so thin that it is almost ridiculous." W.S. Barnes, Jr., added, "There is no question that the vast majority of people who have an interest in the world's champions deplore the trade and consider that Boston gets the bad end of it.... There have been signs that the American League is inclined to use the Boston club for the benefit of the league as a whole, without properly considering the club and its legion of patrons."

As the unofficial defender of his boss' son, the *Globe*'s Tim Murnane increasingly assumed the role of the hatchet man against the departed Dougherty. Beginning his defense of the move on June 20, "the Silver King" started with a relatively muted analysis of the situation, claiming that "Capt. Collins undoubtedly saw that something was wrong and had the nerve to act." The rhetoric raged thereafter as the dissatisfied fandom continued to squeal about the peculiar deal.

By July 10, with controversy concerning the swap still swirling, Murnane fairly roasted Dougherty, positing that "Dougherty on several occasions refused to obey orders and openly refused to listen to manager Collins' suggestions, until it got to be a case of Collins or Dougherty for leader.... Dougherty was moody and a kicker. He was swelled up with his reputation and had lost his usefulness for Boston, and Capt. Collins did right to dispose of him to the club's best advantage.... [He] will soon be forgotten. He was a fine batsman, but a bad, very bad fielder."

Murnane attempted to dispel the rumors that Ban Johnson had engineered the transfer of Dougherty to New York. Yet in this instance, he managed to write one of the poorest columns he ever penned during a long and estimable career, not just because of the caustic criticism of Dougherty, but also because he did not at least once concede that the transaction was a poor one.

The philippic from Murnane clashed with recent lavish praise for Dougherty from his own paper, the *Boston Globe*. On June 9, Dougherty received kudos for being "everywhere, from deep left center to the left field bleachers," while a day later he "made a magnificent running catch." Leading up to the dubious transaction, there is hardly a discouraging word about Dougherty's acumen or attitude.

The trade still did not pass the smell test. Even had Dougherty gotten on his manager's nerves, fielded with indifference, and lacked discipline, at that stage of his career Patsy still had a promising career ahead and had already achieved plaudits for his superior fielding, so it did not equate to trade him for a spare part like Unglaub. And this, to trade a star to the New York team that was only about a half-dozen games behind Boston so early in the season!

Within days, the Boston Americans demonstrated their faith in Dougherty's replacement, Tip O'Neill, by trading him for veteran Washington outfielder Kip Selbach. O'Neill had done very little during that time, but then again, it generally takes more than a week or two to replace a legend. With Selbach, the Americans had a player who once starred and still had enough talent and smarts to at least prove a more competent replacement for Patsy Dougherty than an untried rookie. Knowing the long arm of Ban Johnson at the time, it is quite possible that he forced the Selbach/O'Neill swap on Washington, a cellar dweller clearly going nowhere, to help take some of the heat off Taylor and Collins.

Baseball history is replete with horribly one-sided trades. The Cubs famously traded Lou Brock to the Cardinals for sore-armed Ernie Broglio. Nonetheless, at the time the Chicago front office had wrongfully concluded that Brock would never rise above mediocrity, and they engineered a deal where they received a pitcher who had won 18 games the previous season and had once won 21 contests years earlier.

That was not the case with the Dougherty deal. Unglaub was at best a career ham-and-egger utility guy with no upside whatsoever, while Dougherty promised top five finishes in batting for years to come. Unlike the Tannehill/ Hughes deal, there was no chance that Bob Unglaub would redeem the disaster by outplaying Dougherty.

In his first time back in Boston with his new team, the Huntington Grounds fans cheered madly for Patsy Dougherty, who doffed his cap in appreciation several times. Turning to catcher Lou Criger, Patsy said, "Say, Lou, this is great. Looks like they were trying to make me a wonder. Guess I'll have to make good and crack out a few on 'Cy.'" And after the great Cy Young had caused him to foul off a couple pitches, Patsy did as promised and lined a ball fair over the center of the infield for a single to help lead the Highlanders to a 5–3 win.

Taylor and Collins only escaped a tarring and feathering on Boston Common because their team still stood a very good chance of capturing the pennant, and although no one knew it at that time, Patsy Dougherty had plateaued as a ballplayer and never hit as high as .290 after 1903. The Boston Americans had in essence lucked out in their first major player transaction with their New York rivals. Boston would not always be so lucky.

History has been kind to Taylor and Collins mainly because no one remembers the trade. But once it is analyzed afresh, it still shocks the conscience even after more than a hundred years have passed. Plus, the Red Sox have made so many other ludicrous trades with the Yankees since then that this one stands out as one of the more benign.

The absurdity of the trade continued to nag the Boston Americans all season. By the middle of August, they sat in third place behind the suddenly less-needy New York Highlanders and the Chicago White Sox.

When Jesse Tannehill drilled the first White Sox batter in the ribs and walked another one in the first inning of a game in Chicago on August 17, 1904, it seemed as if the slide might continue. But Boston's stellar southpaw bore down and no other Chicago player reached base all day as he hurled the club's second no-hitter of the season, to complement Cy Young's earlier masterpiece.

Shortstop Freddy Parent and second baseman Hobe Ferris made the most spectacular plays. Tannehill, otherwise, got the White Sox out with his slow curves, which did not result in strikeouts, but rather induced the opposing batters to "offer up easy grounders and pop up weak flies for the gardeners." Unlike Young's perfect game, which unfolded at the Huntington Grounds, Tannehill did not have much time to savor the win as the team had to rush out to take a 10:30 P.M. train back home. However, the win had much more of a positive effect on the team as it used the momentum from the "no-no" to return to the Huntington Grounds and reel off a 14–5 record for their homestand.

Ban Johnson's attempts to improve the Highlanders' at the expense of the Boston Americans succeeded beyond his most idealistic cynicism. New York vied for the lead throughout September, and by the first week of October, Boston held a slight percentage point lead in the race. The outcome of the pennant race depended on Boston winning three of its five remaining games, all of them against the New York Highlanders.

In the first game in New York on October 7, Patsy Dougherty smoked his old team, getting on base twice and scoring two runs as the Highlanders regained first place with their 3–2 victory. The Highlanders had barely made the game, returning from a trip to St. Louis with about three hours to spare and having to wear their dark road uniforms to save time. Looking none the worse for wear, Happy Jack Chesbro started for New York and scattered four hits while Norwood Gibson appeared "frightened" and erratic on the mound, heaving a wild pitch and hitting a New York batsman. Getting behind hitters in the count, Gibson threw straight fastballs down the plate, which the Highlander batters sat on to their delicious advantage.

Hailing from North Conway, Massachusetts, the somewhat-odd Jack Chesbro had established his reputation with some of Barney Dreyfuss' early Pirate teams, but it was in '04 that he became all-world, winning 41 games against only 12 defeats, mainly due to the effects of his beloved spitball. Poetically, Chesbro claimed it was "the most effective ball that possibly could be used," further asserting that he could make the ball "drop two inches or a foot and a half" as reported by the *New York Times*. After defeating Gibson, Happy Jack Chesbro felt invincible.

Jack Chesbro's wild pitch saved the Boston Americans' season. A native of North Conway, Massachusetts, Chesbro was picked up on waivers from New York at the very end of his career and briefly pitched for the Red Sox. Library of Congress.

Serving as a harbinger to the often physically violent series between the Red Sox and the Yankees in the 1970s, Highlander third baseman Wid Conroy tagged Jimmy Collins out in the second inning with such authority that he "tipped the Boston leader over for a complete somersault." Similarly, when New York's Jimmy Williams attempted to field a Freddy Parent ground ball, Boston's Kip Selbach deliberately crashed into Williams, a play deemed so dirty that the umpire called Selbach out for interference.

New York manager Clark Griffith chirped with glee at the victory as his counterpart, Jimmy Collins, became "quite silent," a remarkable feat for a person who affected a rather austere countenance at the best of times. And these were not the best of times as the Boston Americans caught their 11:00 P.M. train out of New York. They returned to Boston for a double-header at the Huntington Grounds, behind in the standings and needing to win three of the next four games to secure their crown.

The next day more than 30,000 people swarmed into the Huntington

Avenue Grounds, a huge crowd for such a small stadium, an aggregation that would have approached a sellout for the future Fenway Park. Not all patrons entered the grounds legally, and small and large boys alike jumped the fence to secure their places at the festivities.

Before the first game of the double-header, Royal Rooter Charles Lavis handed manager Jimmy Collins a loving cup in appreciation for his handling of the team for the year. In the first game, Collins tabbed Bill Dinneen to pitch for Boston, as Clark Griffith somewhat surprisingly chose the previous day's winner, Jack Chesbro, to start for the Highlanders.

Chesbro was not even supposed to be in Boston. Griffith had instructed him to remain in New York for the final double-header, but Chesbro utilized the gentle arts of persuasion to convince his manager to allow him to travel with the team. Once in Boston, Happy Jack asked Griffith who would start on the mound for New York to which Griffith replied, "Well, I figure Al Orth for the first game, and Jack Powell for the second game."

"What the hell's the matter with me?" Chesbro asked. "Don't I work for the club any more?"

"But you worked yesterday," said Griffith. "You don't want to pitch them all."

"You want to win the pennant, don't you?" Chesbro persisted.

And so Griffith caved and Chesbro got shelled, lasting only four innings en route to a 13–2 blowout victory for Boston. New York's other hero from the previous day, Patsy Dougherty, struck out three times. In the fourth, the Bostons rallied, and even after Chesbro went to the showers, the club danced all over the reliever, Walter Clarkson, he of Cambridge and Harvard fame.

In the second game, New York started Jack Powell, a hard-luck pitcher as best reflected in his ultimate lifetime record of 245–254, while Boston countered with the peerless Cy Young. In an oddity of the day, Patsy Dougherty, who had just struck out to end the first game, remained in the batter's box to lead off for New York. The Boston fielders maintained their places in the field, and the next contest commenced.

Powell actually pitched well, surrendering only four hits to Boston as Young scattered six from the Highlanders. Boston's work at the plate proved more telling. In the fifth inning, Hobe Ferris beat out an infield hit and was sacrificed to second base by Lou Criger. Cy Young then aided his cause by flying out to center field. When Honest John Anderson tried to double up Hobe Ferris, who had tagged and scurried to third base, the throw went into the crowd, allowing Ferris to jog home with his team's first and only run of the game.

A nervous Boston crowd squirmed in their seats and along the outfield, hoping Young might eke out the win. Advancing darkness aided Cy considerably as the Highlanders had difficulty solving his dazzling curves. At the end of the seventh inning, the umpires called the game due to darkness, with Boston winning, 1–0.

Boston had the lead in the race as the teams reversed course back to Gotham for the final two games of the year. The next day, 200 Royal Rooters had their pictures taken before they all jumped on a train for New York. Many carried the same suitcases and satchels that they brought to Pittsburgh the year before. Rooter Jerry Watson carried a suitcase so small that one of his friends remarked it "was large enough for two sandwiches and a clean shirt." Manager Collins remained stoic, but did add that "[w]e have the best team and we will more than demonstrate that fact." Collins chose Bill Dinneen as his starter for the most important game of the year, while Griffith went on autopilot and again went with Chesbro.

The Royal Rooters put on a show both before and during this penultimate game as they marched up 165th Street, proudly displaying their Boston Rooters banners. Additionally, they procured the services of a "Mr. Hazard." According to the *Boston Herald*, "Mr. Hazard was a diminutive ebony-hued 'pusson' of 70 odd years, who sported a beautiful blacked fringe trimmed with gray. He agreed to officiate as mascot and scored a great success. He carried a bean pot on top of a pole and was marched in front of the grand stand, much to the edification of the crowd which cheered heartily, while some of the New York players ran their hands through his wool for luck."

Once again, Patsy Dougherty struck out to end the contest as Boston won the first game on October 10, clinching the American League pennant. The pivotal moment occurred in the top half of the ninth inning when Highlander ace Jack Chesbro faced Boston's Freddy Parent with two out and Candy Lachance on third for Boston. The score was 2–2.

The tired Chesbro rang up two strikes on Parent and then made the crucial decision to throw a spitter in hopes of ending the inning. The spit ball has had a long and interesting history in baseball. At its best, the spitter is virtually unhittable, so much so that major league baseball banned the pitch in 1920. Boston fans' hearts broke on August 18, 1967, when a spitter allegedly got away from California Angels pitcher Jack Hamilton and struck Tony Conigliaro so hard in the head that he did not play baseball again until the spring of 1969, and never again played with the same swagger or skill.

In 1904, the spitter was just as unreliable, and Chesbro took considerable time sizing up the Boston batter. Chesbro wound up and let fly a wet one so haywire that it sailed over his catcher's head, permitting Candy Lachance to trot home with the game and pennant-winning run for Boston.

After Dougherty struck out, the Boston players ran about shaking each other's hands as Collins looked ready for bed and Lou Criger was quite "pale." The band sailed into their rendition of "Tessie" as the Rooters sang and the New York fans sat stunned, "as silent as the grave."

Although Boston had clinched the pennant by winning the first game, the two teams slugged it out in the second game of the double-header for 10 innings before New York pulled out the victory in the meaningless but bitterly fought contest. The close pennant race was Boston's only consolation as the National League New York club resisted any attempt at staging a second World Series. Because Boston wanted to play and the John McGraw's club did not, Jimmy Collins and his men declared themselves the greatest team in the world by default.

Assessing the past season, Young and Tannehill not only threw no-hitters, they also won 26 and 21 games, respectively, with ten of Young's victories coming by shutout. Norwood Gibson pitched quite well at times, compiling a 17–14 record, and Big Bill Dinneen won 23 games. George Winter continued to tease with an 8–4 mark for the season.

Chick Stahl bounced back nicely from his previous injury-plagued season with a .290 average and tied teammate Buck Freeman for the league lead in triples with nineteen. Kip Selbach batted only .258, making no one forget Patsy Dougherty. At the corners of the infield, Collins saw his average dip to .276, and Freddy Parent's mark fell to .291. Ferris, Lachance and Criger continued to be appreciated for their defense.

The reprehensible dumping of Patsy Dougherty for Bob Unglaub nearly cost the Boston Americans the title, yet the initially suspect swap of Long Tom Hughes for Jesse Tannehill ensured the Bostons success. Hughes failed in his half-season in New York and never regained his effectiveness elsewhere, while Tannehill regained his form and helped cover up some of the deficiencies of the team's batters.

Most importantly, the series between Boston and New York marked the advent of arguably the most intense rivalry in the history of American professional sport. Boston was a few years away from becoming the Red Sox, and likewise New York still had to shed its clumsy Highlander appellation to be known forevermore as the Yankees, but the rivalry began sizzling in 1904.

7

A Crab Cannot Stem the Tide

With his beady eyes and homely visage, Boston Americans President John I. Taylor sat back in his Boston office, reveling in taking credit for that which he did not deserve, a second pennant for his team. He made a good winner, John I. Taylor did, but then again most people do. And yet he was not a winner; he was simply a man who had been born into wealth and whose daddy bought a baseball team to occupy him.

Like Richard III, hunched over and callous, John I. Taylor had begun to endure a winter of discontent, although he had neither the presence nor prescience to appreciate it yet. His team had won in '04, but it had also grown older, with many of its stars reaching a point in their thirties where irreversible decline set in—Cy Young, of course, excluded. But John I. was not a gracious loser, and as the team aged and other clubs challenged him, he sat back and drank and celebrated and slapped himself on the back and looked forward to overseeing another pennant he did not deserve.

Soon after the 1904 season concluded, the winter hot stove league discussions commenced. Rumors flew about concerning trading George Winter for prodigal son Long Tom Hughes or exchanging Buck Freemen for three-time .400 hitter Jesse Burkett, but nothing came of this. Still, the thought of obtaining the legendary Burkett proved far too tantalizing for John Taylor to ignore, so he countered with promising outfield prospect George Stone and cash for Burkett. St. Louis jumped on the deal. Over in Missouri, Jimmy McAleer relished the opportunity to fleece an empty suit like Taylor, as the scion of the *Globe's* first family began to destroy his own club with drill press precision. For his part, Stone led the American League in hits in '05 and won that circuit's batting title with an average of .358 in 1906.

Although he hailed originally from Wheeling, West Virginia, Burkett has largely been associated with his adopted home in Worcester, where he coached at Holy Cross for a spell. Even today, a successful Little League team and a chapter of the Society for American Baseball Research bearing his name operates in this central Massachusetts city. While Burkett may have welcomed the move, his December proved hectic. He had to rush to Wheeling to attend funeral services for his father, and as soon as he returned to Worcester, he had to turn around and go back to Wheeling because his brother had just passed.

On a superficial level, John Taylor fell in love with Burkett. Nicknamed "the Crab," Burkett more than made up for his sour disposition by batting .338 for his career and registering an on-base percentage of .415. Trouble is, he had turned thirty years old after the 1904 season ended, and his batting averages had dipped over the last few campaigns. Together with Chick Stahl and Kip Selbach, his addition helped form a venerable but very old outfield.

Chick Stahl certainly looked out of shape when the Silver King, the *Globe's* Tim Murnane, visited him in Fort Wayne, Indiana, in January. Occasionally tending bar, Stahl had become quite plump around the midsection. During this period, Murnane's visits to players constituted the *Sports Illustrated* curse of today, and poor Chick must have remembered that one of Murnane's trips to Brookfield, Massachusetts, foreshadowed the terrible tragedy that awaited the family of Boston Beaneaters catcher Martin Bergen, who soon after killed his wife and children.

Off-seasons, Stahl lived with his mother and helped his brother run a tavern in the heart of Fort Wayne, a town of 40,000 with "a Catholic cathedral, a $1,000,000 courthouse and Charles S. Stahl as the three great features of the place," as Murnane described it to his readers. Although Tim's train had arrived in Fort Wayne after midnight, Chick Stahl waited for him, a gesture not out of character for this essentially kind and considerate man.

At his saloon, Chick did not permit any talk of baseball in his presence, having endured enough of it during the season. Like his best friend Jimmy Collins, Chick increasingly looked upon baseball as a hard job, not sport. Murnane reported that although the famed center fielder walked and jogged, his hips carried a surfeit of weight. Given Chick's cravings for alcohol at this time, he probably guzzled more than he could exercise off, and since he owned the bar, he let the good times roll.

One vignette from early in the winter spoke to what people at the time perceived Stahl to be, a stand-up guy willing to help no matter what the risk entailed. As the Silver King tells it, "Stahl had just locked the door at his place of business when he heard the bells ring out a fire alarm and, joining the crowd he was soon at the scene two blocks away to see the flames in close proximity to the hotel Randall, where some of his friends were stopping.... Chick went through the hotel office and up the stairs three steps to a jump, and with his massive shoulders for a battering ram soon had the room doors open and the inmates hustling for safety."

Throughout his life, Stahl repeatedly placed himself into situations like these, in which he heroically bounded into peril with no thought to his personal safety to rescue his fellow man. On one level it did sum up in many ways his good Samaritan nature. Either that, or Chick Stahl had a death wish.

Regardless of what Stahl wanted, the Boston American fans and management lusted after another pennant as if it were their birthright. After trading Stone for Burkett, John I. Taylor largely stopped trying to swap players, although he did sign a local boy, East Boston's Fred O'Brien, as a pitcher. In lieu of transactional activity, John I. surveyed the needs of his team and decided that for too long his club lacked a mascot. So he signed up Battling Nelson, a "fine looking bull pup."

As spring training approached, other dogs on the Americans' roster began to rouse themselves from their slumbers. Collins had taken a laissez faire approach to the conditioning of his men, particularly the veterans, and gave his players the option of joining the club for formal spring training in Macon, Georgia, or fulfilling their own tailored fitness regimes in Hot Springs.

Five veterans took advantage of the curative waters at Hot Springs in an insincere attempt to work themselves into shape, namely Cy Young, Bill Dinneen, Buck Freeman, Lou Criger and Kip Selbach. Dinneen and Freeman spent considerable time cheering the horses they bet on at the race track, and while everyone eventually united in New Orleans for some exhibitions, by that time the five veterans had done little to prepare themselves for the regular season. All of them proceeded to have their worst seasons in years (or in Young's case, ever).

Lou Criger arrived late in Hot Springs in terrible shape, and upon hearing this Collins laughed it off, feeling that "Criger worries a lot ... and imagines he is sick, but a little excitement will make him forget it." Criger failed to answer the opening bell and when the real Opening Day began for 1905, ancient Duke Farrell had to catch.

The Boston Americans had grown complacent, and they needed a manager to demand they dedicate themselves to their profession—not an outrageous request for professionals. Jimmy Collins had made too many friends amongst his players and comforted himself that they would perform for him when the time came, no matter how little they tended to their conditioning. The team was not hungry; it was fat. Collins gave his veterans much leeway and they took every inch given to them to have a good time, gamble on the horses, and sit in hot baths, while the suckers from the other teams prepared themselves for a marathon. A good manager for a team on the way up, Collins needed to discipline his players and keep them motivated, but he mistakenly trusted them to do the right thing.

Jimmy Collins most profoundly wished for Boston to three-peat for the American League pennant, but this year's model lacked the swagger of past ones. Disastrously, his men reeled off six straight losses in defense of their hard-won pennant over New York. It looked good for Boston in the opener when Cy Young squared off against the Athletics' "big Indian," Chief Bender. Down 3–2 in the ninth inning, the Bostons loaded the bases and had Bob Unglaub pinch-hitting for Young.

Unglaub drew a full count, undoubtedly because Collins did not trust

An Opening Day cartoon in the *Boston Post*, depicting all sorts of activity: a championship flag going up in center field, Ban Johnson throwing out the opening pitch, while on the mound the A's Rube Waddell is putting down the Boston batters like the Japanese army is mauling the Russian army at Port Arthur. Someone must have broken a mirror at the game as the team was poised to embark on a seven-year stretch of bad luck. Library of Congress.

him swinging the bat in a clutch situation, as the *Globe's* Murnane called the action: "The big Indian quit like a chicken hawk in the ninth passing three men to first and saving his scalp, and no doubt, a lost game, through the kindness of umpire Silk O'Laughlin, who called Unglaub out on strikes when he should have passed him to first, and thereby forced in another [and tying] run." Not all of the team left the park glum, as during the game Freddy Parent was presented with a toilet set as a gift, an apt metaphor for the campaign to come.

In its first two series, the team lost four games by one run and one by only two runs to stagger back north to see fans at the Huntington Grounds for the first time. In the previous two years, virtually the same roster of players won these tight games, but other teams had made improvements while Boston aged.

After stumbling out of the gate in Washington and Philadelphia, Collins' men came to enjoy considerable pomp and circumstance at the Huntington Grounds on April 21. Collins had some of the boys out at 8:45 A.M., all in preparation for a "midafternoon game." At 12:30 P.M. the gates opened and "[m]en and boys, after getting past the ticket takers, unconsciously gave a vivid representation of Japanese infantry rushing 200-Meter hill. And the rush was not without its casualties in the way of trip-ups, lost dicers and more or less vigorous elbowing and pushing. But not a word of protest, for be it known that the usual Boston baseball gathering—no matter how vast its number—is ever indecorous."

Fans noted the more corpulent frames of the Boston players, a sight that spring training did not apparently alleviate. Some of the spectators speculated that several teams playing on the Boston Common could outplay the defending champions. Boston lost that game, too, as Norwood Gibson surrendered a four-run lead in the eighth inning to keep the club winless.

The wheels fell off the bus relatively early in the season, and most maddeningly, former Boston players haunted the Hub throughout the schedule, including boy wonder Jake Stahl, sold to Washington before the 1904 campaign. Ban Johnson loved the guy based largely on their shared Illinois pedigree and pushed him on the woeful Washington assemblage, where he sparked a change in that franchise's fortunes.

Jake Stahl, a natural leader, led Washington to a surprisingly good start. Unlike Chick Stahl, Jake needed baseball a lot less than the sport needed him, and as his old team in the Hub continued to decline, they needed him back very badly indeed.

A perennial doormat, Washington had permitted Boston to feast upon them in years past, but now Collins' men knew there were no sure wins or patsies on their schedule. Every game was critical. As losses mounted, the team spent the better part of the first two months of the season not angling for the top spot, but ensconced in the basement of the league. Gloom and pessimism set it as the club released Candy Lachance, replacing him with rookie Myron Grimshaw, who did not immediately take to major league pitching, although he did hit a relatively high .290 during his sophomore year in baseball.

Finally, on May 28, Boston tiptoed out of last place by defeating Chicago in front of more than 17,000 fans in the Windy City. Jesse Tannehill bailed the team out of that one, and at 13–19, the "champions" were not that far back of leader Cleveland, owner of 18 wins. Jesse had just recovered from a months-long case of the cramps, a condition for which he treated with aid from a Detroit physician. As small comfort to fans in the Hub, the New York Highlanders now sat in sole possession of last place.

As events had it, the team solved one problem and then faced another challenge as outfielder Chick Stahl battled some type of injury. It is not entirely clear if the affliction was physical or mental, as the *Sporting Life* empathized, stating, "Chick Stahl has not felt as well this spring as in former seasons, and his breakdown was looked for. After a rest, the old reliable will come in handy." The brief comment mirrors exactly the notes section of the *Boston Globe,* and on May 31, Stahl's weakened state was attributed to narrowly escaping typhoid fever, perhaps a euphemism for some other ailment.

Much of the remainder of the spring and early summer involved the club clawing for every victory, not vaulting back to first place, but attempting to work its way up in the standings gradually with the available talent. As the titular champions of the American League, the team management acted like it and rather than commencing a concerted rebuilding process by trading off aging players to contending clubs for their prospects, much like Jimmy McAleer had done with palming off Burkett to Boston, Taylor largely contented himself with holding a pat hand and awaiting his wonderful club's rebound.

In early August, Collins' men finally gave their fans reason for cautious optimism as they crafted a seven-game winning streak at the expense of the St. Louis, Cleveland and Detroit clubs. The team had ended July by winning five of its last seven, as Collins mused about the difference between the 1904 pennant winners and this year's incarnation: "The boys are not playing the game they put up last fall and it's hard to account for their falling off. It wouldn't take very much, however, to put us in the running, for I can see no club with anything on us at the present time."

Murnane quoted two unnamed experts who met at Tommy McCarthy's bar on Washington Street to diagnose the team's ills and possible antidotes. More than likely it was Murnane and McCarthy himself, who saw the needs as follows: 1. A bad need for a first baseman; 2. To get a hitting outfielder with speed; 3. More action on the bases; 4. More variety in play, whatever that means; and 5. Speed in the outfield and on the bases.

On August 8, Big Bill Dinneen pitched dominantly against the Tigers. Suddenly, fans began to talk again about their team making a run for the pennant. Two days later, Detroit ended the streak, but Boston seemed to have gained some momentum. And then they played three double-headers in

Chicago from August 25–27 and lost all of the games, dampening the pennant fever after that.

In these double-headers, Boston wasted some very good pitching performances by Young, Dinneen and Winter, while they threw Norwood Gibson out there with a sore arm and he predictably got creamed. In an early *Globe* article by Melville E. Webb, Jr. (a protégé of Tim Murnane and the writer who prevented Ted Williams from winning an MVP award the year he hit .400), the scribe described the sacrifice of Norwood Gibson, who "had no control, and every ball pitched was accompanied by severe pain."

Webb reserved his harshest invectives for the hitters, who let the team down as they had all season, as Boston lost each of the first four games in the Chicago series by one run. Equally galling, Nick Altrock, the young left-hander that Collins had released in 1903, won two of the games against his old team en route to a 23–12 record for the season. With the "slaughter" in the meatpacking capital of the world, Boston had to win virtually every game for the remainder of the season to repeat as champions, and they simply did not have the firepower to accomplish this goal.

Further, while Boston got older, teams like Philadelphia with Chief Bender, Eddie Plank and Andy Coakley, and Chicago with Altrock and Ed Walsh, successfully transitioned younger pitchers into their rotations and to stardom. After it all had gone irretrievably wrong for Boston, friends of either Collins or Taylor argued that their man had correctly seen the rot that had set in on the club, but that the other guy had obstructed any attempts by their man to repair it.

Historically, it has been more persuasively argued that Taylor missed it and Collins had to stay the course, knowing like a Greek chorus member that doom would result. And yet, even in late August, Collins had defended the continued use of veterans, citing Mack's employment of experienced players over young blood, in obvious denial of how the Philadelphia manager had actually transformed his team.

A further point. Although the decline in 1905 has normally been attributed to the sudden aging of the club, this analysis ignores the strain placed on the club's hurlers. After completing every game he started in 1904, Bill Dinneen never pitched well again. Norwood Gibson's woes sprung from his being a decent minor league talent who sold his soul to the spitter, and later lost any ability he had as his arm became irredeemingly sore.

The ravages of age also were exacerbated by the complacency of too many of the veterans during spring training. Cy Young had gotten his way for years because when the season began, he dominated. But he had not accounted for the fact that even he had to train harder as the years advanced, and his losing record embarrassed him as it should have. The 1904 championship parties had left the team in a giant 1905 hangover, and now with the team a year older, it augured poorly for their chances to rebound in '06.

Because the team went on an eight-game winning streak, Collins' men finished with a 78–74 record, good for a fourth-place finish. In large part, the almost across-the-board decline in the club's batting accounted for the shift from two-time pennant winner to mediocrity. Of the regulars, only Jimmy Collins and Hobe Ferris' averages improved—marginally—over their 1904 production.

The deepening of the dead ball era wreaked havoc on a lot of players' averages throughout the American League; whereas in 1904 the top batter, Nap Lajoie, hit .376, in 1905 only three players batted over .300, and only barely at that. Even accounting for a consistent dip in batting in general, some players plunged even further than this simple explanation warranted, and Boston batters virtually disappeared from nearly all offensive leader categories. Freddy Parent, who hit between .275 and .306 in his first four years in the major leagues, fell to an anemic .234 in '05. Parent proved the most enigmatic because he never regained his swing for the remainder of his career, and the explanation for this plunge is not readily available.

Although he lived 96 years, by his late twenties he had become a poor to mediocre hitting shortstop. Many of his teammates had gotten very old overnight; stars like Collins, Burkett, Stahl and Freeman had left their best years behind in the 1890s and early years of the twentieth century. But Boston seemingly had a solid foundation of younger players with Parent, Hobe Ferris and some of the pitchers. Now Parent had entered a period of ultimately irreversible decline not expected of someone so young. Also, like a later fan favorite at short, Nomar Garciaparra, Freddy Parent had begun the irreversible metamorphosis into a pariah.

Buck Freeman also faced similar futility, although he remained a fan favorite. Chick Stahl too suffered a decline, although he maintained a relatively robust on-base percentage and fielded his position well. But Boston had gone from a team with just enough hitting to win to an aggregation that could not win despite what the pitchers might accomplish. Speculation pegged Chick Stahl playing first base next year, causing Jacob Morse to deadpan, "Some very extensive changes can be expected by the Champions for next season, but nothing as lurid as that." George Stone, the youngster traded for Burkett, starred in his new surroundings in St. Louis. Captain Collins paced the team with an ordinary .276 average.

The pitching, with the exception of 22-game winner Jesse Tannehill, had begun to weaken as well. Cy Young and George Winter each lost more games than they won, while Norwood Gibson gave up nearly a run and a half a game more than he had the previous year, his wildness leading him to a 4–7 record. Throwing the spitball supposedly ruined Gibson's arm, yet Collins may have prevented Gibson's plight because by late August, he despaired of pitching again for the season.

And yet pitch again he did, coming in game after game, throwing fastballs right down the center of the plate, unable to sneak past a curveball or a spitter due to the pain. Today, most competent coaches and general managers would take a player like poor Norwood and have him tested and probably shut down for the season, particularly in a hopeless cause like the 1905 pennant race. Instead, he continued to start and relieve, wild as all get-out, as he exacerbated his condition and hastened his retirement from the game.

Most alarmingly, Big Bill Dinneen went 12–14 with an earned run average that rose even more than Gibson's had, while his strikeouts dipped considerably as well. Had a decent baseball man owned the team rather than a bozo, some trades of still-coveted players for decent return value might have helped rejuvenate the club with youth and at least an upside of potential talent. Instead, Boston let the rot set in.

As if Collins did not have enough problems, Arthur Irwin attempted to lure Buck Freeman and Bill Dinneen to jump their contracts and join his new minor league Altoona entry, causing the *Globe* to deadpan, "Arthur Irwin, with his toy gun, is on the warpath once more." Neither Freeman nor Dinneen were enticed.

When Ban Johnson had forged an American League franchise for Boston, the stodgy National League Triumvirate of owners sniffed at the upstarts and alternately tried to ignore them and drive them out of business; they could do neither. To demonstrate how far the fortunes of both teams had plunged, the two clubs scheduled some post-season exhibition games against each other.

The first World Series it was not. Had the Fates conspired to array the 1892 Boston Beaneaters of Hall of Famers Frank Selee, Hugh Duffy, Tommy McCarthy and King Kelly against the 1903 Americans of Jimmy Collins, Cy Young and Chick Stahl, the games might have been laden with meaning. The Boston Nationals had fallen steeply since their glory days as the perennial pennant-winning Boston Beaneaters, with first baseman Fred Tenney the lone holdover.

Like the first World Series game, heavy betting and some suspect plays accompanied the first game between the nascent Braves and Red Sox. Dinneen dropped a costly and very easy pop-up in the first game, while Jesse Burkett literally somersaulted at one point in what almost certainly constituted a deliberate attempt not to field the ball. Betting went as high as 10–5 and 10–4 for the Boston Americans, which lent further credence that the fix was in.

Billed as a struggle between old Cy Young and young Cy (Boston Nationals pitcher Irving Young), the second contest in this worthless exhibition came as an anticlimax even to the gamblers as the real Cy Young easily won, holding his opposition to only two hits. Either nursing an injury or exhibiting an indifference to the proceedings, Jimmy Collins benched himself and let Unglaub take his stead at third base during these exhibitions, as the Americans went on to win six out of seven of these useless games.

By 1905, manager Jimmy Collins hated team owner John I. Taylor. In

1906, he would hate Taylor even more, as recriminations followed the subpar performance of the squad. Returning to Boston from his Christmas holidays, John I. Taylor denied any friction between he and his manager, asserting that "[t]here is no trouble whatever between Collins and myself. I never have inter-

fered with the management of the team and never have criticized the way Collins has handled things, nor have I criticized the players…. That story about my selling out the Boston team is also absurd. There is nothing to it, and I shall be there next season just the same and so will Collins. I also wish to deny that there is any trouble between myself and Ban Johnson, president of the American League."

That was quite a mouthful, and yet just before New Year's Day, Ban Johnson and Connie Mack took an excursion to Buffalo to visit Jimmy Collins. No details of the meeting immediately leaked out, and indeed, a phony story floated around that Boston had its finger on the trigger to obtain pitcher Rube Waddell from Philly, an absurd rumor since Collins hated flakes like the Rube. For his part, John-

If a picture is capable of saying a thousand words, this photograph captures the essence of Boston owner John I. Taylor more succinctly: deeply suspicious, pensive and ready to pounce. Boston Public Library, Print Department, McGreevy Collection.

son kept trying to persuade Collins to go on a two-week hunting trip with him.

Expecting endless championships, or at the least exciting finishes, the Hub's fandom and its team's management had grown restive by season's end, and John I. Taylor had to deny rumors of an imminent firing of Jimmy Collins. Not only did the demise of the manager seem increasingly unlikely, the press received reassurances from the Taylors that Collins had unfettered access to new players and complete decision-making over personnel, a sticking point in relations between ownership and the field manager. Conceptually, Collins had combined the offices of field leader with something akin to the modern general manager, essentially unifying the roles of his old mentors Frank Selee and Hugh Duffy.

Apparent harmony aside, the rumors persistently hinted of trouble at the Huntington Grounds, with the latest allegations being that the American League (in other words, President Ban Johnson) meant to displace John I. Taylor as owner of the Boston Americans. Denying these accounts, Johnson did concede that his recent visit to Buffalo did address "bridging over some little differences that have arisen between Mr. Taylor and certain members of his club...."

Johnson went on to praise Collins while dismissing the current team ownership as "competent," a characterization he clearly did not believe, while blaming the poor performance of the club on several overweight players. He did choose his words carefully, maintaining, "I am perfectly satisfied that the owners of the Boston club are perfectly competent to take care of their property rights," essentially giving his blessing to Taylor selling the team.

The Taylors did not wish to divest themselves of the Boston Americans, so as Jacob Morse later revealed, a compromise occurred as "Ban Johnson sided with Collins, whom he considered a better base ball man than young Jack Taylor, and at his suggestion General Taylor, to avoid a base ball scandal, ordered the son to take a trip to Europe and remain abroad all season."

At first blush, the move constituted a huge coup for Jimmy Collins, who no longer had to endure John I. Taylor breathing down his neck and insulting his players. Clouds, however, abounded on the horizon. General Taylor most likely did not appreciate participating in the humiliation of his own son and therefore did not have a predisposition to see the manager succeed. Also, Collins' men would grow a year older and pounds heavier in the off-season, with very little in the way of talented, youthful apprentices to begin the transitioning of the team.

With the Boston Beaneaters, Frank Selee keenly evaluated his personnel each year, and had no compunction in replacing older and slower players with new blood, even if it meant offending people like Billy Nash and Tommy McCarthy, for whom he held much personal regard. Perhaps Jimmy Collins meant to follow the example of Selee and implement changes, but in that he found his hands tied by General Taylor with enough rope left over for a hanging should Collins' men falter in 1906.

Ban Johnson's meddlesome ways almost always seemed to create more issues than solutions, and his backroom shenanigans got him a pliant owner in John I. Taylor, but at the expense of the flagship franchise of the American League. The president probably now wished that he had forced Killilea to sell the Boston franchise to Honey Fitz before the 1904 season.

8

Taylor-Made Disaster

The rats jumped the ship or embarked on new ones before the advent of the championship season of 1906. In John I. Taylor's instance, he literally hopped on a boat for a long European tour and did not alight until he had reached London. In a figurative sense, utility man Unglaub acted similarly, repaying his owner's misplaced faith in him by deserting the team and holing up with a minor league congregation in an outlaw league after he presented the management with a "long bill of grievances," not the least of which was the fact he did not play baseball well. If it helped any, Patsy Dougherty experienced the same types of issues with the Highlanders.

Hobe Ferris kicked up a ruckus also, demanding a $500 bonus that John I. had promised him if he played well the year before, an issue that Collins had to smooth over with General Taylor, who managed matters during the period of his son's exile. The pitchers also wanted more money, and Collins ran interference for them also, despite their collectively having a much worse case to make based on their declines in '05.

Even dependable Lou Criger failed to post, ailing from an unspecified element, believed today to have been a morphine addiction. Most turn-of-the-century accounts spoke of his back problems, although the *Sporting Life* notes editor intimated that Criger had entered the private hospital of Dr. Andrew F. Christian, "a noted expert in nervous trouble," of 405 Marlborough Street in Boston's toney Back Bay district.

Seeing its stars get old, the club invited a raft of youngsters to spring training, but soon discovered that most of them lacked talent. On April 12, the *Boston Post* leaked word that Collins meant to release Pop Rising, Harry "Simmy" Murch, Kenney and Ed Hughes (brother of former star pitcher Long Tom Hughes) in what would prove a year-long and largely fruitless audition of young enthusiasts.

Awkwardly, Collins intimated to the sportswriter that he intended to round up the youngsters and "tell them how sorry he was, and all that." While the conveying of the news seems insensitive, the team did offer to transport the released players to Boston, "for none are overburdened by money, and Collins does not want to see them stranded along Broadway." For some, their dreams had shattered, as poor "Harry Murch will return to his Sebago Lake

Opening Day to the disastrous 1906 season. Ban Johnson sits in front to the left with General Taylor (John I. Taylor's father) at the second from the right in the front row. The man seated between them is unidentified. John I. is nowhere in evidence; he was exiled to Europe that year. Library of Congress.

home, fully convinced that he never was cut out for baseball playing." As some major league dreams ended, the club prepared its home grounds for the commencement of the regular season, with fans and scribes alike hoping for a reversal of the team's mediocrity.

Nearly 18,000 customers showed up for the Opening Day ceremonies at the Huntington Avenue Grounds to see George Winter pitch a good, but ultimately losing game against the Highlanders, 4–3. As usual a band led the players out to the flagpole, but instead of lofting up another pennant, Jimmy Collins only raised Old Glory over the park. Massachusetts Governor Guild joined Ban Johnson as honored guests of the de facto team owner, General Charles Taylor.

Patsy Dougherty ruined it for his old team with his stellar play on the field and his timely hitting, while Boston newcomers Myron Grimshaw at first base and Charlie Graham at catcher did their level best to lose the game for Winter. At one point in the pomp and circumstance of the occasion, a horse went wild and ran through the crowd and out of the grounds. Judging by the team the Boston management trotted out to start the new campaign, the horse probably did not wish to witness the horror. Good instincts, that horse.

About this curiously lifeless opening contest, the *Globe's* Tim Murnane cryptically remarked, "I have seem more enthusiastic crowds at the same grounds, but it was after being thoroughly convinced that the boys were the real thing and bound to shine brightly as the season grew older."

On April 30, the Boston Americans defeated the New York Highlanders, a remarkable development because the team had first knocked Jack Chesbro out of the game in the fifth inning and then railed off nine runs in the ninth inning against Doc Newton to win, 13–4. The game proved memorable for another reason—it was the last one the team won for the next three and a half weeks.

The next day Norwood Gibson had difficulty getting the ball over the plate as he contributed mightily to the Bostons' 8–0 defeat. The Highlanders' Bill Hogg encountered little trouble when he took his place on the mound, allowing only one hit for the entire game, with Freddy Parent getting the bat on the ball against the "porcine twirler." It did not take Frederic O'Connell from the *Post* long to panic, as the next day after the hometown team lost, 3–2, he exhorted the players to "[g]et into the game. Use your brains a little and by all means do a little practicing each forenoon on how to bunt the ball." Frustrated, Chick Stahl was thrown out of the game for arguing a call with an umpire.

O'Connell's advice to the team initially seemed reasonable and constructive: bunt more, surprise the other team, utilize the hit-and-run and show some "ginger," or team spirit. As time went by and the slump worsened, O'Connell became more hysterical, advising the team to start pitchers Jesse Tannehill, George Winter or Ralph Glaze in the outfield. O'Connell may have reasoned that since the pitchers could no longer pitch, they might at least make serviceable outfielders with their strong but woefully wild arms.

The fans still seemed to have fun. In a rainout on May 5, during the rain delay the bleacherites ran across the field to the relative safety of the grandstand. "First, one tried to run the gauntlet of [police] officers and was caught at third base because he slipped in the mud. Then another started 'on the hot-foot' with Sergeant O'Neill after him. But O'Neill followed him into the pavilion and made him march back to first base. Then several boys sneaked across and the officers gave up the chase."

Unfortunately, Boston held a 1–0 lead over Washington at the time, and with Tannehill pitching well, had every chance to nip the recent streak in the bud. Afterwards, Collins lamented, "We are not worrying and will be in the thick of the fight." Collins continued to keep the same lineup and the team continued to founder. The inept team ownership provided him with no new resources or players, and though his quiet ways worked wonders for a veteran club constantly in the hunt for a pennant, after 1904 the team needed a motivator and its manager lacked the ability to motivate.

By May 18, the press noted that "Collins seems to be giving way under the intense strain...." Having come to the Boston Americans as a young, handsome man, the years and the unsupportive owners had begun to erode Collins' confidence, and like the portrait of Dorian Gray, portraits of his visage gradually began to degenerate into a morose ugliness. The *Boston Herald* found him "singularly uncommunicative" during this period, as increasingly he bore the brunt for the club's misfortunes. Desperate, Boston fans turned their lonely eyes to President Ban Johnson, but even with Ban's gentle ministrations and nosiness, he could not get Jimmy Collins to talk or his men to win.

On another occasion, hard-luck hurler Joe Harris allowed Cleveland only one run after seven innings, but costly errors by Collins in the next two innings, together with not knowing when to relieve Harris, led to six runs in the next two innings against the Bostons, culminating in a 7–4 loss. After one galling miscue, Collins "actually collapsed, tumbling on the ground after getting both hands on the ball, and then losing it. It was a clear case of being demoralized, and Harris must have been affected, judging from the way he lost his effectiveness.... The large crowd was dumbfounded to see a great player like Collins go to pieces just when he had a game within reach, and sorrow was expressed on all sides at the result." Even Connie Mack shook his head sadly as he peered and pondered the spectacle of his once-proud competitor, now reduced to a laughingstock.

Finding the situation anything but amusing, Ban Johnson attempted to wrest Emmett Heidrick, a good-hitting outfielder from St. Louis. Heidrick had fallen in love, and due to his father-in-law's extreme distaste for baseball, had left the game after the 1904 season. The president met with Collins in New York, and in a telling sign of how little either man respected team owner John I. Taylor or General Taylor, they focused on players the Bostons might obtain from other rosters. In addition to Heidrick, Johnson tried to get a catcher named Ed McFarland off the Chicago team, as Lou Criger remained incapacitated by his appetites and ailments. Nothing much came of these consultations, as clubs around the league did not bend to Johnson's will in the same manner as Taylor did two years earlier in trading Patsy Dougherty for Unglaub.

Johnson supposedly wanted Freeman and Selbach out of Boston as soon as possible, but again, replacements with talent were not readily available. One rumor had Bill Dinneen being traded to Washington for left-handed pitcher Case Patten and utility outfielder Joe Stanley, a deal which would not have done much for anyone. Boston got Patten two years later when he went 0–1 for them and disappeared from major league baseball forever.

Jacob Morse's paper, the *Herald*, leveled harsh criticism against Collins in late May, commenting, "It is high time that Manager Collins put his foot down and assert himself.... It is a fact that Collins was advised long before this season began to get faster men than he has." The piece also skewered Collins because the job had grown too big for him and the club needed the guiding hand of someone like Connie Mack, Hugh Duffy, John McGraw or Clark Griffith.

While Chick Stahl experienced unending torment, the arrival of Rough Carrigan in spring training that year heralded a changing of the guard. In Native American dress is catcher Bunny Madden, with Carrigan in the middle and an unidentified player to the right. Boston Public Library, Print Department, McGreevy Collection.

Comically, while drilling Collins, Morse proposed the lamest of cures for the team's condition: bringing back perpetually disappointing prospect pitcher G.B. Josslyn for another look, although no franchise ever saw fit to permit him to wear a major league uniform, and another recruit named Clay. Of Clay, the *Herald* heralded, "Granted that he is no spring chicken, and granted that he is a poor fielder, no one can deny that he can bat." Criticism is easy but no constructive solution to the Boston American ills lay on the horizon, as the futility on the field persisted.

The nearly month-long winless slaughter finally ended on May 25, 1906, when Jesse Tannehill shut-out the White Sox. It played out so swimmingly that it almost appeared the old pennant-winning club had returned from a long hibernation. Bob Peterson, one of the few players with any intensity in his play, scratched out two of the team's four hits, enough to finally end the horrific skein. Collins did not play that day, being replaced by Bunny Godwin, and saw his team hopelessly consigned to last place with a gruesome 7–27 record.

The next day, the rebuilding of the Boston Americans began in earnest with the outright release of pitcher Norwood Gibson, whom the *Globe* remarked "has proven a costly member for the Boston club, being almost useless for the past two seasons and showing no signs of improvement this year."

Like so many Boston hurlers of the pre–Ruthian era, poor Norwood blew out his arm The housecleaning had begun.

On June 8, the *Boston Globe* all but declared the Boston Americans out of the pennant race as they reported the imminent release of Al Selbach, with the possibility of others to follow. The article is quite remarkable insofar as the Taylors ran the *Globe* and John I. Taylor was running the team into the ground from afar; more optimistic news might have been expected.

Selbach stayed around a bit, but on the next day the promotions of outfielder Jack Hoey and catcher Bill Carrigan were announced, both men personally signed by General Taylor. Carrigan and Hoey had just played their last game for the Holy Cross College varsity baseball team, and they celebrated their graduations by becoming major leaguers. With Hoey, at least, the proposed fix appeared temporary when he announced his intention to quit baseball in the fall of 1907 and enter the seminary to become a priest.

Indicative of the abysmal reputation of the franchise, Hoey almost signed with Hugh Duffy in minor league Providence rather than play in the majors, and Treasurer McBreen had to run out to Worcester to appeal to the prospect to sign with Boston. Hoey nearly accepted the minor-league offer, but his parents, who lived in Watertown, a suburb of Boston, wanted him closer to home.

Across the continent, the California schools had only begun to produce baseball players for the eastern professional ranks, which accounted for cold-weather northeastern schools such as Holy Cross, the Worcester, Massachusetts, college competing at the highest levels of the collegiate ranks. The Holy Cross varsity had been managed in 1904 and 1905 by Tommy McCarthy, who had resigned after the team's captain, Jack Spring, had refused to come out of a game when Mac tried to pull him off the mound. Spring never amounted to anything, but besides Hoey and Carrigan, legendary infielder Jack Barry also played for "the Cross," and like Carrigan, idolized Tommy McCarthy.

Jack Barry played most of his career with Connie Mack's fine pennant-winning Athletic teams, joining fellow fielders Stuffy McInnis at first base, Eddie Collins at second and Frank "Home Run" Baker at third. He joined the Boston Americans late in his career, by which time they were known as the Red Sox, and he managed them to a pennant in 1918. But at this point, the Boston Americans had infused their team with youth with the additions of Hoey and Carrigan.

Hoey received more playing time than Carrigan, but the latter player had the greater impact upon the Boston Red Sox. Born in Lewiston, Maine, on October 22, 1883, William Francis Carrigan was known throughout his baseball career primarily by his nickname, "Rough." As befits a man named Rough, Carrigan was rugged, a good trait to have as a catcher at the turn of the twentieth century, when outlaw attitudes and roughhousing still permeated the game. Not an unhandsome man, Carrigan's face told part of the story as it looked as if he had been hit square very hard by the flat end of a shovel. And although he stood only 5'9", a fairly average height for the period, very few people ever messed with Rough Carrigan.

Rough Carrigan would have been good at whatever he attempted in life. Until Terry Francona accomplished the feat in 2007, Carrigan was the only Red Sox manager to ever win two World Series. After he left baseball for a spell, he returned to Maine to become a very successful banker. While players like Jimmy Collins and Chick Stahl are remembered for the first seven years of the Boston Americans franchise, Rough Carrigan dominated the next seven years, leading to the advent of Babe Ruth with the team.

Carrigan represented promise, but in the doldrums of daily Boston Americans existence, the hunting season on manager Jimmy Collins had begun. General Taylor had executed a master stroke in sending his son to Europe, for as the team collapsed, Collins stood alone to take the blame for the woeful state of affairs. Avoiding the Christmas rush, Jacob Morse opened up on the once-untouchable skipper, letting it out that General Taylor had come to feel that "Collins is not equal to heading the club in all its departments...."

The *Globe*, and by logical extension the Taylors, followed suit, when on July 7, in lamenting another loss by the locals, the newspaper editorialized, "What's the use of anything? Nothing whatever, living is a punishment we all have to bear. When you can not catch the ball—much less hit the leather— mere existence is a frost; life a constant care." By this point of the season, the New York Highlanders had taken the lead in the league pennant race by defeating the last-place Boston Americans (with a record of 18–52) in a double-header.

The column spoke little about what actually occurred on the field, but continued to pontificate, stating, "There is this much apparent with the Boston Americans. It is too late for patchwork. Last year it might have been alright to get a player here and there to bolster up the machine, but now it's too late. The team must be built all over again, move slowly, and leave it to time for the development of a team as will make a race of it in the league. But this cannot be done all in a minute, and seasoned players are hard to get...." Out of touch, Jimmy Collins maintained that his team could still finish in the first division (one of the top four spots) of the American League race.

Most days, the only fielders from Boston's recent pennant-winning clubs were Chick Stahl, who no longer hit like a superstar, Fred Parent, who had forgotten how to hit, and Hobe Ferris, who never learned how to hit. The team continued to fill cracks with players not yet ready to play or not talented enough to prosper in the league. Rough Carrigan filled in sporadically at catcher and certainly possessed the fire needed by his teammates, but he only hit .211 for the year. A week after predicting a first-division finish for his team, Collins boldly promised a good showing in the second division (last four places) by his men in the American League race, while John I. Taylor joyfully announced from London his betrothal to a proper young American woman of means.

In this cartoon, Boston American Nation turns its lonely head to President Ban Johnson, hoping he will restore competitiveness to the local nine. Library of Congress.

This would have been a good time for President Ban Johnson to interfere and force the league-leading New York Highlanders to trade one of their stars to Collins' crew in exchange for, say, Bob Unglaub. Unfortunately, either Johnson did not make the effort or the New York management refused to help and Boston continued to languish. To the credit of the fans, the Huntington Grounds still drew enviable crowds. Even with the horrid dip in the club's performance, Boston only suffered a 10 percent reduction in attendance from the previous year, and the team stood as a threadbare but still proud flagship franchise. Rumors flew about that Detroit star Sam Crawford might join Boston and that Owner Yawkey wanted to sell the club, but this did not come to fruition. Boston would have to wait more than two decades for another Yawkey to resuscitate the franchise with capital and a willingness to spend it on front-line players.

After a season-long absence, fan favorite Lou Criger gamely attempted a return to the lineup, in a home game against Chicago on August 17. He had rehabbed with "specialists" and had worked out religiously at both the Huntington Avenue Grounds and the National Leaguer's South End Grounds. Collins pronounced him fit for a game started by his old friend Cy Young, but Criger lasted until the second inning before he suffered either a split pinky finger or a shearing of a fingernail, depending on the source, and by way of passing the torch, Bill Carrigan replaced him.

A couple of weeks later Criger went back behind the plate, and as Tim Murnane remarked, he "stood out like a stonewall" as he handled Cy Young for the complete-game victory. Had Criger recovered, he may have exerted a calming influence over an increasingly demoralized and rudderless congregation, but he only managed to play in seven games and his three hits did little during that interim to inspire his fellows.

The team suffered from the long absences from the lineup of its injured third baseman-manager Jimmy Collins. Collins was considered the greatest third baseman in baseball history until the advent of Pie Traynor, and missing such a keen fielder and a powerful hitter would have negatively affected any team. But his absences had almost as deleterious an influence on the team as his presence. He often managed games wearing his street clothes, a development that infuriated the Taylors.

By this time, Collins thoroughly loathed team owner John Taylor. Collins had taken the heat by signing off on suspicious deals and serving quietly as the loyal soldier, but now that the team had declined so drastically with little hope of immediate improvement, the abrasive personality of his boss began to wear on Collins, even when separated by the Atlantic Ocean. He began to rebel in multifarious ways. Suffering from a bum knee, probably the result of floating cartilage, Collins left the team in late July and Chick Stahl took over the interim manager chores.

Ban Johnson rushed to Boston, scheduling a summit meeting with Jimmy Collins at the Copley Square Hotel, convincing a thoroughly discouraged manager to stay on. As Jacob Morse later saw it, "Finding himself up against it because of his own incompetency, Collins became more sullen than ever...." Collins did return and pretended to care, then reverted to recent form by nursing his maladies and supposedly missing a game to head to the beach on a sunny afternoon.

On August 28, either league President Ban Johnson or long distance team owner John I. Taylor, wherever he was, had had enough of Jimmy Collins and suspended him from the team. Jimmy had not shown up for duty the past two games, and in light of his other unexplained absences earlier in the month, he left management little choice.

Ban Johnson had come into town that night, met with team vice president Charles Taylor, and most likely called the shots himself. Indeed, when the firing became public, Johnson released a rather long statement, in which in part he excoriated Collins:

> The suspension of manager Collins was not a surprise to me. The Boston club could not have taken any other course, and it is to be regretted that this action was not taken at an earlier date.
>
> When a club manager neglects his charge, a state of demoralization at once pervades a team, and all chance for its success is destroyed....
>
> Weeks ago it was apparent that manager Collins had lost all interest in his work, and didn't seem to care a rap about the success or failure of the club that had been placed in his charge....
>
> Weeks ago it was apparent to every thoughtful baseball patron in Boston that some radical step was necessary to bolster up the club. No action was taken and it was fondly hoped that manager Collins would come to his senses and buckle down to honest work.
>
> This he has failed to do, and his suspension today is a result. Mr. Collins has many splendid traits of character, and no one regrets more than I do his present predicament.

In light of Johnson's de facto support of Collins in the past, the president probably had to deliver a harshly worded indictment of the manager. Johnson may not have respected John I. Taylor as an owner, but Collins had not stayed within proper boundaries in protesting against his boss, so Johnson terminated him to maintain the integrity of the league.

Nothing else much changed, as the club named Chick Stahl the interim manager, a move that in part may have been an attempt to deflect criticism from reaching the team's management. During some of Collins' absences in June, Stahl had run the team and even engaged in a battle with the other Stahl, manager Jake of the Washingtons.

The decline of the team from pennant winner to cellar dweller had happened rather quickly, and yet Ban Johnson did not accept his considerable blame in expediting the process by prevailing upon John Taylor to trade Patsy Dougherty for Bob Unglaub two years earlier. Dougherty could not have solved the club's issues single-handedly had he remained in Boston, but he might have provided stability and at least served as trade bait to lure some talented players to the club.

Instead, Johnson left town with the mess he had partially created, as his beloved New York franchise prospered.

Hot on the heels of Collins' suspension, the very competitive Philadelphia Athletics visited Boston and on September 1 started pitcher Jack Coombs against the Bostons' Joe Harris. On paper it was a gross mismatch, as the Athletics had some players and the horribly disconsolate Bostons had very few.

More glaringly, Jack Coombs was on his way to winning 158 games in the major leagues, winning 31 games once and more than 20 games in a season two other times. Nicknamed "Colby Jack" because he matriculated at Maine's Colby College, Coombs notched 10 wins in 1906, his rookie year.

Harris tooted away on another track. Pitching promisingly in 1905 in a brief stint (1–2 record, 2.35 ERA, 14 strikeouts and eight walks), the local product, a lifelong resident of Melrose, Massachusetts, had begun to establish himself as one of the unluckiest men in baseball history. He would post an atrocious 2–21 record in 1906, and after another disastrous effort the next year, retired with a 3–30 lifetime record as a major league hurler. As a contemporary once wrote, "Joe is a man who requires a lot of work to get all the good there is in him."

On September 1, 1906, it mattered little as Coombs and Harris engaged in one of the greatest duels ever, as both pitchers started the game and ended it 24 innings later for a then-major league record. For perspective, the epic 16-inning battle between Warren Spahn and Juan Marichal in 1963 thoroughly exhausted those Hall of Famers, but Coombs and Harris lasted almost another full game's worth.

Philly scored first in the third inning when their center fielder, Bristol Lord, drove Coombs home with two outs, driving a hot grounder to Grimshaw which the Bostons' first baseman could not get to Harris in time covering first. Boston waited until the sixth inning to strike, when with one out, Parent tripled to right, causing the crowd to cheer "like mad." The redoubtable Chick Stahl then singled to left, bringing in Parent and closing out the scoring for the next eighteen innings. And what a crowd it was—more than 18,000 rooters to cheer for a team hopelessly out of the pennant race.

In the 23rd inning, both teams pleaded with umpire Tim Hurst to call the game because of darkness, but Hurst insisted that the match proceed. Facing catcher Ossee Shreckengost with two outs and two strikes, Harris fired the ball, only to have Schreck single home the ultimate winning run, thus ending the finest game Joe Harris ever pitched.

Matters did not improve much under newly appointed Manager Stahl, and indeed matters reached their nadir as the players' frustration erupted in a game in New York on September 11. In their history, the Red Sox and Yankees have staged a number of donnybrooks: Bill Lee versus Graig Nettles and Jason Varitek's rearranging of Alex Rodriguez' face come quickly to mind. In the late-season game against the Highlanders in 1906, though, it was Bostonian against Bostonian.

Since he had arrived in Boston, athletic right fielder Jack Hayden felt that second baseman Hobe Ferris tried to show him up at every turn, and he did not change his mind when New York's Frank LaPorte hit a short fly to right in the sixth inning. Ferris made no attempt to pursue the ball, and once it fell, Hayden went "leisurely walking after the ball" as an astute LaPorte raced around the bases for a most improbable inside-the-park home run.

Once New York was finally retired, Ferris gave Hayden a real hard time about his loafing, allegedly lacing his repartee with "vile" language. Hayden retorted with "[t]hat was another ball you should have taken. That is the way you have been trying to show me up ever since I joined the team." Once they reached the bench, Ferris let Hayden have it again verbally, and Hayden punched Ferris as many as four times, twice to each side of his head.

The Boston teammates separated the two players as two policemen ran over to help restore order. Cooling down and sitting at the end of the bench, Hayden was shocked to see Ferris break loose from Jimmy Morgan and run over and kick him in the head. Hayden began bleeding profusely from the mouth. Several decades after the event, Fred Parent still vividly recalled the altercation: "Ferris got up, grabbed the top of the dugout, swung in like an ape and kicked Hayden right in the mouth."

A dozen police reinforcements ran to the Boston bench and Mrs. Ferris, in attendance at the game, fairly swooned as some of the policemen handled Hobe "rather roughly." Hayden made an attempt to box Ferris again, but there were too many authorities around for him to be successful. Meanwhile, "[i]nstantly a roar went up from all over the field, and those nearest to the visitors' quarters jumped over the railings and made a rush toward the combatants," as about 500 fans rushed onto the field.

After Umpire O'Laughlin kicked him out of the game, Ferris was arrested and escorted to the 152nd station by the police. Hayden, who attended Villanova and then studied dentistry at the University of Pennsylvania, correctly diagnosed that he had dental issues and left to have his various molars and bicuspids professionally checked. By one account, he had lost several teeth in the altercation. Afterwards, he and his mashed mouth joined Ferris at the police station, where fortuitously charges were never filed while the officer in charge, Captain Cottrell, gave them each a stern lecture. Once released, Ferris protested, "I suppose I am a fool for being in earnest and trying to win. But that is my way. I can't help it."

The next day, the league indefinitely suspended Ferris and suspended Hayden pending investigation. On September 23, Ban Johnson formally banned Ferris for the year, but Hobe got the better of it in the long run as Boston welcomed him back the next spring training. Hayden did not play ball in 1907, and after a brief stint with the Cubs in 1908, this acclaimed pugilist never played major league baseball again. He did, however, receive interest to play football for a Boston team in the off-season.

In a brief editorial in the *Boston Globe*, the writer deadpanned, "It is comforting to think that the disgraceful clash between players Ferris and Hayden in New York didn't imperil Boston's chances of winning the championship this year."

In a chaotic campaign, few bright spots emerged. Myron "Moose" Grimshaw established himself at first base and rapped out a .290 batting average, quite high for that particular time. But like so many other players on the club, the Moose had been born in the 1870s and did not represent much hope for the future. The team needed an infusion of youth desperately, but all too often the youngsters auditioned by Collins and Taylor simply lacked big league talent. In an instance where management did obtain a true athlete like Hayden, they permitted Hobe Ferris to remain on the team even after their altercation occurred. The team had become miserable and unlikable.

9

Chick

On November 14, 1906, Red Sox manager Chick Stahl married a beautiful Boston native named Julia Harmon, and on March 28, 1907, he committed suicide by guzzling down a bottle of carbolic acid. So what happened during this off-season to cause the popular and beloved star to end his life?

It started out nicely enough. Although Stahl had not compiled a stellar record as interim manager at the end of the 1906 campaign, no one seemed to blame him, and the Taylors seemed interested in giving him a real chance to run the team for the next season. After a player's career ended in the late nineteenth and early twentieth centuries, a narrow range of opportunities existed in baseball operations. Having a chance to manage a team by extension granted a man the reasonable assurance that he had a future in baseball once his playing days ended, and the Bostons eagerly extended this promise to Stahl.

Plus he planned to marry a pretty young girl from Roxbury in November, so by outward appearance Chick Stahl had it made. Stahl's wedding certainly received its due public notice, with the *Boston Globe* noting on November 10, 1906, he appeared "the picture of health and happy as a lark" as he prepared for his upcoming nuptials. He demurred as he hurriedly left Boston's Old South Building when asked who would manage the club the next season.

The wedding itself was curious, as chronicled by the few reporters who covered the event. The pre-wedding breakfast took place at Julia's parents' home nearby, certainly a common occurrence of the day, but "there were only a few present." Although Stahl and his wife were both practicing Catholics and parishioners at Roxbury's St. Francis De Sales parish, the ceremony enfolded in the parish rectory rather than the church itself, a most odd development. Stahl's best man, Timothy J. Bresnahan, supposedly a good buddy of his, in reality was one of Julia's relatives.

When ballplayers of this era held their weddings, many of their teammates usually appeared as members of their wedding party or at the least guests, but apparently none of Stahl's friends showed up. The bride did not wear white but rather adorned herself in "a neat-fitting blue traveling suit and wore a beige picture hat adorned with ostrich plumes...."

John I. Taylor and many of the other Boston players lavished the couple with expensive gifts, but to repeat, there is little or no evidence that any of them attended the wedding or were even invited. It is equally uncertain if any of Stahl's family or friends attended the brief service, Stahl projecting himself almost as a wedding crasher at his own nuptials. By one account, after the 10:00 A.M. service, the couple took a coach to South Station for a 10:45 train out "west," with a first stop planned at Syracuse, New York, to pay a visit to Bill Dinneen and his wife. Another version provides the couple with a bit more time to arrive at the train station, and there was also talk that the couple first honeymooned down south.

The couple planned further detours to visit Jimmy Collins in Buffalo, with other respites at Grand Rapids and Detroit, with an ultimate destination of Fort Wayne, where Stahl resided in the off-season and had an "interest in the hotel business." Whether or not he actually doubled as a budding hotelier, he certainly invested his money wisely in real estate and had even bought his widowed mother a home. When Murnane had visited him the winter before, he tended a bar he owned with one of his brothers, so he had a business to fall back on to augment, and perhaps one day replace, his baseball earnings.

Soon after the honeymoon concluded, president John I. Taylor, flush from his ten-month European tour, visited Stahl in Fort Wayne and returned to Boston in early December to announce the appointment of Stahl as the team's manager. Generally a coveted position, the manager's job pitted Stahl hopelessly between the feud involving his employer John I. Taylor and his best friend, Jimmy Collins.

It has become almost universally accepted that at Buffalo the Stahls parted ways, Chick proceeding to Fort Wayne and Julia returning to Boston. This is nonsense, not only wholly unsupported by facts, but actually at total odds with reality. Indeed, just before Stahl departed for spring training, he and his bride attended a party at their friends' home in Fort Wayne, at which time the hostess, a Mrs. Schneider, observed that her guests "seemed entirely devoted to each other." Further, she added, "It would be impossible to conceive of two people happier than they were at that time."

At that party, Julia Stahl expressed a desire to accompany Chick to spring training, but he pointed out the lousy accommodations that awaited them, and the couple decided to reunite in Boston once the regular season began. Stahl returned to Boston, upon which he took a train ride to spring training around February 28, and those in attendance, including Nuf Ced McGreevy, notice he seemed in his usual fine spirits, apparently not affected by anything but happiness.

Once he arrived in Hot Springs, a drastic downturn in Stahl's mood was noticed by several observers. McGreevy sensed that within days Chick became "moody and morose." On the private trolley to the ball field and back each day, he sat alone and kept to himself in the evenings. Except for his time on the ball field, he appeared to McGreevy to be in a "trance."

This did not constitute the first concern Chick's friend had about the state

of his mental health. In his amateur ball-playing days, a period
beginning around 1889, Stahl
experienced severe depression,
spurred on "[s]ometimes [by]
the slightest disappointment ...
and on these occasions his team
mates and manager used to fear
that he had designs on his own
life." While starring with an old
Fort Wayne Pilsener city team, he
pined for his own demise.

Around 1902, Stahl reclined
in a barber's chair and morbidly
observed, "If you would just push
that blade in and cut my head
about half off so I would never
feel it I'd be rid of my troubles."
Stahl almost got his wish. A
scorned woman named LuLu
Ortman believed that he had proposed marriage to her and
reneged; she decided to exact the
ultimate measure of revenge.
Concealing a revolver, Ortman
posted herself at the corner of
Calhoun and Wayne streets in
Fort Wayne, waiting for poor
Chick to stroll by. Only the vigi-

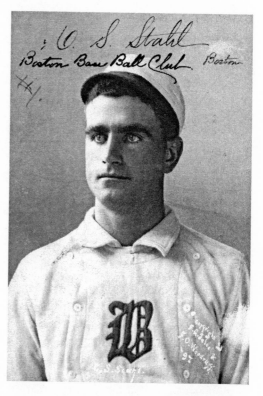

Chick Stahl, at the zenith of his powers with
the Boston Beaneaters, circa 1897. The handsome star had already articulated thoughts of
suicide to his friends, amidst the success he
achieved on the ball field. Library of Congress.

lance of a policeman or the swift response from Stahl himself (versions differ)
saved Chick from becoming the Eddie Waitkus of his day. No charges resulted
as the matter quietly disappeared and scandal was averted, while Ortman
moved to Chicago where she presumably continued to scare the daylights out
of people.

This is a sketchy history of Chick Stahl's mental health, and he most likely
wanted to keep it that way, perhaps recalling Lou Criger's very public treatment in Boston's Back Bay district with a doctor who specialized in treating
nervous disorders. Criger apparently recovered from his issues once he sought
help and committed himself to recovery. Perhaps Stahl heard catcalls directed
at Criger for being "crazy" and did not want to endure the same stigma, so he
plodded on.

In any event, his tenure as team manager at his first official spring training plunged him into a profound and chronic depression, as "he had very lit-

tle to say and seemed to worry all the time." He uttered the type of morose comments he traditionally made as a young man in Fort Wayne, this time before a photographer named Roberts, who had set up a session with Stahl and Jimmy Collins. At the end of session, Stahl lamented, "Well, I guess that will be the last pictures ever taken of me." Having meekly rendered this cry for help, Chick laughed it off and Roberts thought nothing further of the incident at that time.

By the time the team broke camp and headed north to play some exhibitions in Louisville, Kentucky, and West Baden, Indiana, many of his teammates have Stahl under a virtual suicide watch. In Louisville, while rooming with Big Bill Dinneen, Stahl washed his face with carbolic acid and asked, "I wonder if this stuff would kill a man?" "Would it!" Dinneen responded. "Why, a spoonful will kill a dozen men." "Then I have a good mind to take a good drink of it," replied Stahl.

A stunned Dinneen turned to Stahl and postulated, "How would your mother or your wife like that kind of news?"

Stahl thought about it a moment, and conceded, "That's so, Bill. It would kill my mother."

For the rest of the stay in Louisville, Dinneen observed his roommate writhing in pain, moaning and lying in bed and complaining of his head hurting, all the while continuing to articulate a suicidal ideation. Alarmed, Dinneen hid a razor from his distraught friend.

On March 25, Stahl took owner Taylor aside and tendered his resignation as manager, citing the stress that the job had had on him, insofar as he could not eat or sleep and was "wasting away." He suffered from "splitting headaches." Stahl also sent a telegram to his wife in Boston, informing her of his decision. Taylor reluctantly accepted Stahl's resignation but asked him to remain as team captain, which was agreed upon.

On March 26, the team arrived in West Baden, Indiana, and Chick Stahl told Tim Murnane that "[a]nother week of managing a ball team would have finished me, and all day I have been figuring what might have happened if there was a race on." The entire team except for Stahl worked out for two hours that afternoon at the local ball field. Stahl sat alone on the veranda of the West Baden Springs Hotel.

Murnane noted that on the next day, Stahl continued to take on a "troubled look," as he compulsively worried about whether serving as team captain would interfere with his responsibilities of a player. Curiously, Murnane noted that Stahl gave up alcohol about a year earlier and drank nothing stronger than seltzer water. If Stahl did not have a problem with drinking or at least a reputation for carousing, why proffer this observation?

Ordinary bystanders perceived Stahl's palpable gloom. A Cincinnati man, a guest at the West Baden Springs Hotel, penned a letter to a friend back home which in part read, "The Boston Americans are back at the springs again, and poor Chick Stahl is having his troubles. In Louisville he resigned the job of manager, and many a night he does not sleep at all. This looks pretty blue, and I would not be surprised if Stahl took the suicide route before long."

Even young Jack Hoey, the outfielder recruit from Holy Cross, entered into Stahl's confidence, with Chick expressing himself repeatedly on how he wanted to know how to die. It is public knowledge that Hoey intended to enter the seminary to study for the priesthood in the fall of '07, and in many ways he served as Stahl's last confessor. Naturally, the young outfielder attempted to steer his teammate away from such hopeless thoughts. But he did not have the training to treat the underlying mental illness and probably only provided a temporary palliative for what was essentially a terminal condition in the early twentieth century.

On the morning of March 28, Stahl checked out the condition of the local ball field and returned to his hotel room. Dressed in his team's uniform, he drank a bottle of carbolic acid. Immediately, he regretted his decision. Writhing in unbearable agony, he drank some water. Teammates Collins and Unglaub noticed him staggering around and diagnosed what had happened.

Unglaub asked Stahl if he had just digested the contents of the bottle of acid, to which Chick replied, "Yes, Bob, it drove me to it." Collins and Unglaub tried to induce Stahl to cough up the poison and a doctor was summonsed, but in twenty minutes, Stahl is dead.

Since then, people have been left to wonder why.

One important point that either does not appear in any discussion of Stahl's death or is not prominent in such a discussion is the link between Jimmy Collins' dissatisfaction and Stahl's own misery. As his best friend, Collins provided Stahl with companionship and guidance, and indeed he recruited Stahl to jump from the Boston National team to the new American League club. It is difficult to conceive of Stahl jumping teams without Collins' encouragement.

For most of the first six years of the Boston American team, Collins stood as a solid manager of the new franchise and Stahl continued to thrive as a ballplayer under his friend's tutelage. During the latter part of the 1906 campaign, however, Stahl lost his rock as Collins meandered in and out of the lineup, incurring the wrath of John I. Taylor and president Ban Johnson in the process, ultimately culminating in his suspension and Stahl's ascension as manager.

Stahl had little taste for the job, and even though Collins did return to the Boston club in spring training of 1907, he clearly no longer wanted to play for John I. Taylor, not to mention manage the club again and take this source of pressure off of Stahl's shoulders. Stahl suffered throughout spring training and needed Collins' help more than ever, but Collins had problems of his own. In his time of need, Stahl had no rock to cling to in his life.

Speculation concerning Chick Stahl's death has over the past century has become almost a cottage industry. Conspiracy theorists who propose the most absurd explanations for the assassination of President John Kennedy would most likely blanch at some of the theories that have been propounded as to why poor Chick died the way he did.

A popular theory surrounding poor Chick's demise is one that was first propounded by Harold Seymour and adhered to by several authors since, that Stahl had impregnated a Chicago woman and her threats of blackmail drove him insane. No evidence exists to support this theory and it may have sprung from the circumstances swirling around Stahl's marriage to Julia Harmon. Indeed, had this spurned woman existed, would she have not filed a claim against Chick's estate after he died, particularly after she had no compunction of blackmailing him during his life? And yet no claim was ever filed.

As seen earlier, the Stahl-Harmon nuptials had all of the earmarks of a shotgun wedding. Two practical Catholics, one a reasonably prosperous ballplayer, did not get married in their church but hastily exchanged "I do's" in the rectory parlor and then, by one account, rushed from their 10:00 A.M. wedding to catch the 10:45 A.M. train out of town. Stahl had no presence at his wedding, and his wife did not cloak herself demurely in white, but in contrast, dressed rather provocatively.

It is plausible that the "pregnant Chicago woman/blackmailer" was actually Julia Stahl, who may have believed (or convinced Stahl) that she was in a family way and that only marriage would salvage her reputation. If this was a ruse to force Stahl to marry her, he certainly would have known by March that he had been conned, perhaps even blackmailed, into a marriage with a woman who was not pregnant, and whom he did not love and had already wanted to separate from.

Still, the mistake people make in analyzing why Stahl terminated his own life is attempting to apply a reasonable explanation to an irrational act. Poor Chick had evidently suffered from major depression for at least a decade before his death and had abused alcohol for several years, even though he had taken the pledge to quit drinking before his death. He did not have his wife by his side, and he had operated in a deep funk for several weeks. His job as the Red Sox manager brought him stress and no joy, a common experience for men who had to work beneath John I. Taylor. Instead of trying to determine why Chick Stahl committed suicide, perhaps the better question is why he did not do so much sooner.

In analyzing why Stahl ended his life, Ockham's Razor, the philosophical concept that "of two competing theories, the simplest explanation of an entity is to be preferred," has been largely ignored. While Murnane and O'Connell hinted that more than Chick's stress in managing the Red Sox caused him to die, they underestimated the effect that severe mental illness had on the new skipper's life. Ballplayers to this day are blackmailed for one thing or another, but this does not lead them to suicide. Couple a source of stress, whether it be real, imagined or over-blown, to the mind of a chronically depressed individual and the situation worsens considerably. But first and utmost, one must have this insane belief that one's life is narrowing, particularly in a case like Chick Stahl's, where the evidence did not lead to such a legitimate feeling.

The gravestone of Julia Stahl and her family in Boston's Old Cavalry Cemetery. In this ornate stone, Julia's status as the widow of Chick Stahl is proudly heralded. Chick was buried back in Fort Wayne, Indiana, and not in a Catholic cemetery as he had committed suicide, thereby barring him from burial in consecrated ground. (Photograph by Caroline Hubbard).

Sadly, not too long after Stahl's death, Julia passed away as well, under circumstances far more mysterious than her husband's demise. The exact facts are unclear, but by all appearances she had engaged in an all-day bender from Roxbury to South Boston, a distance of a little over two miles. Four men, two of whom were minors, left her for dead in a walk-up of a cold water flat, where she died of edema of the brain. The men were arraigned in South Boston Court for robbing her, not for murder or even assault, and there the historical trail goes cold.

Julia Stahl was buried with full honors of her church in Calvary cemetery in the Roslindale district of Boston. On her tombstone, it is proudly noted that she was the wife of Charles S. Stahl. She died a victim, just like her husband did.

We know how Chick Stahl died, but how did he live? Born in Avilla, Indiana, in 1873, Chick was the sixth son of a rather large brood (24 children) of German-Catholic immigrants named Reuben and Barbara Stahl. The largeness of his family caused Stahl to later quip, "We had just enough in our family to make a couple of nines—eighteen boys and half a dozen girls." He attended Cathedral schools, not as common an occurrence then as later became the case in American cities.

By age 16, his prowess on the diamond earned him a spot on a Fort Wayne amateur team, an odyssey that led him to play on several teams in the Midwest for the next five years. He later played for Roanoke in the Virginia League in 1895, and the next year joined a club in Buffalo, where he attracted the attention of a native of that city, Boston Beaneaters star third baseman Jimmy Collins.

Boston Beaneaters manager Frank Selee liked what he saw. His Boston team had slipped from its premier position in the National League by the mid–1890s due to the aging of such stars as Tommy McCarthy, Billy Nash and Foghorn Tucker, and Selee eagerly sought the ingredients he utilized in all of his rebuilding efforts: youth and speed. Stahl possessed both.

In recent years, Stahl had developed a reputation as a loud party animal, a womanizer and a drinker (if not a drug addict) of the highest order. While he had moderated his alcohol use before his death, many of the other characterizations fall short of the truth. In the late 1890s, *Boston Globe* scribe Tim Murnane observed the coldly efficient and wildly successful Beaneaters as fairly colorless, that "outside of Duffy, Long, Tenney and Bergen, the Boston players are a quiet lot. Two or three of them are likely to drop off into a trance if they are not jolted continually." Far from a bombastic personality, Stahl more closely resembled taciturn teammates like Jimmy Collins, Sliding Billy Hamilton and Kid Nichols.

The Boston Beaneaters achieved a renaissance in the late 1890s at the expense of Ned Hanlon's Baltimore Oriole teams. Stahl rejuvenated the team, hitting over .300 thrice and fielding brilliantly. When Ban Johnson decided to challenge the National League, his Boston boys achieved a coup in getting the popular and talented Stahl to jump leagues. Chick Stahl should have begged onto Duffy's team for reasons that have since become apparent. Historically, much has been made of the close friendship between Stahl and Collins, but little has been said about Duffy's mentoring role with the young Stahl.

Stahl played his first four major league years with the venerable Frank Selee as manager and Hugh Duffy as captain of the Boston Beaneaters, and two better influences a young ballplayer in that rough and tumble era could not have had. Stahl thrived under Captain Duffy, batting .354, .308, .251 and .295 from 1897 through 1900. High-strung in many ways, Duffy had a knack with young ballplayers, a gift that Ted Williams cherished and Johnny Pesky remembered fondly more than six decades after working with Sir Hugh with the Sox in the 1940s. A very pious and patient man with youngsters, Duffy nurtured players.

From his late teens on, Stahl suffered from depression and needed friends, but even more, someone to steer him thorough his often irrational periods of self-imposed gloom. Stahl was a German-American from the Midwest, and Milwaukee provided a support system with the promise of visits to Fort Wayne, relatively close by. Milwaukee offered a chance for Stahl to play in his section of the country in front of other German-Americans for a wonderful fatherly figure like Duffy in the same area of the country as his large family support network. Chick Stahl coming to the Boston American was a huge coup for that new franchise, but it proved the worst thing for Chick Stahl.

Of course, Stahl starred in the new league, and more often than not, in Collins' absences, he managed the club in the stead of his best friend. As Collins became more disaffected with John I. Taylor, Stahl increasingly stepped in until his appointment as interim manager after Collins gave up on the club.

Before his final illness, Stahl had managed the Boston Americans steadily if unspectacularly in the final part of 1906. In one memorable game against Garland "Jake" Stahl's Washington club, intense thunder had erupted in the third inning with the Washingtons ahead, 5–0. Jake wanted the game to conclude as quickly as possible to make it through five innings for a regulation contest. Chick wanted to elongate it and have the likely loss wiped out by the storm before the minimum five innings were completed.

> ...when [the Senators] came to bat in the fourth the enthusiasts at the local lot yelled frantically for them to get out. Manager Garland Stahl's thoughts ran in much the same channel, and he instructed his men accordingly.
> Acting manager Chick Stahl, not to be outdone in diplomacy, put his men through some clever tactics that tended toward delay, and he came mighty near winning out.

While taking over a demoralized and losing team in the absence of his best friend and the presence of an intrusive owner was not an ideal situation, Chick handled it well and seemed to have some fun with it, as illustrated in the shenanigans he and Jake Stahl engaged in. Managing was not Chick Stahl's problem, simple mental illness was, and when it struck for the final time, he destroyed himself, leaving everyone saddened at the loss of such a dear fellow.

Trying to explain why a person commits suicide is rarely successful. Chick Stahl had handled the death of his father in a normal grieving fashion, but any little incident might set him off into despondency. He fought the good fight probably for as long as he could, and unlike his teammate Criger, either did not or would not seek competent (for the era) psychiatric treatment. His death can never be explained, only mourned. Chick Stahl was a great guy, and he left the world too young and too confused.

10

The Year of Four Managers

Haunted by the specter of the death of their manager and great friend Chick Stahl, the Boston Americans meandered toward the commencement of the 1907 season. In their grief, the late Stahl's teammates initially neglected in their calculus of the team's strengths and weaknesses the irreducible fact that in the departure of Chick Stahl, the team had lost one of its only productive players from the previous campaign.

The team named Cy Young as its manager, a title that Cy did not covet, clearly announcing that he only wanted to serve on an interim basis after having seen the strain that the job (and owner John I. Taylor) had placed on Jimmy Collins and poor Stahl. The temporary appointment came about in queer fashion, as Taylor telegraphed the following to Young after the news of Stahl's passing first become known to him: "Just heard the awful news. Wish I had not left. Take care of team until I arrive." Scanning this communication, Young remarked, "I wish Mr. Taylor had picked out someone else for this work."

On April Fools' Day, a day seemingly invented for John I. Taylor, Cy Young captained his team to an impressive 8–1 exhibition win over Cincinnati. Cy pitched and Jimmy Collins played well amidst their pain. Rumors circulated that the team had begun to recruit Jake Stahl as its new manager or that prodigal Jimmy Collins might be invited back to skipper the squad, but no one believed the latter speculation.

John I. Taylor did try to maneuver Young into becoming his manager, but Cy again expressed his profound disinterest in the position, stating, "I can tell you in a few words how I stand on that proposition. I do not think that I am capable of handling your team, and I don't want the job, anyway." Taylor, desperately needing a public relations boost after a horrible stretch during which he (or his unholy spirit) clashed with the popular Collins and after the equally popular Chick Stahl had died, tried to entice the great hurler to take the managerial reins, but Young wisely maintained his bitter disinterest in the job.

Angered and frustrated by an inability to persuade someone to manage his club, Taylor decided to browbeat Parent, who had gone on strike. When no contract emerged from a last-ditch negotiating session, ownership cast Freddy out of the clubhouse and gave him transportation money back to his home in Maine. Difficult as it might be to have any sympathy with management before free agency commenced, particularly in the person of John I. Taylor, Freddy Parent maintained his holdout in stark juxtaposition to a rapid personal decline in baseball skills. He had really begun to play poorly and may have wished to rethink this misevaluation of self-worth.

Exhibiting his innate common sense, Manager Young wisely tabbed himself as the starting pitcher for Opening Day in Philadelphia. President John I. Taylor and his wife were guests of Athletics Owner Shibe. Young pitched well for ten innings and then called in Jesse Tannehill to relieve him, as the club ultimately won in fourteen innings by an 8–4 score. Taylor did not appreciate the victory, but rather was quoted as complaining that "[a] clever manager would have a pitcher warming up right through the game. As it was, Tannehill was sent in to pitch with only a moment's practice." That makes sense—warm up a pitcher for an entire game in the event one needs the reliever in the tenth inning.

During this period, when Taylor spouted his stupidities to the press, responsible people like team treasurer Hugh McBreen feverishly went about luring a new manager to Boston. George Huff from the University of Illinois warranted mention as well as his former protégé, Jake Stahl. Harking back to the glory days of both the Boston Beaneaters and the early Boston Americans, Providence minor league co-owner Hugh Duffy took a train to Boston to interview for the job.

Interviewed by the press, Duffy held court:

> I would like nothing better than a chance to show the Boston public what I could do in the way of managing a ball team, and I fully realize the amount of work any man who takes the Boston Americans at this time is bound to have.... There is some satisfaction in being considered for the management of a ball team that I, more than any other person, was responsible for getting together. I signed up nearly all the original members and have always followed the club's affairs with keen interest. Backed up by the liberal owners of the club, I know that I could, in due time, give the public the kind of ball it has been accustomed to in this city.

The length of the contract—Duffy wanted three years—ended up as the sticking point. Duffy had captained the excellent Boston National pennant-winners in the 1890s and had skippered the Milwaukee Brewers and the Philadelphia Phillies, but his partnership with Fred Doe in Providence may have concerned him even at this juncture. In short time, his relationship with Doe ruptured and Duffy moved on to his next venture, and would not have another chance to manage the Boston Americans until after they sold Babe Ruth to New York. Also, his old teammate, Jimmy Collins, undoubtedly counseled Duffy that running a team for Taylor was a fool's errand.

A week later, John I. Taylor hired George Huff, the director of athletics at Illinois, as the club's new manager. Huff possessed an astute sense for evaluating talent, having scouted for the Cubs and secured for them Frank Schulte and Ed Reulbach, the latter from the University of Notre Dame. Reportedly, Taylor agreed to a hefty salary and a three-year contract to procure Huff, pretty much the same deal Duffy had sought.

Taylor should have sprung for whatever Duffy wanted as Huff proved an embarrassment. Although he had been hired, Huff did not get out to Open-

ing Day for the team, although to the relief of his comrades, Fred Parent ended his holdout and took the field as a right fielder. In Parent's traditional position stood Heinie Wagner, a fine but largely forgotten Sox shortstop and an important link to any possible future rejuvenation of the team.

Born in New York in 1880, Wagner sipped a cup of coffee with the High-landers in 1902 and enjoyed a brief stint with Boston in 1906. But with Parent aggravating management in the off-sea-son and gradually losing his batting eye, Wagner earned an opportunity to vie for the starting position at short. Although he did not hit all that well in '07, he obvi-ously had enough major league talent (while Parent's play had declined so pre-cipitously and with so little explanation) that he became a fixture. Along with Bill Carrigan, Wagner became a building block for the team's return to competi-tiveness, part of a foundation to build around when the stars came back to Boston. Along with later Sox shortstop Rico Petrocelli, he shined as a native New Yorker in the Hub.

While Wagner quietly went about establishing himself, new manager George Huff appointed first baseman Bob Unglaub the team captain, a choice not readily explainable unless one went back to team owner John I. Taylor, who idol-ized this ordinary player or at worst felt bound to see Unglaub succeed at some-

If Boston Americans Freddy Parent had been a gingerbread man, he might have looked something like this. The photograph was ruined several years ago when someone cut out the outlines to the fine short-stop, a man who had outgrown his welcome by the beginning of the 1907 season. Boston Public Library, Print Department, McGreevy Collection.

thing because John I. had, after all, traded Patsy Dougherty for him. General Charles Taylor from the *Globe* had bought the team for his wayward son, John

I. Taylor, to run, and perhaps John I. himself felt enough similar empathy for Unglaub that he effectively let him run his team. Quietly, the team also cut loose former star Buck Freeman.

An intelligent and capable man, George Huff needed little time to appreciate that he had signed on to a team owned by an incompetent know-it-all, with a bunch of miserable players. Other than the undeserving Unglaub, who seemed content to simply occupy space, the entire infield needed a change of scenery. Jimmy Collins hated owner Taylor, Parent really did not want to come back to the team, and Hobe Ferris was just plain mean. Rumors swirled of a trade of Big Bill Dinneen for Washington's player-manager Jake Stahl, but talks stalled and then died, probably because the deal made too much sense for John I. Taylor to be involved in consummating it.

By May 1, Huff was out as the Boston manager. He cited his temperament and his lack of fervor for the professional game as reasons for leaving. Oddly, his departure had been rumored for "several days," strange since he did not manage the team for several days. John I. Taylor did intimate that Huff's old boss "had made extraordinary efforts to induce Mr. Huff to return to the university." A somewhat bemused George Huff occupied the owner's seat as a spectator before he headed back to the University of Illinois on a train. Keeping up the façade that he and John I. Taylor were "best of friends," Huff agreed to serve as a Boston scout, an insignificant development at the time, but one that meant much to the team later with his inking the immortal Tris Speaker to a contract.

Always one to perpetrate an error rather than correct it, Taylor named team captain Unglaub as his new manager, causing the *Herald* to remark, "In a twinkling, as it were, he has risen from the part of 'sub' to manager of the Boston Americans." For his part, Unglaub promised, "I will try for a year anyhow," figuring that after that time, Taylor would have off with his head.

The Unglaub reign as Sox manager is an odd footnote in team history. Perhaps no one player personified the decline of the club as much as the mediocre utility man who had come to the city at the expense of popular Irish-American Patsy Dougherty. The trade was the Danny Cater-for-Sparky Lyle deal of its day. Unglaub had also earned his teammates' open hostility by flapping his mouth with either false or embarrassing information about Chick Stahl after he had committed suicide. Finally, Taylor always seemed to like Unglaub, even after he had once deserted the club for an outlaw team, which gave everyone an additional reason or two to dislike him.

For a miserable team going nowhere, Unglaub seemed the perfect choice. A collective "why does it matter" mentality had set in, with Unglaub unable to make matters better or worse. Privately, Ban Johnson rolled his eyes, seethed at this development, and went about trying to fix John I. Taylor's latest screw-up. Thus, it did not shock baseball insiders when, on June 8, Tim Murnane announced to his readers that "like a thunder clap out of the clear sky came

Two champions, boxing heavyweight John L. Sullivan and Jimmy Collins. By the time this photograph was taken, Jimmy Collins' handsome face was going to hell thanks in large part to working for John I. Taylor. Boston Public Library, Print Department, McGreevy Collection.

the news yesterday morning from the American League headquarters that Jimmy Collins had been traded for John Knight, the youthful third baseman of the Philadelphia Athletics."

The surprises did not stop there. On the same day, team owner John Taylor announced the signing of James "Deacon" McGuire as the new manager of the Red Sox.

The news received wide approbation. Collins did not want to play for the team, and while his hitting had improved, he had clearly lost considerable range at third base since the days that he bedeviled John McGraw and his Orioles by foiling their bunting attempts. In his *Sporting Life* column, Jacob Morse pontificated that Collins "lost many friends by deserting the club last season…" and also believed that the old third baseman had also helped queer a deal with St. Louis earlier. Clearly, a poisonous influence in the clubhouse had disappeared and a respected baseball man in Deacon McGuire had come aboard (with young Knight) to steer the club away from its recent misery. The Boston Americans also lost one of their finest third basemen and (former) managers, before or since.

Because Collins so sumptuously detested John I. Taylor, he essentially blackmailed him on the way out. No doubt learning that Taylor had swapped him for Knight and $7,500, Jimmy told his old boss "that he had to tickle him before he would move," which forced Taylor to inquire, "How much for the tickle?" Collins demanded $3,000 which Taylor agreed to pay, making the departing third baseman the highest-paid player in major league baseball.

Of course, no one reported this, but the developments reflected the fact that the Boston Americans franchise had reached a stage of virtual receivership by Ban Johnson. The general's money had propped up John I. Taylor's sad sack playboy lifestyle for years, but Johnson made a poor enabler and interceded to prevent one of the league's flagship franchises from becoming more of a laughingstock than it potentially might be if Taylor continued to exert his incompetent impulsiveness over matters.

Deacon McGuire was a terrific choice to stabilize the situation. Beginning his career with Toledo in the American Association in 1884, James Thomas McGuire had batted .299 for the New York Highlanders in 144 at-bats in 1906 and had even managed to steal a few bases. Born in 1863 in Youngstown, Ohio, just four months after the battles of Gettysburg and Vicksburg concluded, McGuire would come to bat only five times in 1907, but he possessed a calm demeanor that proved perfect to restore order in the Hub.

Parroting a sentiment that could have as easily been uttered in 2007 as 1907, Deacon came to town and stated right away that "Boston is undoubtedly the best baseball city in the country. The patrons of the game are enthusiastic and understand the fine points of the game better than those of any other place that I know of." This from a man who had already played in Toledo, Cleveland, Brooklyn, New York, Detroit, Philadelphia, Rochester and Washington.

While the Deacon had lost a step and some of the hair on his head, he stood 6'1" and thus towered over most of his players. Unlike Collins of late, McGuire promised to wear the club's uniform to games, although he intended to play far less than Collins did. McGuire had reached a point where he had to alter his career and he fully intended to make good in his new situation. To demonstrate his dedication to the job, he attended a double-header in Providence between that city's team and Baltimore, at which time Baltimore owner Jack Dunn tried to sell him on a player named Beach. The Dunn connection to Boston would, in little more than a half-dozen years, help herald in the golden age of the Red Sox in the twentieth century.

The very next day, another shoe dropped as the club traded Big Bill Dinneen to St. Louis for pitcher Beany Jacobson and $1,500, a swap that had been in the works for weeks. The deal was a typical John I. Taylor blunder: Jacobson's career record was an atrocious 22–26, his record in 1907 at the time of the trade was 1–6, and he had gone 5–23 for Washington a few years earlier. He pitched two innings for Boston after coming aboard and walked three and gave up three runs for a 9.00 earned run average. He never played major league baseball again after that appearance.

In return for these two innings of worthlessness, the club let go of Dinneen, a pitcher who went on to win fourteen games for a poor St. Louis congregation in 1908 (with only seven losses). Dinneen could have netted some prospects from a contending team, a decent ballplayer, or more cash to use to entice players to come to the team. The deal did nothing for the team other than weaken it, and since the transaction had been discussed for some time before Deacon McGuire had been hired, it demonstrated that all too often John I. Taylor made moves without the approval of his baseball men. After this trade, McGuire would not have been faulted had he taken the same train out of the Hub as George Huff had.

To his credit, Deacon stayed, but he had no use for his club's new acquisition, Jacobson. In one game against Chicago, he started Beany, probably on the orders of John I. Taylor, and after seeing the pitcher walk the first two batters, yanked him from the game. Shortly thereafter, he consigned Jacobson to the minor leagues, to a Toronto club that was developing promising catcher Carrigan.

Meanwhile, the team came together to remember their old friend and manager, Chick Stahl, in a benefit at the Huntington Grounds on June 13, against Hugh Duffy's Providence minor league team. It is difficult today to conceive of such an event being held, but in the late nineteenth and early twentieth centuries, major league clubs often scheduled them to benefit the families of destitute former ballplayers. In this instance, Mrs. Julia Stahl, Chick's widow, was the beneficiary of the team's good wishes and financial contributions.

Duffy came to the event, and to demonstrate how seriously the competing clubs took the matter, the game stretched out to sixteen innings; fittingly enough, the Boston Americans did not even win this one. Duke Farrell umpired the game while several St. Louis players watched as spectators. Charitably, Taylor contributed $500 to the cause and canceled an exhibition with another team, which would have netted him considerable money. Every other major league team donated $50, while the Cleveland players rounded up $165, good money considering how much most of their players were being paid. Hugh Duffy and his partner, Doe, brought their club up from Providence for free, with the entire proceeds of the exhibition going to the widow. Strangely, the Stahl family seemed to have little or no role in the fundraiser.

After a balky 1901, the early Boston Americans boasted stellar outfields that centered on Chick Stahl, with Buck Freeman in right field and Patsy Dougherty or Kip Selbach in left. By 1907, that had all changed, with the team sporting Jimmy Barrett in left, Denny Sullivan in center and Bunk Congalton in right.

Originally from Geulph, Ontario, Canada, William Millar Congalton had played briefly for Chicago in the National League in 1902. He reemerged with Cleveland in 1905 and hit .362 in limited service prior to batting .320 the next year as a regular, the fourth-highest average in the circuit. He got off to a slow start in 1907, albeit with only twenty-two at-bats, whereupon the Bostons purchased his contract and he proceeded to hit .282, tenth-highest in league average.

It was a dubious transaction, as many American League transfers in the early twentieth century appeared to be. At the time of the trade's announcement, May 18, Cleveland stood a very close second to Chicago in the pennant race. It made little sense to sell one of the league's best hitters, even if he had not risen above the Mendoza line after only 22 at-bats. One suspects that Ban

Johnson influenced the proceedings to help restore the Boston Americans to some level of competitiveness.

Curiously, at the end of the season, the club released Congalton to a minor league organization, Columbus, apparently based on his slow fielding and poor arm. He did not lose his job because of a poor attitude, "as he was a good-natured fellow and always did his best." Today, he probably would find a roster spot as a designated hitter or bat off the bench, but he never played major league baseball again. In fairness, once George Huff trotted out young outfield prospects for the team, even John I. Taylor could not have failed to see where the failure resided in that area.

A wealth of Bunk Congalton information does not exist to explain why no one wanted him after another productive year. The Boston Americans had committed themselves to rebuilding with a youth movement. Bunk would turn 33 years old before the 1908 season, and quite often ballplayers became quite old quite fast after they reached that age. While that fact factored into the club's thinking, it does little to explain why another team did not snap him up as a pinch-hitter or a utility player. Unlike some of his moronic deals, Taylor exchanged Bunk to Columbus for a pure hitter, outfielder Doc Gessler, and the deal did eventually pay dividends for the club. Sadly, many people who came into contact with John I. Taylor got hurt by him, and compared to others, Bunk may have gotten off somewhat lightly.

Denny Sullivan in center field symbolized how far the team had fallen at that position after the passing of Chick Stahl. Sullivan broke in with Washington in 1905 for eleven at-bats without a hit and then played full-time for Boston in 1907, batting only .245. He had some speed and drew walks well, which helped his on-base percentage, but he possessed no power and by the next year was sold to Cleveland.

In left field, Jimmy Barrett, a native of Athol, Massachusetts, rounded out the outfield, and like his fellow teammates, he batted from the left side of the plate. In 1903 he led the league in walks and on-base percentage with Detroit, but his performance had begun to steadily decline in 1904, even though he still led in walks that year. He barely played in 1906; in 1907, he batted only .244, and by early the next year, he too had vanished.

The infield also had spruced up a bit with the arrival of Knight at third and Wagner at shortstop. Ferris continued to play second and not hit, while Unglaub patrolled first, and his .254 batting average continued to remind local fans what might have been had he never joined the team. Freddy Parent filled in here and there, playing short, in the outfield and even at first base, but he still found his old batting stroke elusive.

The team also began to experiment with new pitchers. It had brought Ralph Glaze aboard at the end of '06 and the Dartmouth undergrad stayed afloat in his first season, compiling a 4–6 record. Tex Pruiett, who was not from Texas, did not fare as well, but Cy Morgan garnered the most interest with a 6–6 record and a 1.97 ERA. Morgan later won 50 games over the next three seasons, but considering the sad state of the Hub's American League franchise, he had debuted in auspicious fashion.

Positive signs did emerge intermittently. For instance, in July the team compiled a 17–16 record for the month, horribly mediocre, but for the first time in several months they had won more than they lost.

Still, the team persisted in repeatedly committing the same errors. Despite being hopelessly out of the race, in late summer the club started Jesse Tannehill, contrary to the team doctor recommending at least two weeks of rest for his sore arm. Tanny pitched a full meaningless game, after which he could barely lift his arm, causing the physician, Dr. Erb, to comment acidly that he was "disgusted." Even Jacob Morse in the *Sporting Life* editorialized, "What is the use of having a medical adviser?" Speculation ensued that the pitcher suffered from rheumatism, to which Dr. Erb replied, "Why, all that ails him is an inflammation in his shoulder...." Nevertheless, because the team had ignored the doctor's orders, Tannehill's season had ended, and like Norwood Gibson before him, the club had ruined his career. The great Tannehill never pitched effectively again, going 3–5 over the next four seasons, only three of which he actually threw the ball to live batters.

The Bostons did not continue their modest success as they finished with a .250 winning clip for the remainder of the season for a 59–90 final record. An optimist might point out that the team had survived a truly horrible year, from Chick Stahl's suicide through a revolving door of managers to win ten more games than the year before, but the team had also divested itself of almost any reminder of glories past.

Heinie Wagner had gained experience at shortstop and would improve in the seasons ahead, and youngsters like Rough Carrigan had obtained valuable seasoning in the minors and stood poised to build on their successes at the next level. Deacon McGuire provided the reassuring influence the team needed and anchored the situation for the next season. But the 1907 campaign could not have ended soon enough for the Boston Americans, at least the few who remained.

After the season ended, the Sox traded shortstop Freddy Parent to the White Sox in a three-team transaction in which New York received Jake Stahl and Boston found a uniform for utility man Frank LaPorte. Besides constituting about the fifteenth transaction involving the Red Sox and Jake Stahl, this development marked yet another sign that the glory years had concluded.

Parent probably sealed his fate when he jerked around management in reporting to the team in the spring, and after another poor year at the plate, Taylor deemed him expendable. Murnane saw another motive, in that "[t]he little Frenchman grew to dislike the methods of Ferris, then came trouble, and now both have parted to go to other clubs."

The trade for LaPorte in turn greased the wheels for Hobe Ferris' departure from the team a month later. Figuring that LaPorte had played second base in the past and could do so again in the future, the Red Sox sold Hobe to New York, which promptly packaged him and two others in a multi-player deal with St. Louis.

While Parent may have overstayed his welcome with his shenanigans during the previous spring training, Ferris's reduced speed and his inability to play nicely with others painted his exit. With scant effort at charity, the *Globe* observed that "Hobe's disposition to make things unpleasant for other members of the team has made the Providence boy unpopular, and it was decided to make a change…." Ferris prospered his first year in St. Louis, where he batted .270, his career high, but by the end of his second year there he had to return to the civilian workforce.

The club also disposed of Myron "Moose" Grimshaw, a casualty of favoring Bob Unglaub at first base. Grimshaw had batted .290 in '06, a fine average for the Deadball Era, and while his average plunged to .204 in '07, so did his at-bats. Analyzing this development is as frustrating as entering into a chicken-and-egg argument. Did Grimshaw lose at-bats because he lost the ability to hit, or did he lose the ability to hit because he had been displaced at first and needed steady at-bats?

Like Congalton, Grimshaw was born in 1875, and he was coming to an end to his useful shelf life. Again, like Bunk, the club shipped him to a minor league club, in this case Toronto, in exchange for the highly touted Bullet Jack Thoney, which meant the deal did not totally lack merit. Grimshaw never worked his way back to the majors, and by 1912, did not report to his team because even he had to admit that he was not in shape. The sense remains that Taylor favored Unglaub over everyone and subordinated the team's best interests to justify the old trade involving Patsy Dougherty. In this instance, it was at the apparent expense of Grimshaw.

That left Lou Criger as the only position player remaining from the 1904 pennant-winning team. As if to underscore his sense of vulnerability, Sweet Lou visited Deacon McGuire in the off-season, and they got along so famously that the catcher came back for yet another year in Boston.

The problem with the Red Sox from the end of 1904 through 1907 was not so much a lack of appreciation for the fact that the team had aged, but the inability to trade the men to other teams for good value in return. The trade of Patsy Dougherty for Bob Unglaub was obviously a farce, and the releases, sales and swaps of their players provided little to restock their squad. Taylor also engaged in wishful thinking that the young ballplayers he signed off college campuses or minor league circuits would provide immediate dividends.

When Ban Johnson had forged an American League franchise for Boston, the stodgy National League triumvirate of owners sniffed at the upstarts and alternately tried to ignore them and drive them out of business; they could do neither. But to demonstrate how far the fortunes of both teams had plunged, the two clubs scheduled another batch of pointless post-season exhibitions against each other.

The Boston Americans still had Cy Young, and indeed he won one of the two double-header games his team took on October 10. The next day Ralph Glaze came in to relieve Joe Harris as the Americans made it five straight in this series, played before less than 2,000 fans at the South End Grounds, one of them being old friend Hugh Duffy.

The series ended with another double-header, in which the teams let in the small boys for free. Denny Sullivan climbed into the center-field bleachers on two occasions to mingle with the 200 young fans, and he instantly became their favorite player. The Nationals failed to win a game in the series, losing and tying in the twin bill, and after the last game the players mingled with the fans and shook their hands, some saying goodbye for the winter, others paying their last regards to those wonderful Boston rooters. Thus ended another annus horibilis for the Boston Americans, but this time hope for the future existed.

The Boston Americans signed—and then almost lost—Texas star Tris Speaker. Although he hit lightly in '07, he quickly became one of the finest center fielders and hitters in baseball history. Library of Congress.

Optimistically, on November 17, Tim Murnane noted the success of one of Boston's players under contract, an "outfielder named Speaker" who had just completed a fine year in the Texas League. Also, in a rare moment of sober inspiration, John I. Taylor decided the team needed a nickname.

11

Red Sox Are Born

The first official name for the team, of course, was the Red Sox, and on December 19, 1907, the estimable Tim Murnane announced the most welcome development: "Pres. Taylor has suggested red stockings to be a part of the uniforms and thought Boston 'Red Sox' might sound better to the baseball enthusiasts than the names now used by many, such as 'The Pilgrims,' 'The Yankees,' etc."

The Boston Yankees?

Finally, John I. Taylor had done something right. Perhaps embarrassed by his son's incompetence and his neighbor's scowls, General Taylor from the *Globe* opened up the purse strings for the purchase of new players, and signings of youngsters from coast to coast accelerated. With excellent judges of raw talent, such as former Boston Beaneater Fred Lake and George Huff, the newly christened Red Sox began to restock and rebuild with some central goals rather than the meandering mismanagement of 1904–1907.

It was an illusion, of course. John I. Taylor did not suddenly gain great insight into managing a business or evaluating talent, but others like his father and Ban Johnson felt embarrassed by him and tried to bail him out of the consequences of his own scattershot actions. As long as John I. wielded any power and exercised decision-making over policy and individual transactions, the Sox knew no worse enemy.

Manager McGuire made the most of his opportunities, and with the infusion of cash and shrewd scouting decisions by Huff and Lake, he had a number of options in the outfield. Barrett and Sullivan from the previous year's squad were still around, but the club had inked promising newcomers Gavy Cravath, Bullet Jack Thoney, Walter Carlisle, James McHale and Doc Gessler. George Huff had also signed two wonderful ballplayers from Texas, George Whiteman and Tris Speaker.

Bullet Jack Thomey certainly did not plan to make it easy on his new employers. Although he had failed in previous major league tryouts with Cleveland, Baltimore, New York and Washington from 1902–1904, over the past three years the young Kentuckian had dominated at the minor league level, making him one of the most coveted prospects in the nation. At spring training in Little Rock, wise acre Bill Hart yelled out during a team practice run,

"Say McGuire, you have more men out here today in uniform than were killed in the Spanish war!" The Spanish-American War obviously generated many more casualties than the Red Sox, but McGuire did have an embarrassment of riches compared with the personnel at his disposal when he first came aboard.

Bullet Jack had a problem, though. While he feasted on competition at his level of play or worse, he never seemed to have the confidence or dedication to make it at the higher plane. In the spring of 1907, he demonstrated this ambivalence by failing to report, with various accounts ascertaining that he wanted more money, thought he needed more minor league seasoning, was out of shape, or more likely, was out of money. Deacon McGuire kept reassuring him that the Sox wanted and loved him, but it took him until well into March to report to the team's spring training site in Little Rock.

One final odd fact about Bullet Jack. Despite his nickname, he did not steal that many bases. And despite the enormous hype, he played poorly.

Confidence did not seem to be an issue for Henry Homer "Doc" Gessler, a life-long resident of Greensburg, Pennsylvania. Although he had not played in the major leagues in 1907, he had batted .290 two years in a row with Brooklyn in '04 and '05. His performance seemingly dipped in 1906 when he hit .250 for the season, but in actuality his on-base percentage with the Chicago Nationals, where he spent most of his time that year, approximated his OBP for the previous two campaigns.

He starred in '07 with Columbus in the American Association, and the Boston Americans astutely picked him up, reportedly for Bunk Congalton and a pitcher. He proceeded to bat .308 for the Sox in 1908, with a league-leading on-base percentage of .394. Never shy to take one for the team, he once led the AL after being hit by sixteen pitches, and while he never led the league in any other category, he once took twenty bases after sacrificing himself to the opposing pitcher's fastballs and curves.

Confidently, outfielder Gavy Cravath strolled into training camp and looked so impressive that John I. Taylor quipped, "If you can make good in your uniform as you do in your street clothes ... you can have my money." To which Gavy (short for *gaviota*, or "bird" in Spanish) boasted, "That's what I came for." Cravath became known for his power hitting in a pre–Ruthian era that was not conducive to the long ball. In June, he would hit a homerun to deep center in Washington, the longest shot to that area of the park that season.

Jim McHale hailed from St. Marys of California, and while he did little for the team in 1908, his one year in the majors, three others from that school eventually did: future Hall of Famer Harry Hooper, his outfield mate Duffy Lewis, and Dutch Leonard. John I. Taylor snapped him up during one of his many trips to his wife's home in California, and predicted great things for McHale if he could hit. He couldn't.

Walter Carlisle never had a chance with his name. He sounded like a

British butler and with a birthplace in Yorkshire, England, and a nickname of "Rosy," one suspects that his mere presence on the roster made Deacon McGuire cringe. The lack of talent did not help either. Picked up from Los Angeles in the Pacific Coast League where he batted .259 and displayed a .955 fielding average, Tim Murnane felt moved to crack, "These averages would not indicate that the young man was a wonder...." He smacked exactly one hit in ten big league at-bats.

Anchored by Wagner at shortstop, the infield began taking on a new appearance as well. Amby McConnell, who had once saved in vain to see one Boston major league ball game as a laborer in Pownal, Vermont, impressed everyone with his skills and professionalism at second base, traits sorely lacking with Hobe Ferris toward the end of his time with the team. Not a bad hitter either. At third base, another New Englander, Harry Lord, from a much more moneyed background than McConnell, joined the club and flat-out hit. In Wagner, McConnell and Lord, McGuire had the nucleus of a fine infield. Standing out in a negative manner, Bob Unglaub continued to occupy first base, but the buzzards had started to circle.

Consistent with management's philosophy to gather as much talent as possible, Taylor traded catcher Alfred Shaw for veteran Chicago catcher Ed McFarland. McFarland, a solid defenseman and a career .275 hitter, had an opportunity to play a great deal or even start, but early on apprehensions arose about his fitness. Manager McGuire said as much at the beginning of the year, when he stated that he had received a letter in which McFarland promised his full dedication to his new club.

The veteran catcher's verve did not even extend into the regular season, for on April 11, after the team arrived in Columbus, Ohio, "McFarland came here all right last night with the club, but this morning turned up missing and has not been located." Alarmed, the club wired for Bill Carrigan to join the team. McFarland did show up at the hotel "late" in the evening of the next day, after the game with Columbus had concluded, no doubt due to his being on an alcoholic bender. The team sent him home for two weeks to "get into condition."

After he dried out, the Sox used him sparingly during the ensuing campaign, as he came to bat fewer than fifty times, but famously in a pinch-hit performance against Chicago in June, he caused the opposing pitcher to throw about twenty-five pitches as the mischievous catcher kept shooting long foul balls in the left field area. Shortly thereafter, he was through, as he had lost the ability to hit the ball in fair territory.

As was its custom, the team relied upon Lou Criger as its starter, and Lou had reason to come to camp in shape after the club also granted his brother, Elmer, an opportunity to stick with them as a pitcher. Criger *frere* did not make the cut, but Lou continued to contribute his stellar defense and maintained his almost total inability to hit the ball when he came to bat.

The Crigers were not the only brothers trying out for the club. Catcher Pat Donahue and his brother both made bids for the team, but only Pat made it. Like Lou Criger, he could not hit. Harry Ostdick, who had played briefly with Cleveland in 1904, had a few at-bats with the team in '08 and did not get a hit or play ever again. Murnane, in particular, liked poking fun at Harry and toward the conclusion of spring training quipped that Ostdick and another recruit "never got off the mark in shape in the spring and cannot be counted on for their best for at least a month or six weeks. This is sure to handicap them, and their chances of remaining with the Boston team are not improved thereby." It appears that the Sox farmed Ostdick to their de facto minor league club—the Providence franchise owned by old friend Hugh Duffy—from whence few in baseball heard of Harry Ostdick again.

That left a very sore Bill Carrigan, vainly attempting to convince Manager McGuire that he was the best catcher by far on the roster. While outwardly supporting Taylor's youth movement, the Deacon continued to count on unreliable veterans like Criger and McFarland. Carrigan seethed, waiting for his chance to convince an unappreciative manager that he could catch, and if truth be known, manage the team better than Deacon McGuire. Ironically, Rough Carrigan later proved he could do that on both scores.

In relative terms, the pitching corps at first blush looked like an oasis of stability, yet even in that department several new hurlers tried out for the rotation. As ever, Cy Young anchored the staff, but Manager McGuire evidenced certain misgivings even with his ace. He mused that "Cy Young, after 18 years of hard service, cannot be expected to keep up the pace much longer, and naturally is something of a problem."

Young got off easy. Commenting upon Tannehill, Deacon let fly that "Tannehill, with a lame arm, has been of little use to the team for the last two years, and cannot be relied upon." Similarly, "George Winter may not play ball this season, and, while a good boy, is naturally losing some of his enthusiasm."

Continuing the brutally frank assessment of his staff, Deacon McGuire intimated that "Ralph Glaze is erratic and hard to size up, when it comes to reliable box work," while "Pruiett complained of a lame arm last season, and while giving much promise, cannot be classed with the topnotch box men."

The quoted portions are Tim Murnane's words, not McGuire's, but were typed after McGuire had pontificated at length to the legendary *Globe* scribe, and they probably did little to ingratiate the manager to his pitchers. Deacon did praise promising youngsters Cy Morgan and Fred Burchell, but his public downgrading of most of his staff does not speak well of his powers to motivate and encourage. Oddly, he seemed intrigued by Joe Harris, a losing proposition if ever there was one.

One towering talent did emerge, as Ed Cicotte, perhaps the most famous member of the team other than Cy Young, made his first appearance in the spring with the Red Sox. Cicotte's fame equaled notoriety, but at this point he was still a church-going French-Canadian Catholic, probably not that different from the departed Freddy Parent. Cicotte threw a wicked knuckleball and later became known for his shine ball, another elusive pitch that he perfected, as remembered by Smoky Joe Wood: "Some of the fellows used paraffin and hid it in their trousers. Eddie Cicotte used it. We called him 'Knuckles.' We called it a shine ball. Rub the ball on the paraffin on his pants." By 1908, he also had a spitter in his repertoire, although this might have been an early version of the shine ball.

Fred Burchell became a manager's favorite early on after pitching briefly with the Boston Americans the previous year. The team loved lefties, and this young man returned the love by winning ten games in 1908. Policeman Ed Hughes and Joe Harris came back for another look but were limited by their inability to win baseball games. Cy Morgan, though, did prove a real find, so the pitching staff by committee approach did work to some extent.

Returning north for a round of exhibitions in the Midwest, the Red Sox stopped by Fort Wayne to play a game or two, weather permitting. John I. Taylor led the players to Stahl's burial plot, at which time he laid down a seven-foot floral arrangement for the beloved Chick. It was a beautiful and classy gesture, but very few players were left on the team that Stahl took north a year earlier and few on this year's edition ever played with him. In the one game the club did manage to schedule against a local squad, the only starters from the last game Stahl managed were Unglaub at first base and Wagner at shortstop (and Wagner probably would not have started in 1907 had Parent not been holding out for more money). For those who remembered Chick fondly, players like Lou Criger and Cy Young, it was a cherished nod to the once glorious past, but this was Deacon McGuire's team now.

Tim Murnane for one noticed a change in the Bostons' spring training routine:

> The old plan of working hard on the field and then running a couple of miles back to the hotel twice each day, is a thing of the past with the Boston club. It has been figured out that the place to train a ball player is on the ball field. At Little Rock the players enter a warm trolley car after their work and ride back to the hotel where warm baths and all the comforts of a club room are to be had, including a rub-down by Prof Charles Green, when the work has taxed the muscles of the boys.

Undoubtedly, McGuire fairly salivated at the breadth of new talent infused into his club by the Taylors' money and astute scouting, but he did not appreciate how deeply his bosses and the fans expected drastic and immediate improvement over last year's product. McGuire wisely did not predict a pennant, but he did stoke up optimism by making grand pronouncements wherever he went, at one point gushing, "I'm getting more stuck on this bunch of ours every day…. I really believe we're going to cut a dash in the American League race and pull down some of these chesty guys who handed us the scornful lip last season. I can't see that we are weak in any department, and when the bunch gets going good, look out."

As a career baseball man, McGuire knew better than to speak so boldly. From Jimmy Collins' example, he should have appreciated that the Taylors loved it when their manager constructed and tied a noose fit for one's own hanging. By talking large, Deacon had to live up to the expectations he created. In a different vein, while the club had spent lavishly on new talent, some players' promise would never be fulfilled. Others needed to adjust to big league hitting and pitching and might not have the experience or temperament to join the Boston Americans as a finished ballplayer, as Freddy Parent had once done.

On Opening Day, neither pessimism nor caution prevailed as the Sox came out in their new uniforms, featuring two red socks emblazoned on each player's breast. Even their mascot, Jere McCarthy, wore the official uniform, as Cy Young started and held back Washington for a victory before the largest first-day crowd in team history. The good karma continued on April 20, when crowds outside the park cheered Thomas Morrissey to his Boston Marathon win (defeating more than 100 other runners) and the Sox behind pitchers Cy Young and Cy Morgan won both games of a double-header against the Philadelphia Athletics.

Almost unnoticed, Jesse Tannehill departed from Boston, swapped to Washington for lefty Case Patten. Patten had won more than a hundred games in his career but had lost considerably more than he won. When he reached his new team, he had nothing to give the Sox. Nevertheless, Boston threw him at the White Sox on June 19 and after the Pale Hose hammered him, the Sox tried to ship Case to New York. The Highlanders pulled out of the deal and League President Ben Johnson upheld their reneging, at which point Case Patten's major league career officially ended. Tannehill did not do much either, so the transaction neither helped nor harmed either team.

Seemingly, Harry Lord led the league in being spiked by an opponent. On the first occasion, on June 24, in a game against Washington, catcher McFarland threw a ball into center field. The Washington baserunner, Muskrat Bill Shipke, rounded second and came hard into third, causing a serious injury to Lord, who was manning his third base post. As Tim Murnane described it, "The spiking was purely an accident, but may put Lord out of the game for some days.... The boys made the usual mistake of crowding around an injured player when Harry Lord lay on the ground after being spiked in the shin by Shipke. The players of both teams crowded around the injured man like a mass play in football, preventing any air from reaching him."

Demonstrating his fortitude, and perhaps not wanting to lose his starting job, Lord came back the next day. In the tenth inning, Lord was spiked again, this time in the left thigh, at which point he had to come out. In his stead, the Sox inserted young Larry Gardner, who only a month earlier had played college ball at the University of Vermont. Taylor wanted him all spring, and as soon as classes ended, signed him as a utility infielder. Destined to become one of the finest third basemen in club history, Gardner played a few weeks in Lord's absence before the club sent him north of the city, to the Lynn minor league entry, for further seasoning.

Another notable addition to the team occurred with the cameo appearances by the handsome young right-hander from Kansas City, Smoky Joe Wood. Years later, Wood confirmed a legend that he had gotten his professional start as a shortstop with a supposedly all-women's baseball team called the National Bloomer Girls. Other men played for that team, but once his season-ending three-week hitch had ended, Wood decided that he wanted to make baseball a career.

He later played for clubs in Hutchinson, Kansas, and for Kansas City, attracting the attention of scout Fred Lake, who purchased his contract. Wood went back and forth with Taylor on the terms, but finally signed with Boston, at which point the extraordinarily handsome rookie admitted, "When I got to Boston, I was single, and you know how women chase after ballplayers. I used to tear around quite a little...."

Dispelling rumors of his professional demise, Cy Young pitched the third no-hitter of his career, against the New York Highlanders on June 30. Like Elston Howard fifty-nine years later, Harry Niles, soon to join the Red Sox, spoiled the perfect game with a leadoff walk. Thereafter, Young silenced all bats, facing the minimum of twenty-seven batters, with Niles having been thrown out trying to steal second base. It had no influence on the pennant race other than to keep Boston in sixth place and the Highlanders in seventh. But it did enhance the legend of old Cy, now in his forty-first year, a man the local papers mistakenly referred to as Denton Tecumseh Young. His middle name was "True," and he had not been named after the equally famous Native American.

By July 4, the club had righted its ship so satisfactorily that Jacob Morse wrote, "Manager McGuire deserves a lot of credit for the way he has guided his boys," with passing praise to the infield, which had begun to gel quite nicely due to Harry Lord at third base and McConnell at second. About Lord, Morse gushed, "He is a quiet, ambitious chap, always giving the club the best he has and is eager to get to the top...." Tim Murnane had similar praise for young Amby McConnell.

With Lord, Wagner and McConnell shoring up the infield, all the team needed was a competent first baseman. The club rectified this flaw on July 10, when it finally regained prodigal son Jake Stahl back to the fold after he obtained his release from the New York Highlanders. Simultaneously, Boston sent cosmic mistake Bob Unglaub to Washington. The idiotic trade of Patsy Dougherty in 1904 for Unglaub presaged the horrible decline in the team's fortunes thereafter, and its loss years earlier of Jake Stahl also hurt the club in so many ways, particularly in the form of leadership and stability.

The *Herald* judged Unglaub the superior player, a view at odds with the historical record. Unglaub never led the league in any category, while Stahl once paced the circuit in home runs and twice led in hit by pitch. Stahl's willingness to take one for the team extended to stealing bases, of which he had over a hundred more than Unglaub in comparing career numbers while Stahl's lifetime on-base percentage exceeded Unglaub's by 45 points!

The *Herald* did point out the recent friction between Unglaub and the Red

Long before the Cy Young Award, there was Cy Young and his giant loving cup, presented to him on his own day, August 13, 1908. Poor Cy looks like he cannot figure out how he is going to get something this big to his house. Boston Public Library, Print Department, McGreevy Collection.

Sox, dating back to replacing him as manager after little more than a month on the job. In contrast, Stahl wanted to return to Boston. Had Jake Stahl returned to the team in late 1906, he probably would have received the appointment as team manager instead of Chick Stahl, and poor Chick might not have sunk into despond and committed suicide.

But for Sox fans, the important thing was a very good player and team leader had returned to the team. Soon after this exciting development, Taylor signed Frank "Heavens for Little Girls" Arellanes, an exciting pitcher from a California outlaw team. Arellanes is principally known today as the first Hispanic-American in Red Sox history, his family hailing from Mexico. And to set the story straight, his reputation as a pioneer needs weighing against the far less savory parts of his reputation, as later came publicly apparent.

With Arellanes aboard, on July 25, the George Winter era in Boston finally came to an end. Wildly struggling with a 4–14 record with a team entertaining ambitions to finish at least with as many victories as defeats, Winter was placed on waivers. Detroit bit, and after some preliminary negotiations, Winter voyaged across one of the Great Lakes to the finest team in the American League. The *Herald* correctly pointed out that "though never a consistent pitcher, [Winter] had periods of great effectiveness...." The *Globe* optimistically predicted that George "will most likely do good work for

Detroit, as it is a run getting team, something that Winter has missed for several years."

With Ty Cobb and Sam Crawford generating runs for him, Winter had every opportunity to thrive, but instead he went 1–5, another sad milestone in his beguiling career. Someone once cracked that a pitcher has to be pretty good to lose twenty games, but George ultimately posted a 5–19 record in '08, his last year in the majors. To the extent anyone remembers him today, he is not considered a talented pitcher in historical terms. He started brilliantly with eight wins against no losses as a rookie, and although he pitched quite well in spots thereafter, he tantalized rather than satisfied his managers and fans in a most inconsistent career. After bouncing around the minor leagues for a spell, Winter's discontent ended and he got on with his life outside of organized ball. As a footnote, on the same day that Treasurer McBreen announced the release of Winter, he also confirmed the signing of Joe Wood.

In a minor deal in mid–August, the Sox traded utility infielder Frank Laporte even up for the Highlanders' utility infielder, the speedy Harry Niles, a trade that Deacon McGuire hated. Niles had spoiled Cy Young's bid for perfect game by walking to lead off the contest, and had led the American League in batting for the first three months of 1907 before his limitations as a .240 hitter sank in.

An inauspicious but much more important debut occurred when young Joe Wood from Kansas City pitched his first game for the Red Sox against the White Sox on August 24. Smoky Joe gave up six runs in four innings before Elmer Steele relieved him. Steele shut down the opposition, but by then Wood had already lost the game.

Commenting on the rookie's first game, Mel Webb from the *Globe* acidly and accurately summed up the performance, writing, "Yesterday he had no particular speed to make his change of pace effective, had none too good control, giving four passes, and showed little in the way of curve equipment except an out and a drop which teased rather than came up with any break or jump."

Another sportswriter provided more balance in analyzing this historic debut: "Wood has a loose action with a natural delivery which produces good speed, and he has a wide curve with a paralyzing break. It was evident that he was nervous yesterday. He certainly showed signs of something better than he exhibited in his first appearance." Wood would perform much better in the future.

Wood had an interesting pedigree. His father was a prosperous attorney in Kansas City, though Wood *pere* once tried to stake a fortune on a Klondike gold drive, only to come back with frozen and near-useless legs. His doctors advised him that "he could be cured if he walked across Death Valley desert with no shoes on. He did and he was cured," as Smoky Joe once related. Clearly, Wood came from a lineage with a high threshold for pain.

But Joe Wood experienced little vexation and much pleasure as he dominated the American Association in 1908 with one of the greatest fastballs in the history of organized baseball. A little known fact is that his son, Joe (not technically a "Junior"; the older Joe was christened "Howard") pitched briefly for the Red Sox in 1944.

Just days after Wood's first game, a self-satisfied Deacon McGuire strolled into John I. Taylor's downtown office to ask for a contract extension, only to have his boss lambaste him for inferior job performance. Stunned, McGuire offered his resignation, which Taylor promptly accepted, intimating that he had had his eye on scout Fred Lake to replace McGuire for some time. Essentially, the move was just another sudden, unplanned reaction by Taylor, who did not understand that it took a bit of time to rebuild a team from the ashes of his own incompetence, Lake, at least, had friends enough to make the move a popular one. In one gracious move, however, Taylor agreed to pay McGuire's salary for the remainder of the season. Flabbergasted, the Deacon told the press, "I flattered myself that I had been very successful considering the handicaps ... starting with a team that was in as bad shape as possible."

A native of East Boston, Lake had served basically as a utility player among the superstars of the Boston Beaneaters of the late 1890s, but got along very well with folks like Hugh Duffy. Unlike many stars of the era, he successfully carved out a niche for himself in professional baseball after his playing career ended.

McGuire wasted little time trying to screw John I. Taylor, despite his receiving pay after being fired. He visited management in New York and then in Cleveland in an attempt to ingratiate himself with those organizations by intimating there might be a way to wrest promising outfielder Tris Speaker from Boston.

Some substance backed up the scheme. George Huff had originally scouted and signed Speaker and George Whiteman from Texas, but after the 1907 season, the Red Sox brain trust failed to send Speaker a contract, thereby technically making him a free agent. This was not a minor hitch. The same type of error caused Carlton Fisk to gain his freedom from the Red Sox following the 1980 season, whereafter he signed with the Chicago White Sox. Parenthetically, Giants manager John McGraw passed on Speaker when he had a chance, indicating the limits of scouting, particularly a hundred years ago.

Criticizing John I. Taylor comes easily, but he probably made the correct decision in tabbing Lake as the new manager. Lake knew the younger players, having scouted many of them, and readily accepted the team's commitment to youth and speed. Unlike McGuire, Lake understood Boston, having grown up and played professional baseball in the city, and he had maintained links with influential folks and many of the Royal Rooters. Taylor may have dumped Deacon for other reasons, perhaps many of them wrong, but even had he acted on whim as was his custom, he chose a very good baseball man to take over his team.

Lake's appointment did not turn around the franchise, as the team limped

Popular Amby McConnell (front, center) receiving a token of Nuf Ced McGreevy's (front, left) appreciation. His debut helped facilitate the rebuilding of the club, but unfortunately for the fans, during McConnell's tenure the rebuilding never ceased. Library of Congress.

to little better than a .500 clip in its remaining games, a feat Deacon McGuire probably would have accomplished had he ridden out the campaign. What sunk Deacon was losing on average more than two out of three games in May and not offsetting this dismal month will spectacular successes. When his final six-game managerial losing streak ended, so did Taylor's confidence in him.

McGuire had taken over the helm and performed admirably during a period of extreme confusion, distress and sadness for the club, all the while stabilizing the situation. John I. Taylor did not appreciate this, and since Lake had his ear, he naturally looked better in comparison to a fellow like McGuire, who did not win with the magnificent team that Taylor's daddy had bought his son.

By season's end, Boston finished in sixth place with a 75–79 record, both an encouraging development given the team's past two campaigns, and a disappointment since Taylor and his family spent so much money to rebuild the club. Cy Young not only notched another no-hitter but led the team with 21 wins. Fred Burchell and Cy Morgan played well, but Smoky Joe Wood's fastballs impressed the fans and scribes the most.

The club fielded one of the finest infields in baseball with Lord, Wagner, McConnell and Stahl, and the outfield showed signs of gelling into a superior unit as well. Tris Speaker did not encounter instant success as he hit .224, but he did have more than one hundred at-bats and played a fine defensive outfield, playing shallow and daring hitters to try to punch the ball past him. Few did. Poised for the 1909 campaign, many rooters and scribes optimistically predicted a pennant for the resurgent Red Sox, a goal possibly obstructed by only the Detroit Tigers and John I. Taylor.

12

John I. Ruins
the Team ... Again

Like a skilled director of a horror film, John I. Taylor enjoyed building up his audience to expect something ghastly to happen, only to let them off easy with a relatively benign occurrence ... and just as the audience relaxes and catches their collective breaths the truly frightening and hideous event suddenly happens.

He performed this feat the previous season when he traded LaPorte for Harry Niles, only to fire Deacon McGuire soon thereafter. Predictably unpredictable, Taylor stoked the hot stove league after the 1908 campaign by trading popular catcher Lou Criger to St. Louis for catcher Tubby Spencer and $4,000 on December 9, 1908.

St. Louis manager Jimmy McAleer waltzed with joy in his room at the Wolcott Hotel when he learned of the consummation of the trade, telling the press that "[n]ow that it's up to me ... the deal is closed for I consider Criger the greatest catcher in the business, and I know that he will be delighted to come to St. Louis this season." McAleer knew this, because he admitted to speaking with the Bostons' player during the past year, a type of business that tampering rules today would strictly prohibit.

In a serious breach of decorum, President Hedges of St. Louis openly bragged about the theft he had just committed, praising it and himself for two reasons: one, Criger embodied a "slashing, brainy catcher," and two, "Boston minus Criger will not finish in the big [ie, top] four" in the American League. Disdain for John I. Taylor had become so open that Hedges exerted no effort to disguise his glee in strengthening his own club and potentially crippling a competitor.

Chicago owner Charlie Comiskey had offered $10,000 in cash for Criger, an exchange that Taylor rebuffed at his own disadvantage. McAleer always fleeced him in trades, plus Tubby Spencer was not worth $6,000. Fans hated the deal, and pitcher Cy Young loathed it even more, making no effort to conceal his displeasure. In all fairness, Criger had hit over .200 only once since 1903 (and would not cross the Mendoza line ever again), and Bill Carrigan had made the Boston Red Sox his club. Someone had to go and it was not going to be anyone with the nickname of "Rough."

Still, Criger had served faithfully in Boston as its main catcher since the inception of the club in 1901 and merited more return in a trade than Tubby and some money. While he battled back pains for years and had to overcome a nasty addiction to morphine, he squatted behind the plate, accepting his assignments when no one else did, often in intense discomfort. While he was not a bad hitter in his initial major league seasons (hitting as high as .279 with Cleveland in 1898), he had almost lost his ability to hit by 1903. And yet he must have seemed like he could hit. At the time of the trade, Jacob Morse noted one fan's reaction with some editorialization "that Criger was the superior of Kling behind the bat, but one must make allowance for the rabid."

As his hitting acumen disappeared, he appeared with each passing year to gain greater esteem among his peers and other club owners. McAleer may have even believed that an old Criger still stood as the finest in the business, and a notorious cheapskate like Charlie Comiskey felt compelled to bid as much as $10,000 for his services, a high sum for the time. Cy Young swore by the guy.

The change blindsided Criger. He had undergone an operation right after the season to remove a growth in his leg and upon his release, he traipsed over to team headquarters with reserve catcher Pat Donahue. Criger told John I. Taylor all about the planned one-month hunting expedition with Donahue, LaPorte and Jake Stahl, and John I. gave a rifle to Criger as a gift. Presumably, Taylor did not tell Criger it was a kiss goodbye.

Burning his bridge to Boston management, Criger published an open letter to his many fans, in which he wrote:

Boston Baseball Fans. I want the Boston fans to know it was no wish of mine to leave Boston. I signed a contract with Taylor in October, and he promised faithfully to never sell or trade me. He gave me a raise in salary and a shot gun, and I thought for sure I would be in Boston in 1909. I assure you I was dumbfounded when I learned of the deal Taylor pulled off.

I love Boston and am sorry to leave, but now that I got my divvy of sales money, I shall go to St. Louis and look out for us. The team that beats us will have to win the championship. I am going to make Taylor sick and sorry of his deal before the year is gone. Am feeling fine at present, and look out for St. Louis when they get to Boston.

Most of the Boston papers adopted a wait-and-see attitude in the wake of the transaction, particularly since it had become very difficult not to love Bill Carrigan as both a catcher and a team leader. Dumping Criger meant Carrigan stood alone as the starting catcher, a welcomed development for many. Collectively, writers and fans alike exhaled a bit, undoubtedly figuring that if the Criger deal was the worst one Taylor intended to pull in the off-season, then prospects for the team still beamed bright for the spring.

But Taylor was not finished. Some folks just love dropping bombshells, and no one ever enjoyed doing so more than John I. Taylor, who shocked the Boston public on February 16, 1909, by trading Cy Young to the Cleveland club

CLEVELAND GAVE UP $12,500 CASH FOR "CY'

Also Gave Two Pitchers Worth $5000, Making Young Highest Priced Player Ever Sold--- Boston Fans in Rage at Deal

The scales of justice did not balance in the Cy Young trade, at least not initially. In this *Boston Post* cartoon, it is apparent the artist believed that Boston traded a horse and got a couple of ponies. Library of Congress.

for pitchers Charlie Chech, Jack Ryan and cash. Losing Criger was one thing, but the dumping of the beloved—and still very productive— Young sent the fans into the streets howling in protest.

The *Boston Post* published a cartoon with the Boston management holding a scale in which a massive bag of money and two small players in the persons of Ryan and Chech outweighed Cy Young with his right hand placed over his heart and a laurel around his head with his "wonderful record." The headlines screamed, at one point insisting that "Boston Fans in Rage at Deal."

Paul Shannon at the *Post* allowed that after the Criger deal, rumors had circulated that old Cy wanted out of town. But Shannon still termed the departure of Cy Young as one that "appalled" people outside of New England, and indeed across America, adding, "No excuse that the Boston American management can make can adequately explain to the fans the great pitcher's sale."

The *Boston Herald*, without venting overt criticism, might have published the worst indictment of the deal, noting that Jimmy McAleer felt upset he had not obtained Young for his club, the implication being that he had swindled John I. Taylor in the past and knew he could make a pigeon of him again. Taylor may have felt this way because he had asked for Rube Waddell, now with St. Louis, straight up for Young. McAleer had turned down this deal, but had been assured by Taylor that he meant to entertain any counteroffers, an opportunity he failed to honor by turning his attention to Cleveland.

The *Boston Evening Record* weighed in against the state of affairs, sensing that while fans regretted Criger leaving town, they genuinely "grieved" at the departure of Cy Young. Fred Lake made a limp-wristed defense of the transaction, arguing that with Criger leaving, if Cy Young had had a bad year in

Boston in 1909, fans would have blamed management because it had dumped Cy's old battery mate, a flimsy excuse if there ever was one.

The *Boston Globe* in its effort to deflect the fan resistance to the move, and by logical extension the latest act of John I. Taylor, took the unprecedented step of quoting sportswriters from competing local newspapers who defended the transaction.

The *Globe* quoted *Boston American*'s A.H.C. Mitchell, an alter ego for John I. Taylor, who delineated what he felt were the reasons for Young's transfer:

> First—Pres Taylor of the Red Sox is determined to have nothing but young blood in his team, as he figures the pennant can come to Boston in no other way.
> Second—It is figured that Young, who will be 42 years old on March 29, and has been pitching ball 19 years, cannot possibly pitch effectively more than a year or two longer.
> Third—Having sold Criger, the old side partner of Young, to the St. Louis club, Mr. Taylor believes that if Young should happen to have a bad year the Boston baseball public would blame it to allowing Criger to go.
> Fourth—The Boston club received in exchange for Cy two young pitchers and a large money consideration.
> Fifth—If Pres Taylor waited until Young lost his effectiveness the veteran would be valueless to exchange for other players. Today the deal is made at top figures.

Secretary McBreen tried to soften the news by employing an old trick of the British Empire: when a fiasco occurs, negate it immediately with a grand victory. In other words, if the HMS *Hood* sinks, it is even more incumbent to "sink the Bismarck." McBreen tried to accomplish this public relations objective by sweetening the news regarding Young with the announcement of the club procuring the services of a young pitcher named Wolter, who had accumulated an astounding minor league record of 27–2 the year before. Boston fans still patiently await Wolter achieving his true potential.

Decades later, when Boston general manager Lou Gorman obtained from the Cubs stud reliever Lee Smith for Calvin Schiraldi and Al Nipper, a scribe likened it to obtaining a horse for two ponies. To most fans and sportswriters in the winter of 1909, it appeared the Red Sox had obtained two ponies for a horse.

Stout and Johnson have maintained that this transaction may have prevented the Red Sox from winning the pennant in 1909. It might have done that, but at the risk of iconoclasm at the time was not a poor one for Boston, it just occurred one year too early. Young would turn 42 years old shortly, and in 1909, he only went 19–15 for a poor Cleveland team. Thereafter he went 14–19 in his final two seasons. Chech had won eleven games and lost seven the previous year with an impressive 1.74 ERA. While primarily a minor leaguer, Jack "Gulfport" Ryan had struck out seven and only walked two during a brief stint with Cleveland.

In first half of the 1909 season, Chech and Ryan did not set the baseball world on its ear, although Chech did win seven games. But later that season, in July, the Red Sox exchanged Chech and Ryan with the minor league St. Paul team for left-hander Eddie Karger and relief specialist Charley "Sea Lion" Hall, both of whom pitched effectively for the team that year, and in the instance of Hall, for several years thereafter. Seen in this long-term light, the loss of Young did not prove all that grievous to the team, particularly since Hall found a niche as major league managers increasingly appreciated the value of having a strong and resilient relief specialist on their staffs.

Born Carlos Luis Hall on July 27, 1884, in Ventura, California (for years reporters had him a native of Kerrville, Texas), Charley Hall fought through some stiff prejudice as a Hispanic-American on his path to a major league career. Any time someone taunted him by referring to him as "Carlos" or "Greaser," he dropped everything and beat the tormentor to a pulp, an otherwise out-of-character reaction for a popular man.

His bark proved worse than his bite as he did not hate all nicknames. Due to Hall's foghorn type of voice, people started calling him "Sea Lion," a sobriquet he took to with marked equanimity. Upon the conclusion of his playing days, he alternated as a policeman, sheriff and jailer in Ventura, California, where presumably he did not have to suffer fools gladly. Fred Lieb always believed that Hall did not fulfill the considerable promise he displayed in the minors, where he posted four no-hitters. But his versatility—he could start, provide long-relief or save games—made him an invaluable fixture on the club's staff over the next five years.

The lefty Karger also contributed in spurts, racking up a 21–17 record in the next two-and-a-half years, often in relief. With the small staffs at the turn of the century, a team needed stars on the mound, and Karger pitched decently, but was no star.

The Sox management maintained the devotion to a youth movement and had made several bad deals in the wake of their plans, but the Young deal does not easily fall into this category. As it transpired, it did not pan out as a spectacular one. Chech only went 7–5 the next season before disappearing, and Ryan never did much, but conceptually the deal made sense when made. Young could not pitch forever, so better to obtain two young arms from Cleveland while he still had trade value than watch him fall apart at a pretty hefty salary as the team tried to soar. John I. Taylor did many stupid things during his ownership of the Boston Americans; trading Cy Young was not the worst of them.

In the winter and spring of 1909, John I. Taylor had become enamored with youth, and Young and Criger contrasted with what he wished. The press and Taylor began to refer to his team as "the Speed Boys," with slick fielders and speedy baserunners garnering the owner's attention. He did not want a bunch of old Dutch uncles like Deacon McGuire, Cy Young and Lou Criger around any longer; after all, they were relics of a previous century. He wanted players that he fancied in their own ways resembled how he saw himself.

Historically, the trade by Taylor of the other Cy, Cy Morgan to Philadelphia for pitcher Biff Schlitzer and cash, has gone largely overlooked, no surprise considering the give-aways in 1909 alone. The Morgan deal deserves attention because the younger Cy won 51 games from 1909 though 1911 while the immortal Schlitzer posted a 4–7 record in the year of the trade. He then disappeared from baseball for five years until Buffalo in the Federal League unwisely permitted him to pitch 3.1 innings and rack up a 16.20 ERA. After Cy Morgan joined the Athletics, he won 16 games that partial year alone, victories Boston sorely needed to contend for the pennant yet did not receive.

Thankfully, not every star left the team. Even John I. Taylor appreciated the excellence of the Grey Eagle, Tris Speaker, who began to realize his enormous potential by batting .309 as a full-time starting center fielder in 1909. Joining him in the outfield as a rookie was Harry Bartholomew

Popular clutch hitter Harry Hooper was inducted into Baseball's Hall of Fame in 1971. Once in the Hall, Hooper did not treat it like a private club, but urged voters to elect Larry Gardner and Duffy Lewis. Library of Congress.

Hooper, a product of St. Mary's College in California, with Doc Gessler at least temporarily patrolling right field. Because Taylor's wife originally hailed from San Francisco, he constantly visited the other coast and sought the cream of the talent, Hooper being just one of his finds, with a little help from Sox scout Charlie Graham.

Trained as a civil engineer, Hooper had begun working for a railroad in the mountains of his home state while also playing local ball, most notably for the Sacramento club of the California League, where he paced the circuit in fielding while also hitting for average and stealing bases. Taylor met with Hooper to hash out a contract in a saloon, to Taylor's obvious approbation, and utilizing some of Charlie Graham's negotiating advice, came to terms for a professional contract with Boston at a significantly higher amount than his combined salary as an engineer and West Coast ballplayer. In his rookie year, he batted .282 in limited duty, charting his destiny as one of the greatest defensive right fielders in franchise history.

A loyal chap too, that Hooper. Years after he was elected to the Baseball Hall of Fame, he hounded the hall's voters to induct Larry Gardner along with an outfielder destined to join the club the following year named Duffy Lewis. Until Lewis hooked up with Boston, Doc Gessler tried to stay happy as a member of the Red Sox, an increasingly difficult task for him to credibly accomplish.

Traditionally, Cy Young had formed the nucleus of the Boston Americans pitching staff. With Young's departure, Lake relied upon youngsters with some mixed results, including Cicotte (14–5), Arellanes (4–3), Burchell (3–3), Hall (6–4), together with the partial contributions of Chech and the overrated Ryan. Smoky Joe Wood started smoking opposing batters by posting a winning record in his first full season.

Describing the velocity with which Wood delivered his pitches to the plate, Cleveland's star Nap Lajoie attributed this success to his "superb stamina, iron nerve, brains and natural pitching skill—the swiftest pitcher I ever faced. It is not exaggerating a bit when I say that at times I was unable to see Wood's fast ball as it sped over the plate." As corroboration, Walter Johnson always maintained that no one threw the ball faster than Smoky Joe Wood. As talented as Joe Wood had begun to demonstrate he was to fans and pundits alike, some scribes, seeking to justify the loss of Cy Young, continued to praise Chech as the true staff ace.

Tim Murnane had to defend John I. Taylor because he headed the sports department for John I.'s father at the *Globe*, but the near-indentured devotion that Jacob Morse (as opposed to the slavish bootlicking of A.H.C. Mitchell) from the *Sporting Life* and *Herald* began to exhibit much more forcefully in 1909 is much harder to explain. Musing about the loss of Cy Young, Morse wrote, "We miss Cy Young of course. Why not? He was a great figure here, but Boston secured a mighty clever young pitcher in his place in Chech."

By late May, Morse touted Chech as the leader of the staff by a wide margin, a curious statement to make with much more talented men in the ranks, such as Smoky Joe Wood and Eddie Cicotte. Morse also gushed over John I. Taylor's rejuvenation of the team, calling it a "huge success." As the summer progressed and Chech's talent did not, Morse finally conceded that Chech was a cold-weather pitcher only, although nary a word of complaint was made about Taylor.

The rejuvenated Red Sox suffered a rash of injuries at the advent of summer, with stellar infielders Amby McConnell and Lord landing on the shelf, while first baseman Jake Stahl ventured back home to mourn the death of his young child. Nevertheless, even with multiple injuries to his roster, John I. took particular pride in his team's prowess on the basepaths, as the fleetness of the "Speed Boys" continued to captivate the public's imagination.

For some years the name caught on as Tris Speaker stole 35 bases, with Lord and McConnell swiping, respectively, an additional 36 and 26 bases. The decrepitude of the late Collins' clubs had disappeared as Taylor's youthful charges created runs and transmitted headaches to opposing pitchers all season.

Supplementing his staff, Taylor signed promising University of Vermont pitcher Ray Collins, a man who once struck out 19 Penn State batters in a game. A teammate of Larry Gardner in college, the much-more taciturn Collins immediately provided quality innings to the team, and in the future, posted numerous Sox victories. Still, even with the encouraging acquisition of Collins, the Sox fielders continued to fall, with utility infielder Charlie French joining the ranks of the physically unable to perform.

Although John I. Taylor made some of the worst trades in Red Sox history, he did not panic when injuries mounted, particularly when the Chicago White Sox offered hurler Sleepy Bill Burns straight up for Tris Speaker. It would have been a steal for Chicago. Burns went 8–14 that year as his undistinguished career petered out, and his everlasting notoriety as a conspirator in fixing the 1919 World Series awaited him. Taylor wisely held his hand for a change and signed two more skilled recruits, pitcher Larry Pape and swift outfielder Duffy Lewis, from his wonderful California pipeline.

Meanwhile, as the team steamed into July, Lord bruised his shoulder, Gessler tore open a finger on barbed wire, and oft-injured Bullet Jack Thoney had to be carried off the field on a stretcher when he ran back to first base after getting his second hit of the game. He slid into first with both feet and broke a small bone in his right leg during a game against Philadelphia in which he chalked up two of his team's five hits. Thoney did not play the rest of '09 and also missed all of 1910. Although he attempted a brief comeback in 1911, his once-promising career had effectively ended.

Mysteriously, Tubby Spencer, the crumby catcher obtained in the Lou Criger deal, disappeared suddenly, supposedly to join an outlaw league in California. Like Charlie on the MTA, Tubby never returned, and his fate is still unknown.

Doc Gessler also took a train out of South Station, receiving his walking papers on September 9 when Taylor shoveled him off to Washington in exchange for hurler Charley Smith and cash. The trade worked almost equally well for both teams, as Smith pitched decently for the rest of the year and through the next, while Gessler played well with his new club but developed premature aging in his early thirties. By the standards of most John I. Taylor trades, it constituted a relative success.

The Gessler trade, as one example, shows why so many of the Red Sox deals backfired over the years. In late July the team leaked to the *Globe* that Harry Hooper might replace Doc in right field. Since Doc no longer would start, he hardly could serve as the team captain, which led the club to publicly speculate that Harry Lord might make a better captain. And by the way, the club felt that even though Gessler excelled at the plate, he lazed in the field.

Taylor then exacerbated the situation by replacing Gessler as captain, which led not only to Doc's humiliation, but caused the team to split into two factions, depending on whether one approved of the move or not. The former captain's emasculation complete, the *Boston Post* concluded that "[i]n short, Gessler ... was not a good man for the discipline of the club, and the development of two factions since he lost the captaincy did not tend to increase harmony in the Red Sox family."

Although Gessler hit .308 the year before (and led the league with a .394 on-base percentage) and had hit .290 for the Sox in '09, the club had a malcontent on its hands that it had publicly humiliated and supplanted with Hooper. Every other club in the major leagues knew the Red Sox had to trade him and not expect an even return. When it came time for trades, John I. Taylor always tipped his hand, and in the Gessler situation, he did not get equal return for losing a talented hitter and team leader. He received Charley Smith.

In contrast to Boston's continuing youth movement, the club picked up Jack Chesbro on waivers in early September and trotted him out to start a game on the last day of the season. Happy Jack pitched six innings, lost the one game he pitched for the Red Sox and never returned to baseball, only five years after he won 41 games in one season for the New York Highlanders.

The team, however, had improved over the year. Young Hooper debuted at .282 with fifteen stolen bases, albeit spending most of his time in left field rather than his more natural position in right. Tris Speaker batted .309, and his .362 on-base percentage constituted the last time until 1919 that his OBP fell under .400 (and after '19, his OBP jumped back over .400 for the next seven years). Had Speaker played with the club since its inception in 1901 and Ban Johnson did not interfere with matters, Jimmy Collins probably would have won another three pennants.

The outfield lacked only a Duffy Lewis, and he was on his way. With Carrigan catching and an infield of Stahl, McConnell, Wagner and Lord, the Red Sox seemed perched on the verge of something wonderful.

And then there were the pitchers. With Arellanes at 16–12, Cicotte at 14–5 and Wood at 11–7, the club appeared on a pretty solid foundation. Charley Hall and Ed Karger looked like the real thing, what the club had hoped it got when it originally traded Cy Young to Cleveland. Wood was solid but still inexperienced, while with Arellanes and Cicotte, one suspected they had way too much street smarts for their own good.

The Red Sox ultimate third-place finish did not prevent them from participating in the postseason, as a series with the National League's third-place club, the New York Giants, had been arranged. This contest should have taken place at the conclusion of the 1904 campaign, but at least the Red Sox players, particularly the younger ones, had the opportunity to take part in a post-season series and gain experience.

Tris Speaker, for one, revealed in the opportunity. Perhaps to remind John McGraw that he had not signed him when Speaker had become a free agent, Tris took the games very seriously and excelled in all of them.

Christy Mathewson, the Giants' greatest all-time pitcher, won the first game on October 8, defeating Smoky Joe Wood, 4–2, but Speaker earned all of the headlines as he swatted two singles and a home run off Matty in addition to stealing two bases. The New York Nationals fans extended two ovations to the visiting Sox outfielder, in some measure because "[h]is homer was the longest hit into the right field bleachers that has been made at the Polo Grounds since Mike Donlin quit the diamond."

The next day Speaker went 3 for 4 at the plate and stole three bases as New York sent in three pitchers to no avail. Cicotte pitched for the Sox and won, stranding twelve runners and demonstrating "how effective the Frenchman was in the pinches." Tongue firmly in cheek, the *New York Times* sports department commented upon the pitching from both teams as "[a]gainst all that talent Manager Lake sent in only Cicotte, whose name, properly pronounced, sounds like a cross between an incubator and a chewing gum ad, but who can pitch some, and then some." Parenthetically, perhaps as a result of the success of the film *Eight Men Out*, Eddie's name rightly or wrongly will go down pronounced as "Sea-Cot."

As a reward, Cicotte departed for his hometown of Detroit to see the Tigers and Pirates in the World Series, only to return on an as-needed basis. It is not known if Eddie bet on any of the games that he subsequently saw. Oddly, the Giants divided their team after the second game, with one squad playing in Jersey while the other combination staged an exhibition in Woonsocket, Rhode Island.

Knotted at one game apiece, the teams trained over to Boston, where Matty should have started again, but perhaps due to the peculiar exhibitions his team engaged in, he did not. With the scored tied 4–4 with two outs in the bottom of the ninth inning, Giants reliever Crandall served up a ball to Speaker that appeared destined to be a harmless single to right field. The ball, however, took an odd bounce and Tris motored around the bases, beating the throw home and winning the game for his team with an inside-the-park home run.

Matty did start the fourth game, but emerging ace Ray Collins shut out the opposition as Speaker went 3-for-4 and prevented a Giant home run by his peerless fielding. Tipping their cap, the *Times* proclaimed, "Speaker was again the star of the game." In the first four games, he had hit eight singles and two homers in seventeen at-bats. No superlatives needed for that sustained performance, the numbers stand to this day.

In what proved to be the final game, the Sox scoured their bullpen, sending in Pape, Wolters, Mathews and Sea Lion Hall to face the Giants' Crandall, and the Americans won game, set and match behind their star outfielder's triple, single and sacrifice fly, winning the last contest by a 5–4 margin. Only 769 fans braced the cold to see the end of this series, but almost all constantly cheered Tris Speaker, who ended up with a .600 average, turning an otherwise meaningless set of games into a showcase of his greatness.

The Red Sox had finished third in the American League race and had dominated their New York counterparts in their competition against each other. For the first time since the heyday of Jimmy Collins and Jesse Tannehill, the team had closed on a truly high note, and no one could ruin the accompanying karma. No one, that is, except John I. Taylor.

13

John I. in the Hands of an Angry Lord

Fred Lake ran the Red Sox competently in 1909 and had them poised to challenge the Detroit Tigers for the pennant in 1910, with one minor hitch. Incompetent John I. Taylor fired him during the off-season. By November 1909, Lake had drawn a line in the sand, demanding a raise to $6,500 a year. The sticking point concerning money seems nonsensical since Taylor's old man had spent thousands of dollars the past few years trying to buy every marginally talented ballplayer from Portland, Maine, to Portland, Oregon. But with John I., one never knew, least of all John I. He simply may not have liked the way Lake asked for a raise.

Poetic justice in part explains Lake's demise. After all, he had served as John I. Taylor's chief adviser at a time when Deacon McGuire had cause to feel that as a manager, his word should have had more influence than that of a scout. Once in power, Lake discovered what McGuire had learned too late, that Taylor played folks off each other and tended to listen to people who flattered him, or at the least, did not come to him with daily concerns and needs like a manager had to. When it came to baseball managers, Taylor treated them like the wives of King Henry the VIII, entities that lost their luster once they had ascended to the throne, or the manager's office, as the case may be.

The firing makes little sense when one considers that Lake had done a good job with the team and John I. Taylor at least believed that his men could win a pennant in 1910. So why break up a good thing with a manager over relative chump change? The answer, of course, lies in the utter lack of management skills and perspective that John I. brought to the job. Hearing that the Sox had dropped Lake, the Boston Nationals promptly procured him as their manger for the coming year.

In his stead, Taylor tabbed Patsy Donovan, a native of County Cork in Ireland and a resident of the industrial mill city of Lawrence, northwest of Boston. Donovan compiled a long and fairly impressive career as an outfielder, batting .301 and tabulating more than 2,200 hits. As a manager in St. Louis, Washington and Brooklyn, he enjoyed far less success, but seemed willing to spend a lot of time in the Red Sox's office downtown during the off-season

Why is Fred Lake so happy? Probably because he is no longer working for John I. Taylor, and has been hired to manage the crosstown Boston Nationals club. Library of Congress.

and by nature posed no threat to John I. Taylor. After inheriting Collins, having Deacon McGuire foisted upon him by Ban Johnson, and seeing Lake get too big for his breeches, Taylor now had his perfect manager—a yes man even less distinguished than he was.

The Detroit Tigers had won the last three AL pennants behind Ty Cobb and Sam Crawford, but in this campaign, Connie Mack's Philadelphia Athletics loomed as the more formidable challenger for the crown. Traditionally, Mack won games behind great pitching, and certainly with Colby Jack Coombs (author of 31 victories in '10), Sox cast-off Cy Morgan (18–12) and future Hall of Famers Chief Bender and Eddie Plank, they remained strong in the box.

More dramatically, the A's had improved in the field as they started Home Run Baker at third, Jack Barry at second and Eddie Collins at second, having assembled three-quarters of what became known as their vaunted "Hundred Thousand Dollar Infield." With right fielder Danny Murphy continuing to play well, the club had a rare combination of staunch pitching, slick fielding and timely hitting to rely on. Few clubs approached their balance, although certainly on paper, the Red Sox had accomplished that and some. Tellingly, Philadelphia had the clever Connie Mack at the helm while Boston had less perceptive people in positions of power.

Indeed, these upper-level types in the Hub began to spout off even before the opening pitch had been thrown. Treasurer McBreen anticipated a higher finish for the club than the previous season, while John I. Taylor boasted that he could "see nothing but the Red Sox" for first place in the American League, a bold boast given recent history, but an appreciation in part of the talent the club had assembled. Fred Lieb quoted Taylor later as waxing, "I believe my 1910 season was my biggest disappointment. I thought our young Speed Boys had arrived and confidentially expected to win the pennant, but we just couldn't get anywhere."

While Taylor and McBreen may have boasted, no one in the spring training camp came off as loud as rookie George Edward "Duffy" Lewis, an Irish-Catholic from California, who like Harry Hooper played his college ball at St. Mary's. Not known as a bigmouth, Duffy Lewis' loudness resulted from his brash, playboy style of dressing, arriving in his first professional camp not as a meek rookie, but a fashion plate decked out in a velvet vest "trimmed with diamond buttons." The veteran teammates almost rode him out of camp after seeing his Great Gatsby display.

He never dialed it down. One of his favorite ensembles featured a lavender shirt, purple slacks, a rust-colored sports coat, black and white shoes and a gray yachting cap. On less flamboyant days, he wore a flashy yellow shirt, yellow trousers and socks and his reliable rust-colored sports coat. Had he added a splash of plaid or calico to the mix, it is quite likely the combination would have clashed severely enough to spontaneously combust into flames.

His vanity extended on the field as well. One day he had cut his hair very short, so short that Tris Speaker decided to take off Duff's hat in front of the crowd before a ball game, which vexed Lewis so much that he whipped a bat at Speaker, a blow that knocked his fellow outfielder from the lineup for a number of days. This did little to hurt Lewis' standing on the club since he was John I. Taylor's pet, a feeling that Duffy reciprocated. Duffy remembered years later, "John I. was a good boss.... Maybe he was sharp at times, but he always bought the boys suits of clothes wherever they had big days."

Flashy threads aside, Duffy Lewis worked his way that spring into a starting position in left field. He distinguished himself as one of the finest fielding left fielders in major league history, joining Speaker in center and Hooper in right field as defensive stalwarts.

Despite the high expectations surrounding the club, its players barely scraped out records above a .500 winning percentage in April, May and June. One of the reasons for this disappointing start, McConnell, "not in the best of form," was sent home to Utica by the Red Sox in early May to recuperate. Supposedly, Amby suffered from stomach problems, and he had not hit well of late. In his absence, management, in accordance with established custom, swooned over every utility player or spare catcher that went on a temporary run of good hitting, which no doubt added to the young second baseman's indigestion and alienation from the team.

To bolster its bench, the club purchased utility infielder Clyde Engle from New York on May 10, with both Donovan and Captain Lord endorsing the acquisition, "finding the New York club in doubt as to his ability." Engle had played some left field for the Highlanders and some third base in the minors, and he hit lefties well, so he came to Boston "as an extra infielder." Captain Lord soon rued this acquisition, but at the end of May he seemingly had little to worry about with he, Speaker and Larry Gardner the only regulars on the club with averages exceeding .300.

But the slow start transcended an injury to one player, particularly since Amby's replacement, Larry Gardner, was a far superior baseball player than the talented McConnell. Gardner had not yet fully committed himself to third base, his natural position, with his superior fielding abilities allowing him to master second base.

William Lawrence Gardner, from Enosburg Falls, Vermont, did not rescue John I. Taylor from Ban Johnson's doghouse, but in time he made the Boston fans forget Harry Lord. After brief stops in Boston in '08 and '09, Larry Gardner stuck with the club in 1910, batting .283 as the starting second baseman, a one-year assignment before settling in at the hot corner.

A native New Englander like Lord, Gardner's roots ran very deep; one of his ancestors fought in the Battle of Bunker Hill. Gardner's grandfather lost a hand while working in his mill. As a young boy, Gardner watched with his grandfather as the mill became engulfed in flood waters until it came off its foundation and floated down the river. Gardner *grand-pere* "never turned a hair. He always took things philosophically but never went into the same line of business again." A chapter in his life had closed. Other folks had it tough, and he got on with his life.

Gardner's parents were the tiniest couple in Enosburg Falls, and Larry never topped 5'8" in height, but he loved playing baseball at a very early age (his parents discouraged him from playing football). His mother felt that "Larry was always an obedient boy, so I encouraged anything he took up and to this day he has shown a deep appreciation for his own home...." A good-looking chap, he sang pretty well too, although no matter what his mother might claim, he never perfected walking on water.

A most pleasant person, he attracted friends everywhere, and in an era and on a club where religious lines often dictated friendships, his best friend was Harry Hooper. This friendship lasted a lifetime. Several decades later, on Hooper's induction day into Baseball Hall of Fame, Gardner sat proudly in the crowd. No less a baseball man than Smoky Joe Wood felt that Gardner, too, belonged in the Hall, saying, "We had a third baseman on the Red Sox. A clutch hitter all through his career, and you never hear his name mentioned. I wouldn't trade him for ten Frank 'Home Run' Bakers. His name was Larry Gardner. A hell of a ballplayer. Loved the game."

Having a gamer like Gardner in the lineup undoubtedly sparked his teammates. In July, the team soared, winning almost 70 percent of its games. A cynic might remark that the schedule played into the team's hand, as the Red Sox did not have to play any games that month against the league-leading Athletics, a club against whom the Sox won only four of 22 games in 1910. But this stretch of good feelings for Boston actually followed the team winning the last two games of a series against Philadelphia in June.

Amazingly, the Sox reeled off this remarkable run despite the fact that ace Smoky Joe Wood sat out injured during this entire period. In the middle of the month, his leg was still "badly swollen" and he had to use a cane to ambulate. Captain Harry Lord had also fallen victim to a pitch thrown by Washington's star Walter "Big Train" Johnson, causing Jacob Morse to lament, "Harry is a man not to be spared or replaced." No wonder so many Beantown scribes and fans anxiously awaited his return, seemingly the final piece of the puzzle needed to overtake the A's. By July 26, the Red Sox held on to second place, seven games behind the Athletics in the loss column.

It was a wonderful stretch, and in a column dated July 24, Tim Murnane unofficially typed out the pitchers' records during this skein:

C. Smith:	4–0
Karger:	4–1
Hall:	4–1
Collins:	3–1
Cicotte:	3–2
Arellanes:	2–2

The news kept getting better, with Joe Wood returning on July 30 to pitch a four-hitter, albeit in a losing cause, to the New York Highlanders. Smoky Joe received a "great reception from the fans," who had every reason to calculate that if the club had such a magnificent string without their ace fireballer, then they surely would overtake the A's with Wood very soon.

There was a built-in problem with this wishful thinking. Murnane's numbers belied the fact that Karger and Charley Smith simply were not very good pitchers and that over time their records would even out. Murnane did not know this yet, but Arellanes had only one good season in him, and 1910 was that year. Charley Hall was a very good pitcher, but he was ideally suited for relief, which made his starting numbers deceiving. While Eddie Cicotte is remembered as the doomed 1919 Black Sox pitcher that should have made the Baseball Hall of Fame, in Boston he was very inconsistent. Collins shined from 1912 to 1915, but early in his career, he still experienced the normal bumps and growing pains.

Returning Wood to the rotation helped, but the staff around him simply did not match up well against the excellent group that Connie Mack had every day during the year. And it cannot be repeated enough that at any given time, Sox owner John I. Taylor's impulses might unleash on his team in ways that ensured defeat. And as July changed into August, his dark side prevailed again.

During John I. Taylor's long tenure of incompetence, it is difficult to discern the precise point at which league president Ban Johnson irreversibly decided that Taylor had to go. It may have occurred with the trading of star outfielder Harry Lord to the Chicago White Sox in August 1910.

One of the truly bright points of the club's effort to rebuild after its horrible 1906 and 1907 campaigns, Lord had starred at third base and as a batter, so much so that he was the team captain in 1910. The previous season constituted his breakout year as he batted .311 and stole 36 bases.

Born in Kezar's Falls, Maine, in 1882, Harry was a lord born to the manor as his father accumulated piles of money, lavishing it on young Harry, who attended Bridgton Academy and Bates College. Raised as a prince, Harry Lord turned into a bit of a princess as the years passed, and yet as he hit and fielded, his teammates followed him.

Third base was indeed the hot corner during John I. Taylor's ownership. Jimmy Collins had hated Taylor almost as much as Lord later did, but while Collins largely kept his thoughts to himself, Lord made no secret of his feelings toward management. Lord had battled some physical issues during the season, including malaria spawned during spring training and a injured finger once the regular season commenced, and yet he had not relinquished his position.

Having fallen in love with mediocre Bob Unglaub years earlier, Taylor now turned his affections to the new object of his unabashed awe, utility player Clyde Engle. It might have been possible that Engle was an even worse player than Unglaub, but this did not deter Taylor, who loved him all the more for his flaws. Engle soon began to start at third base in lieu of the very gifted Lord. John I. Taylor loved the third baseman he was with while forgetting Lord's contributions.

Lord also wanted to take over the manager's job from Patsy Donovan, and probably could have performed better than his lackadaisical manager, but John I. Taylor wanted a "yes man," not a challenger to the throne. Around this time, Fred Lieb wrote an article in which he maintained that Lord "probably takes baseball a good deal more seriously than many other stars...." Coming from money, Lord also appreciated that any time he wished to walk away from the game, he might do so with little or no financial repercussions attached to such a decision.

By the middle of the summer, Lord pushed for a change of scenery. John I. Taylor brashly broadcast the fact that he meant to trade his disgruntled captain, albeit only for someone of the caliber of the White Sox's Ed Walsh or Detroit's Ty Cobb. Lord had established himself as a star, but not a player the caliber of these future Hall of Famers. As a result, no deal resulted on these terms.

Deciding to make a bad matter worse, the team did not showcase Lord, but continued to start Engle to the frenzied frustration of the captain. Admittedly, Lord was a prima donna, a fact demonstrated throughout his career, but all the Sox had to do was to keep a temporary peace while they shopped him in order to get optimum value in return in a trade. This the Sox did not do.

On August 11, the axe fell when the Sox traded Lord and Amby McConnell for lame-armed Frank Smith and utility player Billy Purtell, a completely one-sided deal in favor of the White Sox, causing Chicago manager Hugh Duffy to crow, "I had no idea we could pull off such a trade as this." Hugh Duffy played a critical role in building the original Boston club in 1901, and now nine years later as the manager of the White Sox, he fleeced the franchise that he largely created.

A firestorm greeted the trade of Lord and McConnell from fans and most of the non–*Globe* press alike. John I. Taylor's family money had insulated him from accountability for years, but just as the club seemed to be poised

A lord born to the manor, Captain Harry Lord rebelled against manager Patsy Donovan and owner John I. Taylor and his disastrous trade to the White Sox probably triggered the ultimate overthrow of Red Sox management by Ban Johnson. Library of Congress.

to win another pennant, Taylor's idiotic trade wiped out half of his infield while receiving very little in return. In the past, the Taylors might have blamed it on the manager, but since Jimmy Collins' departure, a revolving door had sent managers coming and going with no good purpose, resulting in the fans blaming the owner.

The press, too, may have been cowed by General Taylor and Tim Murnane at the *Globe*, but they also competed against that institution and smelled the blood of John I. Taylor' self-induced wounds. Public outcry had reached a sufficient pitch that it began to reflect itself in editorials masked as sports commentary. Without the press in line, little stood between Ban Johnson and his long-shelved wish to purge the team of dilettante John I. Taylor.

The *Post* led the charge, quoting venerable wise men from the city. Percy Lowell offered that "[t]he management of the Red Sox have been getting away with these deals long enough," while Tom Connolly had given up on the hope for another pennant "until there is another change, and that will have to be at the top." Added Jim Ward, "Take it from me the Red Sox outfit will never win a pennant."

The *Boston Evening Record* criticized Lord for going back to Maine with his broken finger instead of staying with his team as captain and a coach. The newspaper had much more severe words for the team's front office, because it "was a deal that does not reflect credit on the judgment of the management of the Red Sox." The *Record* in many ways topped the coverage of its local competition, some of it either beholden or afraid of General Taylor at the *Globe*, with other writers prepared to tar and feather the General's son, John I., on the Boston Common.

The *Record* carefully detailed the major transactions of the club under Taylor's stewardship and persuasively argued that the Red Sox had let go during that period the equivalent of a pretty talented major league team. The wholesale slaughter of his team clouds the sheer individual and collective lunacy of the deals that John I. hatched. On the Chicago White Sox alone, Lord and McConnell joined expatriates Patsy Dougherty and Freddy Parent. Cleveland had Cy Young, and St. Louis had Criger, who unlike Tubby Spencer could be located. Cy Morgan now starred for the A's, while Charlie French and Pat Donahue served valuable utility roles for other teams.

The *Record* only neglected to place on the other side of the ledger the relative swill the Sox received in return for these ill-conceived moves. With the exception of the Sox ultimately and indirectly obtaining Charley Hall for Cy Young, the team received nothing useful in return for sacrificing so many of its stars and productive role players. "Mistakes?" wondered the *Record's* scribe. "Why no other team in the American League within the last 10 years has made so many mistakes as the Red Sox management has in the last 18 months."

The dumping of Lord and McConnell by the Red Sox proved to be the watershed event in the long reign of error of John I. Taylor. In the past, the friendly members of the press might crucify Jimmy Collins, whisper about the deceased Chick Stahl, or crow that the largesse of the Taylors was buying wonderful talent for the team, guaranteeing a return to prominence for the Sox.

The departure of Lord and McConnell gave lie to all of the excuses and wishful thinking, for the only star in the Red Sox firmament was John I. Taylor, and he did not shine brightly. As long as he owned the team, he meant to fire managers with abandon, make knucklehead trades, and hope that a loyal press corps might continue to convince the public that the team had a plan, that the emperor did have new clothes and they were spectacular. John I. Taylor had offended the Lord, but more importantly, he had alienated the loyal rooters who just wanted to cheer on a winner.

For a spell after Lord left, John I. Taylor's luck held, as the Red Sox remnants deflected some of the outrage by performing well. For instance, Sea Lion Hall nearly pitched a no-hitter against Cleveland on August 27, the lone hit coming off a fly ball by opposing relief pitcher Elmer Koestner. At this juncture, while the Red Sox had shaved a bit off the loss column since their trade of Lord and McConell in their race against the Athletics, they had achieved a very respectable 70–48 record, sitting securely in second place. When the White Sox came to Fenway immediately after that one-hit game for a three-game series, the Red Sox quickly won the first two contests of the series to extend their winning streak to eight games.

And then the bottom fell completely out. On August 31, the White Sox shut out Boston by the score of 8–0, and then the Hub's favorite baseball team inexplicably went on a 9–23–1 run for the remaining two months of the campaign.

What happened?

In one sense, the team may have collectively experienced a delayed reaction to the trade of Lord and McConnell, having given up too much in leadership and talent, with newcomers Purtell and Smith getting in the way. Once the team got over the stunning fact that the management had triggered another horrible trade, the players may have given up, a belief that Stout and Johnson espouse.

Those wonderful pitchers that carried the club in the absence of Smoky Joe Wood through most of July proved most human as the season wore on. Vexingly, the return of Wood did not produce the dramatic results needed to keep the team in contention and the fans' attention away from missing Harry Lord and Amby McConnell. While their young ace returned to battle and posted a magnificent 1.69 ERA for the year, he only won twelve games against thirteen losses, highlighting again in part what happens to a team when a very good hitter like Lord is swapped for a banjo hitter like Billy Purtell.

By way of illustration, the Sox lost a close game to the Athletics on September 8 at home, a fairly unremarkable event. But at this point, New York moved into a tie with Boston for second place. The game highlighted one of the chief reasons the club had gone into a tailspin. Ed Karger threw a good game, but the lineup that backed him consisted of Moskiman leading off, followed by Purtell at third base, Speaker in center field, Stahl at first base, Lewis in left field, Wagner at short, Engle at second base and Kleinow at catcher.

Ideally, the lineup to face the powerhouse A's that day should have included Harry Hooper in right field, Gardner at second or third base, Carrigan catching, and Harry Lord or Amby McConnell rounding out the infield. Not to mention Fred Lake managing instead of Patsy Donovan. Obviously, Lake and his former charges Lord and McConnell had left the team, but injuries to other starters expedited the Red Sox tailspin in '10. And when injuries occurred, the Sox lacked adequate replacements and had to dig down real deep to find even reasonable facsimiles of ballplayers to draw on.

John I. Taylor failed to appreciate that the Red Sox were not his. Sure, he held the title of president and he sent men and managers to the plank with impunity, but in his three years as a fan of the team, during the stewardship of Somers and Killilea, he had to have understood the very special nature of the club in all New England, almost from its outset. Even though the Beaneaters (later the Braves) had won several National League pennants in the 1890s, most fans almost immediately deserted that organization the moment the Boston Americans came to town. It was love at first sight, and it has never ended, over a century later.

Guiding the Red Sox is a trust, not sacred but special, a commandment that the person or persons operating the team treat the club with reverence and the same level of love that its rooters extend to it. John I. Taylor had repeatedly engaged in tests of wills with good baseball men and winners like Jimmy Collins, Fred Lake and Harry Lord and disposed of them to the detriment of the most deserving team and set of fans in American baseball history. He had, in essence, sinned against the light. Maybe the trust was sacred after all.

At about this time, Boston's Cardinal O'Connell boldly proclaimed, "The Puritan has passed. The Catholic remains." Now Catholic and Puritan alike had had their fill of John I. Taylor. And a lonely Boston American fandom turned its eyes toward league President Ban Johnson, who spent his winter sharpening his axe, patiently waiting for the turn to wield it against John I. Taylor.

A clever strategist, Johnson waited, formulating contingency plans to solve what ailed Boston at a time, place and manner of his choosing. He let John I. Taylor twist in the wind as the locals became more frustrated and disillusioned with his ownership while the team limped to a dreadful finish.

The Sox closed out this most perplexing of seasons on October 8 with a double-header loss to the Highlanders at the Polo Grounds. Wood lost the first game, backed by a largely unimpressive contingent of fielders, including Purtell at third, Engle in center field, Bradley and Moskiman sharing first base, and Kleinow catching. For the second part of the twin bill, the Sox did not trot out anyone nearly as distinguished as Smoky Joe to the mound, choosing to start Chris Mahoney in a "who cares" final game. He was backed once again by an even more sad-sack crew, with Bertram Roe Lerchen spelling team captain Heinie Wagner at shortstop.

After this brace of losses, the Sox closed out in fourth place, 20½ games behind the leading Athletics.

Curiously, the Red Sox season did not end with the disheartening losses to the Highlanders, who were occasionally referred to as the "Yankees." On October 10, the team split in half to play an exhibition game in Burlington, Vermont, before the governor, many legislators and other Green Mountain Boys in squads managed, respectively, by Ray Collins and, his old University of Vermont teammate, Larry Gardner. Collins' team lost, 4–1, but some of the faces that had seemingly disappeared from the team of late, among them Rough Carrigan and Tris Speaker, turned up for perhaps the first fun game of baseball the men had played since the Lord fiasco exploded.

Had John I. Taylor participated in the event in any meaningful way, it is likely the two squads would have accomplished the metaphysically impossible, with both sides losing.

14

The Odyssey

Clueless concerning how to place a consistently winning team on the field, John I. Taylor decided to commence the 1911 season by putting on a show. While manager Patsy Donovan spent much of the winter at the Red Sox headquarters whittling, hobnobbing with old ballplayers and umpires and, in general, acting the part of the town coot, Taylor commissioned Norris "Tip" O'Neill, the president of the Western League, to arrange to ship the Sox to new spring digs in California.

The trip, with all of its detours projected to be about an 8,500-mile venture, billed as the "longest ever undertaken by a baseball team in the history of the game." In lieu of fielding a competitive club with a secure team manager, John I. Taylor had unconsciously taken a page out of the P.T. Barnum philosophy of entertainment and fronted a circus. The *Globe*, because its writers had to, promoted the spectacle while others openly ridiculed the useless undertaking.

Taylor loved California and visited there with his wife at every opportunity he had. The club, and more properly O'Neill, chose grounds at Redondo Beach and lined up scads of games on the West Coast featuring split squads, one taking a proposed northern route and the other a southern path. Theoretically, each half would scrounge up games in venues heading eastward while the team returned to Boston to start the regular season.

Redondo Beach promised a sunny climate and a prolonged vacation for the club while removing players from the sources of temptation that had been carefully cultivated in years past in Little Rock and Hot Springs. As part of the attractions available, the Sox players and family could fly down a water slide and enjoy hot water baths and rubdowns. In an attempt to keep the players focused on baseball, Redondo Beach in that day was "far enough from a big city to be safe from its nightly allurements, yet near enough to permit daily trips with no inconvenience." In other words, try to keep the players away from prostitutes and camp followers.

A lousy owner, John I. Taylor did make people laugh, quite often on purpose. For instance, he eschewed training in the usual southern haunt because of what he termed "Hot Springs rheumatism," a nice way of saying syphilis and gonorrhea. He also heard with mixed emotions the news that Bullet Jack

Thoney intended to train at Redondo, offering, "I have tried the boy out twice, and might as well make it three times. He cost the Boston club $12,000, and I would like to get a little of my money back if possible, so I will take another chance." Bullet Jack never did live up to his lofty expectations, high price tag and cool nickname.

The trip west also took on the trappings of a victory tour as ports of call were made to pick up players along the way and hopefully garner some press in the process. The club also charted a special train with six cars—one for dining, one for observation, one for storage/buffet/library, and three for sleeping—to house an estimated 75 ballplayers, Sox employees and members of the fourth estate. A few Royal Rooters, namely Mike McGreevy, Joseph Burns and James Donahue, bummed a ride with the other invited guests. For entertainment, someone suggested packing a piano and encouraging pitcher Bucky O'Brien, a somewhat minor figure in professional singing, to act as cantor, along with Larry Gardner, Hugh Bradley and Martin McHale.

The excursion turned into a bit of an odyssey, leaving Boston at 1:00 P.M. sharp on February 18, with team secretary Edwin Riley, a few sportswriters, some Royal Rooters and ballplayers Rough Carrigan, Bunny Madden, Hugh Bradley, Larry Gardner, Martin McHale, Bucky O'Brien, Christopher Mahoney and some chap named Nourse aboard. By design, the first circuit of the trek meant to travel only as far as New York City, arriving by late afternoon or early evening.

The next day Riley took the players to Jersey City, where they met Smoky Joe Wood, Heinie Wagner, Jack Kleinow, Walter Moser and a southpaw recruit named Thompson and his wife for the next leg. At that point, Riley turned around and went back to Boston. Arthur Cooper then took charge of matters with two representatives of the Rock Island Line. If all went well, the party had scheduled a stop in Philly to pick up a couple more Sox.

On February 20, the team steamed into Chicago in the morning and met Ed Cicotte, Ray Collins and a bunch of rookies at the Great Northern Hotel, drawing compliments from White Sox team owner Charlie Comiskey. After rendezvousing in the Windy City and perhaps catching some real sleep, the club, now totaling almost 79 members in the party, flew off for California. If nothing else, the venture allowed the teammates to bond while traveling to camp at the same time, as opposed to the more general practice of individuals arriving when they felt like it. From Chicago, the players got their kicks on a line somewhat parallel to the soon-to-be legendary Route 66 to the American Southwest.

As the train steamed into El Paso, Texas, for Tris Speaker, Ed Karger and "also Stansfield," the *Globe's* Tim Murnane permitted his prose to veer almost into poesy as he gazed upon the beautiful snows lining the Texas horizon and observed the stark beauty of the desert in winter:

Redondo Cal. Mar. 1911

Gardner Bradley McHale — O'Brien

From left to right: Gardner, Bradley, McHale and O'Brien, the singing Red Sox. After the 1912 World Series, the band dropped Gardner and added a fellow Irishman as they headed off on a vaudeville tour. Boston Public Library, Print Department, McGreevy Collection.

The party rose with the sun this morning, to look out on a sea of glittering snow without a tree to break the monotony of the vista or relieve the eye. The Badlands of New Mexico are indeed well named.... Icicles two feet long hung from the eaves of the few houses we did pass.... The country was full of jackrabbits and their tracks along the railroad interested the boys.... I am writing this with the train speeding down the mountainside at a rate of a mile a minute, with big snowdrifts in the gulches with the scrubby trees filled with snowballs, like trees in the blossom at springtime.... The sun has been as bright as burnished silver nearly all day....

The men seemed to enjoy getting caught up and bonding together. On George Washington's birthday, Bucky O'Brien and his Red Sox Quartet sang "patriotic songs."

Once the train steamed into Redondo, the club had all of the natural surroundings and rudimentary theme park rides at their disposal. On February 24, Donovan scheduled a four-hour morning workout and a light two-hour

Boston Red Sox players relaxing at Redondo Beach, California. In the background is the water chute that injured pitcher Smoky Joe Wood. Boston Public Library, Print Department, McGreevy Collection.

afternoon practice. Smoky Joe Wood and Clyde Engle injured themselves on the water chute and had to take some time off. Murnane approved of the facilities because of the wonderful hot springs and the lack of a vivacious night life that the old Hot Springs haunt had provided.

There was an obvious disconnect between the owner and his players. John I. Taylor loved California, but had alienated so many of his men and the Boston fans that he dared not take this dream vacation with a team he so loved and so badly misunderstood. Back in Boston, in full Captain Queeg mode, he fired off a missive warning players to be more careful after learning of Smoky Joe Wood's incident on the water chute. In Boston he continued to brood, wondering why he could not be one of the guys.

Meanwhile, the ballplayers, deprived of much of their ability to cavort around saloons and cathouses, walked along the beaches for miles and at night gathered together staring at the large fire at the hotel, writing home and talking ball. Despite precautions, some women probably found their way onto ballplayer bunks in old Redondo.

After the initial amusements, arrangements had been made to ship most of the regulars up to Oakland with Manager Donovan to play a schedule of games. A second group, largely comprised of players not expected to make the major league club, stayed around L.A., with Rough Carrigan leading them. Already, Carrigan had exuded leadership skills and a rare ability to elicit respect from his fellow players.

While Hot Springs and Little Rock had more entertainment for young men than Redondo or Oakland at that time, particularly with women with flexible consciences, the cities also had much less rain. The California spring training of the Red Sox essentially devolved into one long rainout. The team did get a game against St. Mary's, where Duffy Lewis and Harry Hooper once played, and the college boys ended up taking that one. Somehow, in the near-absence of conditioning and exhibition games, a skilled second baseman named Steve Yerkes emerged.

Steve Yerkes briefly tried out with the Red Sox in late 1909 before returning to the minors the next year under one of the Sox's various agreements, this one with the Worcester ball club. A sometime Jerseyite, occasional Pennsylvanian and a student at Penn for a spell, he traveled quite extensively in his minor league years, wearing the cap of the Millville (New Jersey), Stroudsburg (Pennsylvania), Newburn, Altoona, Wilson (North Carolina) and Chattanooga clubs. Donovan liked Yerkes enough to promote him in 1911, primarily as a shortstop instead of a second baseman, his natural position.

Unlike the Boston Americans' old second baseman, Hobe Ferris, Yerkes did not court controversy nor project as a very colorful player. He helped solidify an infield decimated by the senseless loss of Harry Lord and Amby McConnell, and his presence at least allowed Larry Gardner to make the permanent switch to third base. Perhaps after the dissension that marked the John I. Taylor era, having a rather dull but dutiful infielder like Yerkes was a positive development.

The emergence of Yerkes aside, like so many matters dealing with baseball that John I. Taylor dabbled in, the trip made no sense. Spring training in San Francisco, where the regulars primarily gathered, is almost as cold and difficult a venue to train in the late winter and early spring as Boston, Massachusetts. In one stretch, the regulars did not play a single scheduled game. In supposedly sunny Redondo, meanwhile, Carrigan's crew only managed to fit in one game due to the inclement conditions outside of their hotel.

One poor prospect, Herman Priepke, became deathly ill as a result of a severe cold he contracted in Oakland while participating in this dreadful exercise. No sentimentalist, Taylor sold him to the Utica minor league club, where he never played due to his inconveniently dying. The California odyssey injured some of the players and caused one fatality. All in all, not bad for a John I. Taylor operation.

Even A.H.C. Mitchell, more of a Taylor apologist than Tim Murnane, conceded that the "California venture is a frost." In addition to losing out on conditioning the players, the escapade made it difficult to evaluate the talent on hand. With the team heading back east, its management was convinced that Engle and first baseman Hugh Bradley were legitimate front-line starting talents instead of role players at best.

Befitting a team that had very little spring training conditioning, recurring injuries ravaged the Boston Americans throughout the season, taking shortstop Heinie Wagner out of action for much of the year. Rather than blame Taylor and his wacko tragic mystery tour, A.H.C. Mitchell excoriated Wagner, claiming that the late Chick Stahl, Bob Unglaub, Deacon McGuire, Fred Lake and Patsy Donovan "all told him to go easy on his arm."

In cataloguing these managers (leaving out Cy Young), Mitchell did not once figure out that maybe Wagner and all of the other players had too many managers and too few new owners; that might risk incurring Taylor's wrath and jeopardizing Mitchell's chances of procuring employment with the club at some later date, a development which did occur years later when the club finally rewarded Mitchell for his water-carrying efforts by giving him a post. Mitchell was one of the few people who was a company man before he even joined the company. His bootlicking is remembered, not his often-prosaic sportswriting.

Unfortunately for Mitchell and Taylor, Boston players continued to drop all over the place. And when additional players fell, it no longer became credible to blame their ailments on their failure to heed the warnings of the ghost of Chick Stahl.

In addition to injuries, Patsy Donovan fretted about his pitching staff, a legitimate concern for a club that had barely eked out a .500 record the previous year. John I. Taylor did not think much of his pitching staff before the 1911 season began, and he probably thought even less of it as the weeks progressed. Eddie Cicotte's performance continued to vex, as this wonderful and commanding presence kept trying to come to the fore and yet never really did on a consistent basis in Boston. Cicotte closed out the books for the year at 11–15, a reverse of his previous campaign's record.

Management pounced on its troubled hurler on May 9, when John I. Taylor and Manager Donovan met with Cicotte in New York and read him the riot act. The club also made no effort to hush its displeasure when management leaked the story to the *Globe*, intimating that the Sox only intended to allow Cicotte to travel with his teammates if he promised to get into shape. Back then, that often meant laying off alcohol, although as reported management supposedly mandated that the hurler work out mornings so he could make it into the later innings refreshed.

Obviously the club took the matter very seriously, making his following the program a condition of Cicotte staying with the team. Had Eddie been a lesser talent, he may have been released years earlier, but just about everyone back then had faith in him, if only he harnessed his ability. Clearly, patience had worn thin, and he never did pitch with much devotion that year.

Heading into June, the Red Sox had ten fewer wins to their credit than the first-place Tigers, yet stood right on the tail of the second-place Philadelphia Athletics, with young pitchers sharing the laurels. Joe Wood excelled on several occasions, including May 30, when he slightly out-pitched Walter Johnson. A month and a half later, he harnessed his speed as he fanned 15 batters, allowing only one hit in the ninth inning in a July 7 game against the St. Louis Browns. Smoky Joe Wood had not yet arrived as a full-fledged star, but he had set upon the right course to that goal.

On a lesser level, spitballing Brocktonian Bucky O'Brien absolutely mesmerized a strong Athletics squad by shutting them out in August. He contin-

The team takes a day trip to Los Angeles, a city supposedly strictly off-limits once the sun set. Boston Public Library, Print Department, McGreevy Collection.

ued to baffle opposing lineups with three key performances over the next month. O'Brien shut out Philadelphia on September 9, bailed Cicotte out of a bases-loaded jam in the seventh against Washington four days later, and then on September 17 shut out Cleveland.

The Sox also scored a minor coup by signing Olaf Henriksen from the local Brockton minor league roster, and he paid immediate dividends within a week of his promotion by winning a game for Boston against Detroit with a triple. At 5'7½", Henriksen was dwarfed by the stellar outfield of Lewis, Speaker and Hooper, but for a change, John I. Taylor seemed to bring up a prospect purely with the idea of providing pinch-hitting assistance, with the occasional assist when one of the regulars needed a rest or incurred an injury.

Mistaken at the time by some as a native of Wareham, Massachusetts, Henriksen originally hailed from Kirkerup, Denmark, and carried around the incongruous nickname of Swede. He hit pretty well in his utility role until 1915, when he suddenly and irreversibly developed Parent/Criger syndrome, the sudden inability of a Red Sox to hit the ball. But before Parent/Criger set in, he had a memorable role to play the next October.

Despite the infusion of talent from Wood, O'Brien and Henriksen, the Sox settled in a malaise, and by September 2 their record stood at a quite ordinary 62–60, barely holding onto fourth place over Cleveland and Chicago. Thereafter, the club eschewed mediocrity for an abysmal level of performance while the team won only ten games in the entire month of September. The total collapse of the club appeared unlikely at this juncture, particularly since on the second of September, Boston finished a series at home against first-place Philadelphia in style, winning, 7–4, behind new pitcher Larry Pape and one William Carrigan, "a Lewiston, Maine, tobacco merchant" as Tim Murnane dubbed him.

Boston fielded a pretty good lineup that day, with Harry Hooper, Tris Speaker and Duffy Lewis in the outfield and Larry Gardner and Steve Yerkes running down ground balls. With the exception of Engle at first and a youngster named Thomas Lonergan at second base, the team had gelled on the field.

Behind 3–1 in the bottom of the sixth, Boston loaded the bases behind a walk to Lewis, Gardner being hit by a pitch in the shoulder, and Yerkes trying to sacrifice the runners over but gaining first on a botched throw by the A's. In came the redoubtable Carrigan as a pinch-hitter for fellow catcher Alva Williams. The A's pitcher, Krause, tried to smoke Carrigan inside and Rough tomahawked the ball to the left field fence, scoring two runs and advancing Yerkes to third base with the double.

Gentlemanly Connie Mack then strolled to the pitcher's mound, and after diagnosing Krause, called for a reliever, former Sox hurler Cy Morgan. According to Murnane, "Cy looked as if he liked the job, for he hummed a bit of a favorite song as he strode across the field and bit a husk of licorice stick. The crowd is never so happy as when it sees the minstrel pitcher facing the Boston players." Cy heaved the first pitch to Boston's Thomas Lonergan five feet over his head, scoring Yerkes from third. Later, Sox pitcher Pape aided his own cause with a long, lazy fly to left that scored his battery mate with what proved to be the game winning run.

Then disaster struck. If the Boston season had started off like an odyssey with a worthless cross-country trip to California and back, catcher Bill Carrigan had performed like Achilles in *The Illiad* all year, beating back gods and mere mortals and keeping his teammates in the fray through his leadership and clutch hitting. He willed the team to victories that its underperforming pitchers had let slip away, and his thrilling double off the wall on September 2 was no exception.

But then two days later in an otherwise uneventful game against New York, Rough Carrigan led off first base and scampered to second on a sharp drive up the middle by Larry Gardner. The ball shot past the pitcher but the Highlanders' shortstop, Johnson, scooped the ball and raced to tag out Carrigan, who in trying to avoid the fielder twisted his leg into the bag and broke two bones in his right leg. Carrigan fell like a sack and lay on his back, ultimately being removed from the field on a stretcher after a doctor had been summonsed to examine him.

Rough's year had ended as his doctors placed his leg in a cast, leaving him with little to do but spend his free time with Heinie Wagner, the latter recovering from a bad sprain. Carrigan batted .289 for the year, leading the team and providing peerless service behind home. The Sox had a few good backups—rookie Les Nunamaker, Kleinow and Bunny Madden—but there was only one Rough. Most galling, the New York shortstop had tagged him out on the play in which he was injured. Off went the team on a seven-game losing streak as Rough gritted his teeth as his broken bones mended.

In his history of the Red Sox, Fred Lieb devoted merely a page and a half to the 1911 Sox, naturally choosing to focus instead on the exciting pennant race and World Series of the following year. He paints a poignant picture of John I. Taylor obliviously parading dignitaries through the new Fenway Park in December 1911, while all the time Ban Johnson hatched a plan to take the team away from him in the very near future.

This version does not correspond with the facts, unless John I. Taylor did not read his own father's newspaper. Taylor did walk Ban Johnson through the Fens around Labor Day, and history should have instructed him that when Ban came to town, it generally foreshadowed the occurrence of notable events.

In mid–September, the bomb dropped on John I. Taylor when Ban Johnson, AL secretary Bob McRoy and Washington manager Jimmy McAleer came to Boston and met Taylor at the Parker House to negotiate new ownership of the Red Sox. Johnson had never thought much of Taylor's baseball acumen, and as he saw another Red Sox rebuilding era in the offing unless he terminated Taylor, he brought two of his most trusted friends into his conspiracy to buy out the Sox.

As the newspaper account made clear, Johnson had let Taylor know that he, Taylor, must divest himself of his shares of stock. In the final settlement, McAleer became the team's president, Bob McRoy its treasurer and Taylor the vice president, even though the latter still controlled in some form half the shares of stock of the team (McAleer, McRoy and some Chicago "investors" held the remainder). On paper he still should have been able to exert controlling influence over the club or at least tried to pit McAleer and McRoy against each other, but in reality Ban Johnson had emasculated him, a long-overdue chore in the estimation of the American League president.

Lieb proffered two explanations for the seismic shift in team ownership: "Ban [Johnson] got tired running to Boston and 'straightening things out for John I. Taylor'; another was that with the new park about ready to open, General Taylor thought it a good time to get out." Most likely, Johnson wanted control of the team. Jimmy McAleer had no money after playing ball and managing for his adult life, and McRoy did not have a lot stashed in the couch cushions either. Charles Somers and Henry Killilea they were not, and yet, they did have the friendship and solid backing of Ban Johnson. In an age when many transactions smelled, the deal clicked, with the assistance of Johnson's Chicago friends.

McAleer and McRoy, again in theory, supposedly intended to let the season run its course and take over the day-to-day operations of the club in 1912; in reality, quite the opposite occurred. Both new owners immediately cast about to re-install Jake Stahl as manager and first baseman of the nine, enticing the financially astute Stahl with shares of stock. Patsy Donovan was kicked downstairs, hanging on as a team scout, far removed from any significant say in the operation of the franchise. Stahl signed on, and reportedly scratched out a percentage interest in Red Sox stock on the way back in.

The move against Taylor had probably been meticulously planned by Johnson and others for quite some time so that when the coup occurred, the blow to John I. would be brief and clean. Taylor probably did not see it coming, evidenced in part by his purchase of land in Toga, Texas, for the Sox's planned permanent spring training site, a development noted in the *Sporting Life* in its September 11 edition, just days before Ban Johnson lowered the boom. Even John I. Taylor would not have passed papers on land in Texas and announced the new site plans to the press had he any inkling that in a few days he would effectively lose his team.

Since the sale of the Red Sox had been in the works for "several months" before September 1911, the last spring training of John I. Taylor takes on more of a bittersweet aspect. Clearly the man failed at running a team, but he dreamt a lot and the trip out west was based in large part on some misplaced romantic notion of how things might be. In practice, it rained all the time and it was much colder in San Francisco and Oakland than the old stomping grounds in Arkansas. The excursion did little to prepare the team for the 1911 season, and the lack of adequate preparation contributed to the club's rash of injuries once the real games started.

But Taylor's romanticism did give the team Fenway Park, a venue cherished by Sox fans long after Taylor's death. He ran his teams into the ground, but created a "lyrical bandbox." It is a very mixed legacy, heavily weighted to the negative, but say this about John I. Taylor—he knew how to put on a show.

During the season's course, the Sox dumped Charley Smith, Freddy Smith, Ed Karger and Frank Arellanes. Fred Lieb theorized that Taylor had become "peeved" with the staff and decided to toss the four of them. In some of those instances, by that time it mattered little what Taylor thought of anything concerning baseball and the Sox in particular. He was just another fan as far as Jimmy McAleer and Bob McRoy considered the matter.

On paper, the release of Arellanes, sold to a Sacramento farm club in April, seemed the most questionable. Although he had posted a 4–7 mark in 1910, his ERA had only dipped slightly from his 1909 mark, when his record stood at 16–12. Perhaps during the course of his West Coast voyages, Taylor had chanced upon some unsavory aspects of the hurler's personal life.

This disturbing predilection came to the public's attention at the conclusion of the 1914 baseball season, by which time Arellanes was both married and a fixture in Pacific Coast minor league baseball. In October of that year, police in Portland, Oregon, arrested Arellanes, a handful of other ballplayers, an actor and a merchant for allegedly contributing to the corruption of a 14-year-old girl, with Arellanes allegedly the "worst offender." Specifically, the authorities charged him with statutory rape, for which he faced a potential 20-year sentence if convicted.

It allegedly started when Arellanes offered the young girl a "hot bird and a cold bottle," and then went out with her for a night on the town. Arellanes denied the charges, protesting that he "was not one of these 'chasing' fiends." He need not have worried because the judge at the trial treated the matter as a farce, banning the public from viewing the trial, even though he knew the legal decisions on this issue were to the "contrary" to his order. During the trial, the judge permitted defense counsel to beat up on the young girl while she testified. Another young girl scandalously found it amusing that one of the middle-aged lawyers did not know what a "pecan punch" was.

Not surprisingly, Arellanes walked after the jury came back quickly from their deliberations from this sham of a trial. Not even the judge believed in Arellanes' innocence as he sternly warned him from the bench "to mend his ways and never appear in court charged with acts of this kind or he would be punished without mercy." Why did the judge read the riot act to a man found innocent by a jury of his peers?

Arellanes did not outlive the trial for long, as he died four years later during an influenza outbreak, passing away on his seventh wedding anniversary.

As Arellanes faded in 1911, Smoky Joe Wood won 23 games, which was very good, but lost 17, which was not so terrific. Ray Collins showed some signs of life at 11–12. The club had collectively limped to 78–75, fifth-place finish.

By October 9, most of the Red Sox, once numbering almost twenty players, had vacated their digs at the Putnam Apartments on Huntington Street. Catcher Les Nunamaker, who had flirted at times in his rookie year with a .300 average before dipping to .257, paid his respects to the last two remaining veterans, Bill Carrigan and Tris Speaker, before departing for his Nebraska home.

Speaker meant to stay only a brief time as he read his magazine and recovered from a leg injury caused from being hit by a pitch a couple days previously, which was close to a groin injury according to Tris' delicate description. He hoped to catch a few games of the World Series as an esteemed spectator on the way back to Texas. For Rough, he had at least another three weeks before he could even contemplate traveling back home to Lewiston, Maine, to complete his recuperation from his broken leg.

Rough traipsed across his room on crutches, his plaster cast installed five weeks earlier still in place. He had lived through six chaotic years with the club, and still remembered playing for Chick Stahl and suiting up near Jimmy Collis. How long ago that must have seemed to him. Confined to his room for the previous five weeks, he eagerly awaited his freedom from the Putnam and the memories of so many vexing campaigns with the club. But Bill Carrigan never wasted time. He thought about games past and next year, and perhaps hoped that with new ownership and a new park success might return for the Boston Americans.

After Speaker healed and departed, Rough sat alone, the personification of all that was good and still is today about the Boston Red Sox and their drive to win. He embodied the bitterness and eternal hope of his fellow New England fans, pissed off about the season past but convinced that next year would be different—had to be different. While his teammates attended the World Series as spectators or went hunting and fishing, the heart and soul of the Boston Red Sox pulsated, ripping itself apart and then soaring again, just waiting for that next chance. If Rough Carrigan had anything to say about the matter, in 1912 the Boston Red Sox would become the champions of the world.

15

New Owner, New Park
and a Pennant

Today, the type of takeover by Ban Johnson, Jimmy McAleer and Bob McRoy would spawn endless litigation, but by March of 1912, the most significant legal battle confronting the Boston Red Sox was a $2,000 suit brought by a fan, Joseph A. Paes, who had been hit by a ball thrown by one of the ballplayers during warm-ups in the previous year. Paes suffered slight physical wounds, but had allegedly sustained "physical and mental anguish," and had also lost out on seeing the ball game, which appeared to be the only damage he might have legitimate cause to complain about. Like all true fans before and since, Joseph A. Paes had his priorities straight.

Happily, so did Red Sox management, which pushed relentlessly to ensure Fenway Park's completion by April 9 to accommodate a planned exhibition with the Harvard varsity. The cost of construction approached $300,000 as laborers and architects feverishly planned and built last-minute punch list extras, with the hope of housing as many as 40,000 fans, assuming some might be allowed to roam onto the field, held back by ropes, in the event of a particularly momentous contest.

Almost one hundred years after its construction, Fenway Park to the casual observer stands out as an unspoiled treasure, not only the same bandbox in which Ruth and Williams and Yastrzemski played, but one unchanged since its inception. Most surprisingly to many, the massive left-field wall, nicknamed the "Green Monster," simply did not exist for quite some time after 1912.

In the Dead Ball era, most batters did not hit the ball far enough to straddle the more modest porch, so there was no need for any high structure to somewhat offset towering shots punched toward it. In lieu of the Green Monster in left, there was Duffy's Cliff, a ten-foot slope leading up to the fences, named after its first great defender, Duffy Lewis.

Relatively unheralded in comparison to his Hall of Fame mates Speaker and Hooper in the outfield, Lewis mastered this extremely difficult handicap in left. He learned how to storm up the cliff after balls, intuiting that backpedaling only made the job of shagging flies more difficult. As an additional indicia of Lewis' peerless patrolling in left, he had to adjust each of his throws to

After the one-year hiatus in California, the Red Sox went back to the South and their grinding hikes to practice and back. Pictured here, from left to right, are Marty Krug, Duffy Lewis, Harry Hooper, Larry Gardner and two unidentified Sox. Boston Public Library, Print Department, McGreevy Collection.

the infield based on how many feet above sea level he was when he ran down a ball. To his enormous credit, Lewis calibrated each throw to the infield and by all accounts delivered it with laser-like accuracy.

Another feature about Fenway Park in 1912: no one wore pink hats. In addition to constructing Fenway Park and fending off Paes, the new Red Sox administration began issuing press releases and dropping news items virtually every day after the New Year. One of John I. Taylor's *faux pas* from the past campaign involved turning over promising pitcher Hugh Bedient to Providence, after which time he became the property of Jersey City, with no strings attached. Recognizing Taylor's mistake, McAleer and company sent out feelers to Jersey City, whose management demanded seven players in exchange from the Red Sox. Jimmy McAleer gulped, and then closed the deal, regaining the rights to a young right-hander who in his rookie season of 1912 won twenty games for the Boston Red Sox.

McAleer and Stahl did not stop there, signing Olaf Henriksen as a spare outfielder and gaining the rights to another St. Mary's of California product, hurler Hubert "Dutch" Leonard. For his part, Stahl ran spring training much differently than the Disney vacation during Patsy Donovan's final campaign. Gone were the fun rides, replaced by runs to the ball field and long hikes, some stretching out to fifteen miles a shot. Assuming more of a leadership role, Rough Carrigan accompanied McAleer to a league function out west and then joined Stahl early in spring training like a good company man, even accompanying him on some of his ridiculous hikes. Carrigan knew how to play the game outside of the ballpark with even greater skill than he did between the base lines.

After relaxing in the heat of Hot Springs, the team returned by rail to Back Bay station for the inauguration of Fenway Park on April 9, in an exhibition against Harvard. The park had not yet been completed, with some runways and more than a hundred of seats needing installation. Snow flurries and freezing weather dampened the novelty of the new ball field, as only 3,000 spectators came out to see the Red Sox beat the Crimson, 2–0. Huge pots of coffee kept the workers and presumably a few fans from freezing.

Then it was off to New York for a three-game season-opening series against the New York Highlanders, beginning April 11. Smoky Joe Wood started wildly for Boston, and New York led until the ninth inning when the Sox plated four runs, setting the tone for the type of year the men intended to have thereafter. Wood had matured in the off-season, as evidenced by his not becoming unhinged after his poor first inning. Of more importance, he had the backing of an infield that rivaled the fielding of the outfield constellation of Duffy Lewis and Hall of Famers Speaker and Hooper. Stahl settled in at first base, replacing the unsuccessful "position by committee" approach of Donovan, while Yerkes and Wagner formed an effective keystone combination. Good-natured Gardner starred at third base.

The next day, Bucky O'Brien scattered six hits and Jake Stahl had four of his own off the New York pitchers to win game two. The Sox completed the sweep on the third day. Trailing 4–2, in the fifth, the team exploded for six runs, with backup catcher Les Nunamaker tripling in Gardner and Wagner. Charley Hall shut down the opposing batters the rest of the way, causing the *Globe* to gush, "The Red Sox look like the Speed Boys of two years ago. They played all the games with the pepper that was lacking last year." After only three contests, pennant fever had officially gripped the Hub.

It got even more virulent after the Sox christened Fenway Park on April 20, fittingly enough with another game against New York. Rain had canceled the first two attempts at play, while the entire nation ran to scan the newspapers to check for survivors of the sinking of the *Titanic*, which began to plunge into the ocean after striking an iceberg on April 14. Sox owner Jimmy McAleer devoured the papers for days, seeking information concerning four friends, passengers from Ohio, until he learned that they had perished.

The national mourning did not deter the eventual start of the home season on April 20. The rain abated and the players ran into a field of mud as

Boston Mayor Honey Fitz threw out the first ball while his doting daughter Rose and over twenty thousand fans looked on. The overflow crowds bustled for space in the outfield, roped in with the ground rules dictating that all hits counted for doubles. This proved a huge boon to New York since none of the Highlander hits got much past the infield while the Sox runners repeatedly banged the ball into the crowd but had to stop at second base on each occasion.

Spitballer Bucky O'Brien started and fast became a victim of the usually sure-handed Steve Yerkes, who booted three balls hit his way. Buck eventually gave way to Charley Hall, who kept the team in the game until the eleventh. With Yerkes on third base, Tris Speaker won the game for his team by drilling a pitch so hard to the New York shortstop that Yerkes had scampered home by the time a handle had been found on the ball.

In time the New York-Boston baseball rivalry developed into the most intensely fought one in sports history, but in '12 the Red Sox captured nineteen out of twenty-one ball games. As usual, the Bostons had to get past the Philadelphia Athletics, well managed by Connie Mack and featuring talented hurlers like Boardwalk Brown, Cy Morgan, Colby Jack Coombs and Byron Houck. And if these staff members let old Connie down, he could always call on future Hall of Famers Chief Bender, Herb Pennock and Ed Plank and the vaunted "One Hundred Thousand Dollar Infield." If they had a weakness, it was in the outfield, where nobody bested Speaker, Hooper and Lewis, although Rube Oldring was an extremely good player.

Another surprising entrant in the sweepstakes in '12 was the perennial doormat Washington Senators, whom Jake Stahl had once managed and incrementally improved as a brash, young player-manager. Bob Groom came from nowhere and won 24 games, after which he returned from whence he came, while Carl Cashion picked up ten wins and Long Tom Hughes netted another thirteen for the club as he began to phase out of a largely disappointing career. Chick Gandil played a fancy first base and Clyde Milan led the team in center field and batted well. The superstar of the Senators was Walter Johnson, who breezed to 33 victories and led the league in ERA and strikeouts while posting another superior campaign by one of baseball's greatest pitchers.

In 1912, Boston traded seven players for Hugh Bedient; the deal worked quite well for the club as he won twenty games for them in his rookie season. Interestingly enough, although Bedient started nearly twenty games, he had no shutouts to his credit. Even Buck O'Brien with his often-unpredictable spitter earned a couple that year.

Bedient often pitched quite well, winning a twelve-inning game against Chicago on July 19 by a score of 2–1 and giving up only two hits against New York on September 2. On the latter occasion, the only real ripper came off a hit by Hal Chase with two out in the ninth, with the other official single occurring when Harry Hooper slipped and fell approaching an otherwise sure out. Slip or no slip, even in the two-hitter, a run scored.

Like Charley Hall, Bedient also chipped in effectively in relief. He struck out a fair share of batters with 122 in '12 and maintained a decent ERA, particularly since he had no shutouts. It is difficult to discern today why he eventually had only a four-year big league career, with the final one a poor valedictory in the upstart Federal League, but he possessed a steadiness early in his career that belied his age and relative lack of experience.

It is always wise to keep an eye on the quiet ones, though, as Hugh Bedient shocked the local sportswriters and fans alike by marrying in mid–July, something a renegade like Long Tom Hughes had once done, but for proper Bostonians and good teammates was simply not allowable. Accentuating Bedient's wallflower personality, no one on the Sox seemed to have seen it coming, causing A.H.C. Mitchell to surmise, "It must have annoyed his team-mates when the team was going so well to have one of their regular pitchers get married in the middle of the playing season."

That may have been the only shocking event in Hugh Bedient's life. Dull as a cow, he navigated his way through life with a fixed set of values imprinted on his compass. After a brief and unsatisfying flirtation with the Federal League, he received an offer from Miller Huggins in New York to pitch for the Yankees, an opportunity he declined as he enlisted to fight in World War I, because he "thought it was a bit more important."

He finally gave up his ballplaying career a decade later, even though he had posted a 3–0 record in the early part of a season with Atlanta: "I just can't explain why I quit, but I felt the strain of trying to produce every fourth day would be a little too much so I came home." Maybe he felt that way as a thirty-six-year-old player almost ten years removed from any major league experiences, but in 1912 his dullness belied a gift, an imperturbable nature, most valuable if needed to pitch in a big ball game, which became an increasingly likely scenario as the season unfolded.

Jake Stahl had no mercy on Bedient for his B.B. gun wedding, putting him into games right away in all types of situations to emphasize that the team came first. Bedient had no proper honeymoon, but since he continued to win ball games, his fans forgave him and wished him well. The quiet pitcher did things on his own timetable and upon the directions of his conscience, and then settled down for awhile and went about his business, which is how he handled the remainder of the games on the schedule.

The puzzle called Eddie Cicotte greatly assisted Bedient's cause. On a team with strong fielders at every position (and perhaps the finest defensive outfield ever) and terrific hitters led by Tris Speaker, Cicotte should have posted a winning record based on the efforts of his teammates alone, but he simply failed to do so. Most vexing, A.H.C. Mitchell felt at the time that Cicotte had more natural talent than anyone in baseball, but simply did not apply his talent to the cause.

On July 9, the Red Sox sold him to the White Sox, supposedly for only $1,500, a paltry sum even in that era. Whispers abounded that management felt he had no "stuff" and had lost his nerve, although the advent of such pitchers as Bedient and Ray Collins had squeezed him out of the rotation so thoroughly that he had no way to pitch effectively on the rare chance that Stahl trusted him in a game. He also had garnered a reputation as an unlucky pitcher. In any event, Cicotte closed the book on his Boston career with a 52–46 record, his destiny of becoming one of the craftiest hurlers in history and a conspirator in throwing the 1919 World Series awaiting. For the good and the bad, Eddie Cicotte needed a change of scenery.

In a foreshadowing of the effect his greed had upon his life, Cicotte at first threatened not to report to Chicago unless he received a cut of the very modest purchase price plus a share of the anticipated World Series money for Red Sox players. Revisionist history has portrayed Eddie Cicotte and his seven friends on the 1919 White Sox as basically innocents screwed by the penurious team owner Charlie Comiskey, but the famed pitcher's departure from Boston in '12 belies this. Eddie Cicotte was first and foremost out for the coin, and if he had to blackmail his new team or his old teammates, he would do so. No one doubted his underlying talent, and as the phenoms of 1912 faded one by one, Cicotte continued to get stronger until he ruined his own career.

Dumping Cicotte demonstrated the depth of the club's staff, and unlike year's past, the Philadelphia Athletics simply did not sail ahead of them at will. Marginalizing Cicotte coincided with the Red Sox embarking on a tear from June 8 through July 1, when the team posted 20 wins and three losses. In one of the notable games before 20,000 vigorous Chicago fans on June 15, Buck O'Brien bested future Hall of Famer Ed Walsh.

With Boston holding a bare percentage point lead on Chicago and Washington before the contest, the White Sox management procured a band to distract and dishearten the Sox, beginning with Ed Walsh coming onto the field to the strains of "For He's a Jolly Good Fellow." When O'Brien panicked a bit in the sixth inning, letting in three runs to tie the game, the band played the "Turkey Trot." By then, O'Brien had lost his catcher, after Carrigan took a pitch to the head while batting and did not answer the bell. But Buck steadied and helped his own cause in the seventh by singling Heinie Wagner from first to third, whereafter clutch-hitter Hooper singled home the eventual game-winning run.

As the summer wore on, the Athletics played the role of also-rans, competing for second with the resurgent Senators. During the Sox's wonderful stretch, Washington managed to split a series, but that meant little because before and after those contests Boston feasted on the New York Highlanders, hammering them game after game by lopsided margins.

One key acquisition the Sox made shortly before mustering Cicotte out came with the announcement of the purchase of Cleveland second baseman

Neal Ball, the man who made the first unassisted triple play in baseball history, against Boston no less. Ball had hit .296 the season before but had precipitously lost it at the plate, and yet his coming to Boston signified the club wanted no injuries to its infielders to impede the quest for a pennant. Having Neal Ball meant the club had insurance against ailments with a player fully capable of handling himself in the field.

Carrigan, right, boxing Buck O'Brien, circa 1912. It is not known who won the match, but the safe money would have been with Rough. Library of Congress.

It also meant that unlike in years past, a clear role had been assigned to a veteran utility man rather than create a situation where the owner fell in love with a ham-and-egger during a brief hot streak at the expense of alienating the true star, such as Harry Lord. Ball was there if Jake Stahl needed him, but in terms of starting—barring an emergency—Ball was not wanted.

The new Sox manager simply knew how to use his players for optimum advantage to the team. Hugh Bradley was never going to be a very good first baseman, but when Stahl needed a break, he called upon his sub, who performed adequately when summonsed. Similarly, the club purchased catcher Forrest Cady's minor league contract. He filled in for Rough Carrigan and stuck with the Red Sox for six years, the greatest seasons for the franchise in the twentieth century.

The Sox subs certainly pitched in and did not disrupt the team with delusions of personal grandeur. But the team thrived on the performances of its stars, none of whom shined so brightly at bat or on the field as Tristram Speaker, who enjoyed his best year at the plate. He hit .383 for the year, more than forty points higher than his previous best, and one of the highest averages of his illustrious career (he never hit .400, although he batted .344 lifetime, the same as another legendary Boston outfielder, Ted Williams). Speaker led the league with an .464 on-base percentage and for the only time he paced the circuit in home runs with a Dead Ball era-respectable 10 round-trippers.

Even allowing for Speaker's excellence, the pitchers on the club accounted for the difference between their team and the very talented Athletics and persistent Washington team. It was against Washington that staff ace Smoky Joe Wood shined the brightest.

Perhaps the greatest pitching duel in baseball history occurred at Fenway on September 6, when the Senators' Walter "Big Train" Johnson squared off against fellow speedballer Joe Wood. Johnson, of course, had one of the most brilliant pitching careers ever, winning 417 games, second only to Cy Young all-time. Smoky Joe had the 1912 season, and on this day in Boston, he had the opportunity to claim his spot as the greatest hurler who ever lived.

Or was it? Historically this game has entered the pantheon of great pitcher duels, but largely forgotten is the fact that in late June, the two fastball artists faced each other in the extreme heat of D.C. with little attendant pre-game hype, and Wood won, 3–0, over Johnson. At that time, the game meant much more. Boston had a comfortable lead but had not run away with the pennant, as the club had done by the time the two immortals faced each other in September.

In the second, more-publicized matchup, the fans crowded the park, causing the police all types of problems until they roped a number of the cranks into left field. Bob McRoy estimated that it was the highest attended weekday (non–World Series) game ever. The ancient Romans had gladiators and lions, the Fenway faithful that day witnessed something much more profound.

Johnson only surrendered five hits and Wood gave up six to the Senators, although he struck out nine to the Big Train's five. What ultimately tipped the scales in Wood's favor was not so much what he did, but what he had: the Senators had some very good hitters, the Red Sox had Tris Speaker.

It was Tris Speaker who came to bat with two outs in the sixth inning, Johnson having retired Hall of Famer Hooper and Steve Yerkes with little difficulty. It appeared to be much the same work after Johnson made Speaker look foolish while chasing an inside pitch and then painting one clearly outside for two quick strikes. Tris Speaker detested looking bad, so when Johnson got just a bit too cute, Tris laced the ball over third base. The ball did not stop until it reached the edge of the jumping and cheering crowd in left, and Tris trotted to a double.

Duffy Lewis then came to bat and, unlike the great Speaker, presented nowhere near an impressive challenge. Knowing that Lewis liked to hit the ball to left, the Senators' outfield shifted in that direction. At that point, as Mel Webb saw it, Johnson bore down and pitched even harder and faster. Lewis lunged at one ball and pushed it to right field, for him a sure sign he had started late on the pitch, and it flew over the head of Washington first baseman Chick Gandil.

Despite Washington having committed to the shift, the shot did not look fatal to right fielder Danny Moeller.

> Moeller, who had been almost in center field, was off with the crack of the bat. The ball was almost black, and many in the crowd could not see it, but they did see Moeller legging it toward the foul line for all he was worth. Faster and faster he came, and nearer and nearer the ball came to earth. Finally, with one frantic plunge, Moeller dove after the ball. For an instant it seemed he had caught it, but the ball just touched his finger tips and dropped onto the sod.

With two out, Speaker had sped off second base once Lewis got wood on the ball. By the time Moeller retrieved it, Speaker quite fittingly stood on home plate as the one immortal who had scored that day. The crowd sensed that only one run would score that day. Once it had, the fans also knew that on September 6, 1912, Smoky Joe Wood had bested the great Walter Johnson, and that Joe Wood was the greatest pitcher who ever lived or ever would live.

Smoky Joe Wood might have been the finest hurler on September 6, but he continued to pitch an enormous amount of innings that season, long after most people had conceded the pennant to Boston. For the year he threw 344 innings, almost 70 more innings than he had ever thrown in one season. Like Big Bill Dinneen in 1904, he needed rest but received none.

The warning signs were all in place. As early as September 15, the *Globe* reported that Jake Stahl had decided to give his starters some rest to prepare for the upcoming World Series, a reasonable approach given how hard everyone had worked to obtain supremacy in the American League and the primitive state of sports medicine at the time. The club had called up a young lefty named Ben Van Dyke from Worcester, presumably to soak up innings and give the starters a chance to rest and recuperate, a good idea since Smoky Joe began to suffer from tonsillitis. Other than perhaps being one of the few Red Sox players in club history deemed better looking than Smoky Joe, Ben Van Dyke had done little in his major league career, hurling 7⅓ innings for the Phillies in 1909.

In the first game of a double-header, Van Dyke did just that, relieving Charley Hall in the second inning against St. Louis. Stahl then reversed his decision from the previous day and stuck Wood in there for the remainder. The umpire mercifully called the game due to darkness after eight innings, giving Wood his American League record-tying 16th straight win. Wood had no business pitching that day, not only because of his tonsillitis, but also due to the fact that he had already thrown way too many pitches when the games actually counted.

Pitching "as white as snow" as the game lengthened, Wood "was forced to pitch for all that was in him to save the game, and his uniform was as wet as if dipped in the river, when he got through." Murnane felt that at the end of this ordeal, Wood needed at least a week's rest to recover. Unfortunately, Stahl did not heed this sage advice, starting his ace five days later, at which time the hurler lost his first game in 78 days, thus failing to surpass Walter Johnson for sole possession of the consecutive win record. Even though the club had clinched, Smoky Joe came back again shortly thereafter to heave a two-hitter against the hapless Highlanders, a pointless exhibition if ever there was one. To top it off, as Jake Stahl was killing his ace's career softly, Joe began to receive death threats by mail, thought to have emanated from a New York Giant fan.

On a poignant note, Smoky Joe Wood, one of the best interview subjects in baseball history, once related to Tim Murnane, "I could curve a ball when I was 7 years old. I never was shown anything about pitching. I devised and developed every curve and shoot that I use."

This fairly innocuous comment suggests two things: Wood may have been this country's most notable baseball prodigy before Babe Ruth, and that at an early age, he may have unwittingly fostered the arm troubles that eventually beset him. Every Little League coach who gives half a whit about the welfare of his or her young charges will instruct an adolescent not to utilize a curveball or other breaking pitches because the strain it potentially can place on a young arm.

No Little League existed during Wood's boyhood and adolescence, but later his great nemesis, Walter Johnson, warned him not to snap the ball as he released it toward the plate, feeling that it placed too much stress on the arm. Unlike the delivery of a giant farm boy like Cy Young, who never threw a pitch in spring training until he had trained his legs into top shape, Wood's arm bore the full thrust of each pitch, and the torque on his arm must have been fierce. He did not listen to Johnson's advice, after which Johnson prophesied a short career for the Sox star, but perhaps due to his youthful devotion to the curve, he had already shortened his playing days.

There are many explanations why Wood never replicated his 1912 performance while contemporaries like Walter Johnson seemingly possessed rubber arms in comparison. It may well be that by age 23, Wood's right arm was much older than that. As a much older man, Wood revealed that he had seen an x-ray of his right shoulder: "It was bone against bone. It still pains me. That's why I had to throw out the first ball at Fenway Park left-handed."

Oblivious to the strain on his ace's arm, Jake Stahl persisted in sending Wood out to take his regular turn in the rotation, a practice that produced a 34–5 record for the right-hander that year. Bedient and O'Brien won 20 games apiece, with Charley Hall chipping in at 15–8. The Red Sox won an incredible 105 games that season, the most ever at that time and a mark not eclipsed until the 1927 New York Yankees dominated the game.

The Sox needed all of these strong young arms with the looming World Series against the New York Giants and their pitching staff of Christy Mathewson, Rube Marquard and Jeff Tesreau, a front line which arguably provided a fairly even match for Boston. While Christy Mathewson might offset Smoky Joe Wood, the Giants had no equivalent for the massive talent named Tris Speaker.

16
The 1912 World Series

Alighting at New York's Grand Central Station from their special car on the Knickerbocker Limited early in the evening of October 7, the American League champion Boston Red Sox players cautiously surveyed their surroundings. Allaying the possible fears of young team mascot Jere McCarthy as well as Mrs. Jake Stahl, Mrs. Duffy Lewis and Mrs. Sea Lion Hall, the ballplayers received an almost immediate and thunderous welcome from their fellow traveler fans and the hordes of New Yorkers who secretly loved the Olde Towne Team the best.

Kicking off the rust since their last supporting appearance in the '03 Series, Mike McGreevy and 300 of his Royal Rooters, bedecked in red and carrying megaphones with a band in tow, followed close behind, joined by such Beantown celebrities as Mayor Fitzgerald and Governor Eugene Foss. Meanwhile, the ballplayers hustled into taxicabs and headed to their lodgings at the Bretton Hall Hotel on Eighty-Sixth and Broadway, with a goal to get between the sheets of their beds by 10:00 P.M.

Many New Yorkers thought the Red Sox had many more fifth columnists on their side than those cheering at Grand Central, principally in the person of *New York Times* sportswriter Hugh Fullerton, who had for days confidently predicted a Sox victory in the Series.

Three years after the peculiar post-season exhibition between the third-place Red Sox and Giants, the two teams met for the World Series. Little had changed with the Giants on the field, with Fred Merkle replacing Fred Tenney at first base and Chief Meyers taking over the catching chores from George "Admiral" Schlei, but that had proven enough to propel them into the 1911 World Series. In the past year, the Giants repeated as champions and vastly improved their fortunes through the addition of a rookie right-hander from Ironton, Missouri, the 6'2" and 220-pound "moist baller" Jeff Tesreau, who led the National League in ERA at 1.96.

Of course, the Sox had significantly improved as well, primarily through the subtraction of owner John I. Taylor. On a more positive note, the outfield had tightened up its defense even more with the addition of Duffy Lewis, and the club's young pitchers had ripened, pretty much at the same time. And as John McGraw understood all too well, his opposition still had Tris Speaker, who had only improved during that interim.

When the Royal Rooters sang "Tessie" they were not honoring Giants pitcher Jeff Tesreau, seen at right. Shaking hands with Tesreau is none other than Smoky Joe Wood, coming off a 34–5 regular season and primed for World Series glory. Library of Congress.

Hoping to confound Jake Stahl, the Giants' John McGraw tabbed Jeff Tesreau as his starter over Christy Mathewson for the opener, while Smoky Joe Wood permitted the ice water to course through his veins in anticipation of his Series debut. The Giants could have warmed up their entire staff to little effect as the greatest pitcher on October 8, 1912, was none other than Smoky Joe Wood.

And yet, for the first five innings, Giant Jeff Tesreau held the Red Sox hitless. His teammates in their batting, meanwhile, had chiseled away at Wood, tagging him for two runs in the third when Red Murray doubled to center, scoring teammates Devore and Doyle.

In the sixth inning, Tesreau showed signs of fatigue, and in the seventh Tris Speaker laced a shot between left and center fields that rolled to the Polo Grounds fence, giving him a triple. Duffy Lewis grounded out to drive in his hallowed teammate, and Boston had its first run. In the eighth, Boston tossed Tesreau around for another three runs and a 4–2 lead.

In the ninth inning, behind 4–2, with one out and no runners on base, the Giants rallied. Fred Merkle hit the ball to right as did the next batter, Herzog, and "Meyers good Indian that he is pummel[ed] the sphere to right and Merkle scores. The crowd then broke out into real baseball insanity...." Wood's

Sox mates gathered around him, hoping to steady their indomitable ace, providing shelter from the storm as over thirty thousand energized Giant fans pounced for the kill.

McGraw sent in a pinch-runner for Meyers, and with runners on second and third, lonesome Wood faced Giant infielder Art Fletcher, a good hitter and over the course of his major league career a five-time champion in being hit by pitches. Would Fletcher take advantage of Wood's nerves and lean into a ball to load the bases, all the while taking one for the team? For Wood's part, he "wavered and it looked as though he was going to crack. His face paled and his jaws were set tightly as he faced the frenzied multitude which howled for his downfall."

Channeling his adrenalin, he stared down Art Fletcher and blew fastballs past him until he struck out, causing a collective groan to emit throughout the crowd, with the exception of the Sox, Mayor Fitzgerald and Nuf Ced McGreevy's bold three hundred. Next up was pitcher Otey Crandall, who hit .313 during the regular season, McGraw figuring he needed no pinch-hitter. The crowd commenced to screaming again, hats were thrown into the air with blissful abandon and "[c]ushions were thrown from the stands onto the field by hundreds."

Jake Stahl walked over to Wood to calm him down. There are several quotes concerning exactly what he said, but the gist of it was to remain in control, an easy thing for a manager to say. Wood did what he did best, which was to throw fastballs, although the *Times* intimated that at least one pitch was "saliva moistened." With two strikes, Wood may or may not have resorted to the spitter, but he whipped it shoulder-high to Crandall, who had not completed his swing by the time the ball rested safely in Red Sox catcher Forrest Cady's mitt. Strike three and game one to the Red Sox, as a throng of disappointed Giants fans rushed onto the field, not violently, but with the need to somehow avert the despondency that had consumed them. Back with his teammates, best friend Tris Speaker strolled up to Wood and gave him the biggest prize. "You were great, Joe. Great! I'm proud of you."

Boston 4, New York 3: Boston Leads Series, 1–0

The next day's contest resulted in an eleven-inning 6–6 tie as Mathewson started for the Giants and Ray Collins went for the Sox, playing at friendly Fenway. Before the game, manager Jake Stahl received a car from Mayor Fitzgerald, paid for by his friends and admirers in the Hub. The Sox initially hopped on the Giants' great hurler, touching up "Matty" for three runs in the first inning.

After seven, Boston led, 4–2, the game seemingly in hand, an enthusiastic crowd basking in success. Fred Snodgrass started off the eighth batting for

New York and hit a liner that the normally sure-handed Duffy Lewis actually caught, then dropped, permitting Snodgrass to go to first. Larry Doyle then came up and singled to center, bringing his teammate to second, as "[t]he great crowd, which had been chilly and undemonstrative, suddenly waked up and became frightened." Becker forced Doyle at second and Red Murray hit a ground-rule double, at which time Stahl pulled Collins for Sea Lion Hall.

Hall went right to work, inducing Fred Merkle to pop up, and it looked like déjà vu when he got Herzog to hit a high foul ball near home, seemingly the inning-ender, and Rough Carrigan charged after it. This being October in New England, the ball started whirling back and forth with the whims of the wind until Carrigan took a stab at it with his glove. As the *Times'* Hugh Fullerton witnessed it, "The ball hit in it, rimmed around like a golf ball on a long putt, rolled out, and Carrigan leaped and cursed wildly." On the next pitch, Herzog whacked the ball to left, scoring two runs and making it a whole new ball game. Hall retired Chief Meyers, but New York now led, 5–4.

In the bottom of the eighth, Matty quickly dispatched Yerkes and Speaker, but Duffy Lewis rapped a ground-rule double into the bleachers. Larry Gardner hit a ball just through the Giants' infield to score Lewis and knot the game at 5–5: Jake Stahl then singled and promptly stole second, eyeing Gardner at third base with Heinie Wagner at bat. On the verge of another Sox breakthrough, Matty methodically struck out Wagner to end the inning.

The ninth passed uneventfully for Boston and eventfully for New York, which loaded the bases but did not plate a run. Each team scored once in the tenth, as the Back Bay skies grew darker and darker. Speaker hit the ball sharply to the outfield, and while rounding third for an inside-the-park home run, Giants third sacker Herzog bumped Spoke to try to knock him off balance. It worked by throwing Speaker off his stride, with Giants catcher Wilson awaiting at home with the ball, poised for a tag out. Not to be denied, Spoke drilled the catcher, causing him to drop the ball and allowing the Sox to score that crucial run.

Before the eleventh inning, Tris Speaker lept into Buck Herzog's face, accusing the Giants' third sacker of blocking him from scoring after tripling in the tenth, a moot point since he scored on Wilson's error at home. Speaker would have ripped his head off, but Heinie Wagner pulled him from the fray as Larry Doyle restrained Herzog. Bedient came on to relieve Charley Hall while Matty stayed in the game for the Giants, but neither team scored, thanks largely to Carrigan throwing out Giant runners who tried to challenge his arm and steal a base. With darkness having engulfed the Fens, umpire Silk O'Loughlin called the game, 6–6, with the teams returning to Fenway the next day, this time hopefully for a game that counted.

The draw did benefit the Red Sox, as the great Mathewson pitched 11 innings to no avail, a point not lost on the normally more diplomatic Jake Stahl, who observed, "I think to-day's game, while it did not end in victory, shows that we can hit the New York twirler, whose work to-day must have tired him out." Whether it did or not remained to be seen, but unofficially, Matty had tossed 128 pitches in a futile effort, and McGraw did not go four deep with his staff like Stahl did with the Sox.

Boston 6, New York 6:
Boston Still Leads Series, 1–0

Having rendered the wonderful game the day before a nullity, the Sox and Giants squared off on the tenth of October with Rube Marquard, owner of nineteen straight victories during the regular season, going for the Giants, and the less-heralded Bucky O'Brien starting for the home team. On paper it might appear to be a mismatch since Marquard had a Hall of Fame career and a 26–11 mark in 1912, but Marquard was now generally considered to be over-rated and his regular season ended with less fanfare than it began, tallying seven wins against eleven defeats. Marquard only accumulated a 201–177 career record, and in the last eight years of his career, he only posted winning records in two seasons (17–14 and 10–7). But he was a character and a lady's man, and as a New Yorker, he seemed far grander than he was.

O'Brien is a largely forgotten figure today. In 1999, a Suffolk County pro-bation officer in Massachusetts was arrested and pled guilty to stealing numer-ous wills of dead ballplayers, many of them Hall of Famers, but several of them ham-and-eggers like Bucky O'Brien. Still, he did win twenty games in this championship year, and since he hailed from nearby Brockton, he had plenty of friends and family at what was then estimated to be the best attended game in Boston baseball history.

Having awarded Jake Stahl an automobile the day before, Tris Speaker received a new Chalmers, which he drove crazily around Fenway at a high speed to the delight of the Sox and foes alike. On a more technical note, the sides agreed before the contest to a new ground rule—if a ball hit a policeman in fair territory, the ball remained in play.

This arcane rule mattered little as the game turned into a pitcher's con-test, or more accurately, Rube Marquard's outing, as he mesmerized Boston with his speed. Buck O'Brien flailed along wildly all day, in trouble with at least half the opposing batters. Luckily for O'Brien, New York did not capitalize all that much on his slow fastballs and dry spit balls, as Boston headed into the bottom of the ninth trailing only 2–0.

Leading off for Boston, Tris Speaker lofted an easy infield pop-up for the first out. Duffy Lewis then beat out an infield hit and scored on Larry Gard-ner's double. Coaching third base, Heinie Wagner initially held Lewis at third, and while he eventually ran home on the play, the delay prevented Gardner from stretching his double to a triple.

Jake Stahl then hit a sharp drive up the middle and Marquard made a great stop on it, electing to throw to third for the tag-out on Gardner, who went on the pitch, as Stahl sat on first base as a result of the fielder's choice. Olaf Henriksen then pinch-ran for Stahl, a wise move as Heinie Wagner came to bat and beat out an infield hit, with Henriksen advancing all the way to third. Wagner then stole second.

That is how matters stood, with runners on second and third base and two outs, as Sox catcher Forrest Cady, a man described by Tim Murnane as "a farmer's son with a strong heart and a mighty punch," walked to the batting box. Marquard sized up his opponent and threw him a fastball that Cady hit squarely. For "four seconds" the game stood in doubt as the ball shot between Giants outfielders Snodgrass and Devore in left-center before Devore, with his back to the plate, threw both hands over his head and came down safely with the out. The Fenway crowd had gone wild, anticipating the winning run of a pitchers' duel, only to lose out on the last pitch. The Series now stood 1–1 with the teams due the next day at the Polo Grounds.

New York 2, Boston 1: Series Tied, 1–1

For five innings in the third "official" game, the Giants "looked as if [they] had about as much chance as a sober man on the midnight to Boston" against Smoky Joe Wood, in Hugh Fullerton's colorful phraseology.

While the Royal Rooters triumphantly belted out "Tessie," the Giants wasted another strong pitching performance from their own Tessie, Jack Tesreau. Larry Gardner touched him up in the second with a triple and scored when Tesreau's pitch to the next Boston batter hit the edge of home plate and bounded away from catcher Chief Meyers. He also coughed up a run in the fourth when the Red Sox took advantage of some more quirks, but had commanded the game admirably until McGraw pinch-hit for him in the seventh.

It became interesting in the seventh when the Giants came to bat. With one out, and a dark mist hovering over Fenway, Wood began heaving a very dark and muddy ball, which Herzog hit into the stands foul. With a clean white ball, Herzog saw the next pitch clearly and singled. Fletcher then doubled Herzog home as Moose McCormick came to bat for Tesreau. The Moose hit sharply to Steve Yerkes at second and had an infield hit. At that point, John McGraw, coaching third base as managers often did in the early twentieth century greatly aided the Hub's cause by sending Fletcher home, a huge gamble that failed for the third out of the inning.

The Red Sox added an insurance run in the ninth, and while it appeared on some occasions that Wood might break, shortstop Heinie Wagner bailed him out with terrific fielding and accurate throws. The day itself was misty and dark, which permitted Wood to rely more on his curves than his heat, but ultimately Jeff Tesreau was simply not as good a pitcher as Smoky Joe Wood.

Boston 3, New York 1: Boston Leads Series, 2–1

Prior to the Series, John McGraw had crowed that Boston only had one pitcher, Smoky Joe Wood, but in Fenway on the twelfth of October, Hugh Bedient proved him wrong by outwitting Christy Mathewson by the tally of 2–1. Thousands came to the park and hundreds of thousands sat or marched as Columbus Day was celebrated with parades and the like despite the foggy, cold and damp weather.

On paper, Mathewson should have had no problem out dueling Bedient, and he only gave up the two runs. But Bedient, buoyed by the crowd and inclement weather conditions, which proved to be a great equalizer, pitched just a bit better. The Giants' Larry Doyle and the Red Sox' Larry Gardner both made costly errors for their teams, but they essentially offset each other as Boston hit more advantageously for the crucial win at the Polo Grounds.

Boston 2, New York 1: Boston Leads Series, 3–1

Leading three games to one in the Series, the Boston players embarked on their train ride to New York in high spirits, figuring that New York had had it and only awaited the formal *coup de grace* from Smoky Joe Wood. At this point, owner Jimmy McAleer—according to sacred Sox lore—accosted Jake Stahl and suggested that Buck O'Brien start, reasoning that he had more rest than Wood and had pitched well against the Giants.

Stahl listened to the suggestion at first with incredulity and then with resignation. After all, it was McAleer's team, although he seemed possessed by the buttinski tendencies of the unlamented John I. Taylor. It is unclear how hard Stahl fought for Wood, but on the pecking order of the Red Sox, he was fated to lose as long as McAleer wanted it more.

McGraw had erred by starting Jeff Tesreau in the first match of the Series, and in a fit of hubris, McAleer had just compelled Stahl to commit a similar strategic error by starting a pitcher much less qualified than Smoky Joe to nail down the Series.

O'Brien lost the game early for his teammates. With men on the corners and two out, he made a motion to throw the ball to first base to catch the runner sleeping off base, when as Tim Murnane described it, "He held the ball, making a balk, the like of which I have not seen before this season, forcing the first run over the plate and taking all the sand out of him." He then demolecularized, serving up two doubles and two singles and watching with horror as Steve Yerkes botched a double-steal attempt by the Giants, to allow four more runs to cross the plate. O'Brien's manager did not want to start him and many of his teammates resented him for an assignment he probably had nothing to do with and did not want.

Ray Collins came in to relieve in the second and did not let another run cross home for the rest of the game, but the fatal blows had occurred. Boston chipped away and got some of the difference back, with Engle pinch-hitting for O'Brien and doubling home two runs, before Marquard shut down the Sox the rest of the way. As one of the club's only consolations, the Royal Rooters marched around the Polo Grounds after the game, singing "Come to Boston and See Joe Wood." More importantly, the management of the Red Sox and the Giants got together simply to toss a coin to determine which city would host the final game of the World Series, if necessary, and Boston won the toss.

New York 5, Boston 2: Boston Leads Series, 3–2

The train ride back for the Red Sox was chaotic. Supposedly, Joe Wood's brother Paul had lost a lot of money betting on the game in addition to the blot on the family pride and socked Buck O'Brien, giving him a black eye. The next day it would be Wood versus Tesreau, with one major equalizer. The overzealous Boston fans negated the normal home-field advantage with their antics.

Ninety-two years after the event, the Boston band the Dropkick Murphys focused on the events of the Ides of October, 1912, in their remake of the classic song "Tessie":

> The Rooters showed up at the grounds one day
> They found their seats had all been sold
> McGreevy led the charge into the park
> Stormed the gates and put the game on hold
> The Rooters gave the other team a dreadful fright
> Boston's tenth man could not be wrong.

Bob McRoy had inexplicably decided to sell to the general public the few hundred seats in left field normally allotted to the Rooters. The Rooters, led that day not by Nuf Ced McGreevy but by Johnny Keenan, had marched onto the field with their hundreds of minions waving tiny red stockings and singing "Tessie." They were accompanied by a twenty-five-piece band while heading over to what they believed to be their reserved seats, only to see them populated by other fans.

The situation rapidly swirled out of control. Captain Thomas Goode attempted to explain how the tickets had gone on sale to other patrons, while Keenan, Hubie Curley, William Shea and Jack Killeen tried to keep their troops, many of them undoubtedly inebriated, in check. The Rooters somehow

This is the event that spurred the remake of "Tessie" as Boston Riot Police try to quell the Royal Rooters after club owner Bob McRoy denied them their usual seats. In many ways this event marked the high-water mark of the Rooters as the large Fenway Park lessened the volume and influence of any one group. Boston Public Library, Print Department, McGreevy Collection.

squeezed themselves into the area, but the other fans became quite agitated as their views became adjusted. Every time a Rooter tried to lean his head over the fence in front of him, "he was unceremoniously shoved back by a policeman." Accelerating the chaos, the other fans began to swear and say other hurtful things to the Rooters.

And then, the *Globe* reported, "Like the imbecile who cries 'fire!' in a theatre someone in the crowd yelled for everybody to leap the fence...." Scores of Rooters, boys from the band, and other jerks "stampeded" onto the field, and "[i]n an instant, the police, at first swept off their feet by the sudden push began to assail the trespassers...," urging them to return to their places behind the fence. Just as this crisis had seemingly passed, another section of the fence gave way, with panicking people running onto the field, trampling each other while many sought refuge in the area of the visitors dugout.

Enter the cavalry. "From far down the field a shout went up, and mounted policemen in full gallop were seen racing up the field." Accompanying the charge of the light brigade was another group of uniformed policemen who went after the latest mob invading the field, as Johnny Keenan did his part to try to get everyone to love each other again, to no avail. Seeing the mounted police, several fans in the stands began tossing "bags of peanuts, scorecards, canes and miscellaneous weapons and missiles" at the policemen. The second Boston Massacre seemed set to commence.

Grabbing a microphone, Johnny Keenan wisely prevented mass arrests and a likely Boston forfeit of the game by loudly beseeching his followers and the other troublemakers to move back to the stands and not to blame the police. Captain Goode appeared, and perhaps realizing he could identify practically all of the rowdies, the crowd dispersed, and over the course of fifteen minutes returned to the stands.

Tired, and perhaps a bit shaken by the near riot before the game, Joe Wood took the mound and after thirteen pitches, the Giants tallied six runs. The fans and management had not prepared for this unlikely event. Their ace had appeared omnipotent, particularly after he reeled off sixteen straight wins late in the season and had so far humbled the opposition in the Fall Classic.

The *New York Times* parodied the feelings of the Fenway faithful, greeting Smoky Joe "[w]hen he walked to the pitching mound this afternoon Wood wore a halo. Not since the days of the great 'Charley' Nichols had there been such another idol in this hero-worshipping city." Charley Nichols, better known as "Kid," had won more than three hundred games, primarily with the Boston National teams of the 1890s. But the *Times* hinted at perhaps another fate for Wood: "He is not tireless like Walter Johnson or 'Ed' Walsh. He needed a good rest, he didn't get it and he cracked." Wood had pitched an ungodly number of frames during the regular campaign, a feat made more dubious since his team had run away with the pennant quite early and did not need him to throw as much as he did. Maybe Smoky Joe had had it—certainly most New Yorkers believed so—as they awaited with glee the mismatch between the immortal Christy Mathewson and Boston's "speedy Frenchman," Hugh Bedient.

The contest came to be seen almost immediately as a watershed event for the Royal Rooters, who had become bigger than the game they were cheering in. The next day the *Globe's* Lawrence J. Sweeney penned their requiem:

> The Red Sox Royal Rooters of 1912 are a thing of the past. They have passed into history, for today, if any of them attend the final game, they will do so individually. There will be no Royal Rooters Band, there will be no parade, no flying of colors, singing of songs or cheers.

The rumors of the Rooters' demise were a bit exaggerated, but the beginning of their end had come. They had become bigger than the show, and in Fenway, there were just too many seats for too many fans for the Rooters to exert the type of influence they had. Plus, they had shot their bolt during the World Series and had looked bad in front of many of the fans who formally supported them or at least tolerated them. McGreevy's saloon was near the old Huntington Grounds, not so close to Fenway, and when Prohibition became the law of the land at just the point the Red Sox began the curse of the Bambino, the Royal Rooters were truly dead. Their members increasingly left Roxbury for the suburbs, caring more for their spacious new lawns than their old team.

Rooters or no rooters, Game Seven still awaited the Boston Red Sox and New York Giants.

New York 11, Boston 4: Series Tied, 3–3

In the final game of the Series, relatively few turned out for the game, given the cold shoulder turned to the Royal Rooters and, perhaps, due to the Rooters nearly rioting. Stahl went with Bedient, a good pitcher that year but hardly an immortal like his opponent, Christy Mathewson. Through seven innings, Bedient pitched well enough to lose, coughing up only one run in the third inning when Red Murray doubled home his teammate, Devore, with two strikes and two out. Many folks thought of Matty as perfect, a Frank Merriwell brought to life, and through six innings that is how he pitched.

In the seventh, Olaf Henriksen pinch-hit for Bedient with Sox at first and second. Laboring with two strikes, Henriksen plunged at a Mathewson pitch, clearly outside, driving the ball down the third-base line and scoring the lead runner, Jake Stahl. And then matters simmered down until the tenth inning.

Joe Wood had come in for Boston in the eighth and pitched effectively, if quite tiredly. In the top of the tenth, Murray doubled and Fred Merkle, the Giants' first baseman, singled him home to stake out a 2–1 lead. Wood hurt his hand stabbing at an inning-ending shot from catcher Chief Meyers, and although he posted the last out, his injury took him out of the game. More importantly, if the Sox could not at least tie the score in the bottom of the tenth, no one from the Red Sox would pitch again that season.

The bottom of the tenth inning felled the Giants. Engle led off, pinch-hitting for Wood. Wood must have been hurt fairly seriously, because not only did the Sox potentially need him in the eleventh in the event they tied the game, but Wood was such a good hitter, a point he punctuated by playing the outfield and batting decently once he left Boston. Engle lifted a ball to left-center field and Snodgrass settled under it for what appeared to be a routine fly ball out. Snodgrass, however, bungled the play, with the certain out bouncing in and out of his glove, giving Engle renewed life as he raced safely to second base with the potential tying run.

Up came Harry Hooper, one of the greatest clutch ballplayers in Red Sox history, and risking nothing, Mathewson threw every pitch to him low, hoping to induce a harmless grounder to the Giant infield. Hooper tried bunting and when that did not work, he hit the ball sharply to center, straight to Snodgrass, who speared it for the first out. Snodgrass had choked on Engle's fly, but redeemed himself with a much tougher catch off Hooper.

Inexplicably, Matty continued to telegraph his pitches by throwing everything low to the next Sox batter, the light-hitting Steve Yerkes, and in the midst of working Yerkes too fine, walked him. At this point, McGraw should have relieved Mathewson with either Marquard or Tesreau, both of whom he had throughout much of the game warming up, but he did not.

Having walked an ordinary batter like Yerkes, Matty now had to face a fellow immortal, Tris Speaker. Matty seemed to have bested his foe by tossing a slow inside curve that Speaker popped up harmlessly in Fenway's narrow foul territory, between first and home. As the *Times'* Hugh Fullerton called it, "Anyone could have caught it. I could have jumped out of the press box and caught it behind my back, but Merkle quit. Yes, Merkle quit cold. He didn't start for the ball. He seemed to be suffering from financial paralysis…. Mathewson saw the ball going down. [Giants catcher] Meyers saw it would fall safe, and they raced toward it, too late, and the ball dented the turf a few feet from first."

Whether Merkle, Meyers or Matty should have caught it, Tris Speaker supposedly told Mathewson, "Matty, that play will cost you the game and the series." And it did, as Speaker ripped a single to right field, plating Engle with the tying run. Mathewson now had men on second and third with only one out. Again, why not relieve him with a fresh Marquard or Tesreau? Duffy Lewis came to bat and again, Mathewson threw him nothing good, with each ball pitched "less than a foot from the ground." Duffy took his base on balls to load the bags for Boston.

Thus far during the inning, Mathewson had allowed each Boston at-bat to culminate in either a walk or a ball hit into the outfield. With the bases loaded and one out, either result meant the end for the Giants. A fresh hurler like Tesreau or Marquard may have been able to strike out the side, but they remained on the side as McGraw continued to keep Matty on the mound.

Larry Gardner came to the plate to face an exhausted Giant pitcher, who continued to throw low for two balls. Gardner missed the next pitch, but Matty then departed from his low ball strategy to pitch one around Gardner's knees, and Larry rapped it to "deep right field" where Devore settled under it. Pandemonium broke out at Fenway once the fans saw the trajectory of the hit. Everyone knew that even if Devore caught it, Yerkes had plenty of time to tag up and scamper home with the game-winning run, which he did the moment Devore's glove cradled Gardner's fly.

For decades, scribes fixated on Snodgrass' muff and Merkle's "boner" as the classic moments in the Series, spending little time discussing how competent the Giants fielders were in comparison to those of the Red Sox. Snodgrass committed his team's sole error in the final game, while Larry Gardner alone booted three chances and his teammates erred another couple of times, a huge burden for Bedient to overcome. Buried under the traditional blaming of Snodgrass and Merkle is the fact that the Sox players performed very well in the clutch and that John McGraw probably should have relieved Mathewson in the tenth. Jake Stahl had out-managed the great John McGraw.

The Red Sox reigned supreme again, for the first time since their pennant-winning run a decade earlier when John McGraw refused to play them in the

World Series. Unfortunately, cracks and fissures in the team soon became evident, or at the least more pronounced. Wood and his friends and family had a problem with Bucky O'Brien, Jake Stahl had issues with intrusive owner Jimmy McAleer, and religious differences threatened to divide the club. The worst strain of all may had already occurred—the destruction of Smoky Joe Wood's magnificent arm.

Boston 3, New York 2: Boston Wins Series, 4–3

17

Smoky Joe Goes Skiing Downhill

Rifle through any period in Boston Red Sox history and just about the time when the team seemed to be on the brink of a dynastic roll, internal dissension threatened to undermine the situation. The 1913 season proved no different. Hurt feelings emanating from the events of the previous World Series had exacerbated latent tensions between some of the players, and the Royal Rooters had not forgotten their poor treatment in ("official") Game Six and blamed part-owner McRoy.

Strange bedfellows spawned the success of the Sox in '12, but by the spring of the following year, Jimmy McAleer began to eye Jake Stahl in a way much like a predatory bird draws a bead on road kill. In the meantime, McAleer forgot that he brought no money to the Sox and had come aboard only through the good graces of Ban Johnson.

Unlike Patsy Donovan, Jake Stahl had no intention of hanging out at headquarters in Boston over the winter while entertaining members of the fourth estate or old ballplayers like Hugh Duffy. He had married money and did not even stay in Chicago over the winter to overlook his banking interests. Instead, he spent the off-season in his father-in-law's estate in California, enjoying the life of the idle affluent.

Back in Boston, Jimmy McAleer curried favor with the press and attended Winter Club (a precursor of today's Bosox fan club) meetings, letting every member of the Knights of Columbus know that he had nothing to do with the lockout of the Royal Rooters in the recently concluded World Series. Press releases did not emanate from one central source, and all hands in the organization did not read off of the same page. There was Jimmy McAleer's take on things and Stahl's independent view on matters, with McAleer maintaining the inside track at all times by remaining in Boston and representing the perceived interests of the club's large Irish-Catholic fan base. Unbeknownst to him, Jake Stahl was on safari to stay.

A cynic might suggest that McAleer had painted Stahl's exit from the time the last out of the World Series was registered, if not sooner. Surely, he did not operate with the utmost of tact when he touted in the off-season the endless prospects of a local first baseman, Roxbury's own Hal Janvrin.

In retrospect, Janvrin's career amounted to little more than a useful utility player's contribution. He played in the majors for ten years, toiling briefly for Boston in 1911, and hit .232 in ten seasons, almost all as a substitute. But leading up to his proper rookie season, McAleer built Janvrin up as the next star of the club. Early on in spring training, Stahl gushed, "Janvrin is a young wonder and I think he will stick with the team this time."

Spring training did not get off to a wonderful start as players wandered into camp in dribs and drabs, reminiscent of the final days of Jimmy Collins. The club had invested in a facility at Hot Springs, but the players did not eagerly line up to enter the oasis, and Ray Collins held out for more money.

More importantly, the specter of hard feelings in the World Series managed to infect the club's spirit as the new season beckoned. In particular, Christy Mathewson had stated in his column in New York that he had heard "gossip" that Joe Wood and Buck O'Brien had clashed during the Series, a rumor that most people gave credence to. Both Sox hurlers did their best to squelch it, with O'Brien arguing that "Mathewson has always been a knocker; he evidently takes himself seriously and should be stopped or get out of the game. He puts everything in the way of gossip, and gossip is a hard thing to tie to." More succinctly, Wood added, "Mathewson is still sore over and is trying to annoy someone." The Sox hurlers mused about filing a defamation lawsuit against Matty, which went nowhere.

Smoky Joe Wood ran into misfortune from the outset of spring training when he blistered his hand badly in early March. In the middle of the month, he strained an ankle, which kept him out of Stahl's extended hikes through the countryside. Smoky Joe had banged himself up two years earlier during the club's ill-conceived odyssey in California, but what should have alarmed the management even more was the fact that he pitched 344 innings the previous year, almost 70 more innings than in 1911, and that figure excludes the World Series.

To the Sox' credit they did not stand pat in the matter of pitching talent, having learned the lesson with the flame-outs of Bill Dinneen and Long Tom Hughes during their last World Series defense.

Having mined St. Mary's in California successfully in the past with Harry Hooper and Duffy Lewis, the Red Sox took on another former scholar-athlete, pitcher Hubert "Dutch" Leonard, destined to be one of the team's most effective hurlers for the next five years. The *Sporting Life* noted early in the year that "Leonard, the youngster, is showing a lot of class." The Sox had worked out an option with Denver of the Western League the previous year when he had led his team to a championship, so McAleer wisely recalled him to the parent club.

Dutch Leonard would become one of baseball's all-time pariahs, a notoriety he earned by finking out Cleveland's Tris Speaker and Smoky Joe Wood (by then an outfielder) and Detroit's Ty Cobb in their attempt to throw a game late in 1918 in order for the Tigers to finish in third in the AL race that year.

Late in his career Leonard had pitched for Detroit, by then managed by Cobb, who cut him in 1925 due to his poor ERA (albeit with an 11–4 won-lost record). Apparently acting out of revenge, Leonard told all to Commissioner Kenesaw Mountain Landis and produced an ambiguous but incriminating letter that caused Landis to quietly ease out Speaker from his position as manager in Cleveland and Cobb as the Tigers' skipper after 1926.

Ultimately, Landis held a hearing at which Leonard refused to testify, leading Landis to allow Cobb and Speaker back into baseball. Someone may have bought Leonard's silence; after all, he loved money, and he invested wisely in a grape ranch in California where at one time he owned 2,500 acres of farmland and lived like a prince there with a grand manse. Indulging his love of music, he accumulated more than 150,000 record albums during his lifetime, presumably enough to drown out the hatred of his fellow former ballplayers.

In 1913 in pennant crazy Boston, Leonard's reputation was not yet tarnished in anyone's eyes and his presence in spring training constituted but one of many promising young arms the team brought to camp that year. Six other prospects—Earl Ainsworth, Earl Moseley, Grover Brant, Al Watkins, George "Rube" Foster and Joseph Martina—were out to prove they were the next Joe Wood.

Ed Moseley initially vaulted to the head of this class of prospects, posting an 8–5 record as a rookie. He had some very good starts in August and September during games against the Tigers and the Athletics, and yet he must not have felt appreciated, as he jumped to the new Federal League the next year. The Sox seemed to have wanted him to walk. He played on four major league teams in three leagues over a four-year span, winning one more game than he lost, and at all times appears to have been the greatest obstacle to success in his own career. Since he won the ERA title for Newark in his second year in the Federal League, he is the answer to some trivia question, but ultimately he betrayed his own potential.

Not so with George "Rube" Foster from Oklahoma. He only went 3–3 in '13, but Murnane considered him a "clever right-hander" who might benefit by sitting for a bit and learning the trade. He got bombed by opposing batters on a couple of occasions, and yet had some good outings too, enough to spare his job and permit him the opportunity to become a big winner for the team in ensuing campaigns. Rube did not disappoint.

One Sox prospect did not break camp with the team and did not take the news well at all. Everett Scott fielded the position of shortstop better than most anyone who ever lived, but while Stahl kept junky utility infielders like Clyde Engle, he cut Scott, who promptly "verbally undressed everybody in the clubhouse," according to Bill Carrigan, who witnessed the tirade. The normally calm and respectful Scott had a point, and when he returned and made the team the next year, he proved so durable that he proceeded to establish the all-time consecutive games played mark, since surpassed only by Lou Gehrig and Cal Ripken.

Jake Stahl might have taken Scott's protestations with equanimity, but on a personal level he seemed hell-bent on disappointing management and fans alike with increasing complaints about his legs. He had come from California much lighter and in better shape than the condition he appeared in during the previous spring training, and he had participated in forced marches and hikes all spring. But Stahl pulled up lame, with a leg or toe problem, depending on what source once believes, once the season commenced. In the case of Jimmy McAleer, he did not believe Stahl's complaints at all.

Bill Carrigan for one saw spring training that year as most antithetical to good conditioning. Years later he related to Boston sportswriter Joe Cashman that "[r]ight after leaving our Hot Sprints training camp ... we ran into a flood in Memphis," which caused the cancellation of several exhibition games, with the team ultimately trying to work itself into shape at the University of Illinois batting cages.

Playing in the last exhibition against Holy Cross College, Stahl tried unsuccessfully to steal second, as he "tore the nether part of last season's traveling pajamas." The next day he injured his right leg when a thrown ball hit him in the shin, an injury that was projected to keep him out of action less than a week. He may have experienced pain in his legs all spring, and rather than rest, he climbed hill and dale. In the regular-season opener against the Athletics, the player-manager did not play at all. Smoky Joe Wood started and the club lost, 10–9.

Opening Day proved an inauspicious start and the Sox reeled thereafter, staggering to a 6–8 record, bad enough for sixth place in the American League. Stahl bemoaned his staff woes and played Janvrin and Engle in his stead; they both stunk. In desperation, Stahl sought elastic stockings that he presumably intended to wear to restore the youthfulness of his legs, as he mused about perhaps playing in the warm weather.

The sense of despair worsened when on April 29, 1913, the club leaked that it was trying to trade for New York Highlanders star first baseman Hal Chase. Much has been written about Chase, who was one of the greatest fielding first basemen in history and also quite often a very good hitter when he tried. He also cheated his talent by finding every opportunity to lay down and fix major league ball games, finally fading away for good after his role in the 1919 Black Sox scandal unraveled.

His manager in New York, Frank Chance, could not wait to get rid of him, and purportedly the Sox needed only to cough up three players. New York wanted Rough Carrigan badly, which would give the Highlanders not only a terrific player and team leader but an honest and hard-working man, the opposite of Hal Chase. The Sox offered catcher Les Nunamaker, infielder

Neal Ball and spare outfielder Olaf Henriksen, essentially a one-sided deal in favor of Boston, even given Chase's utter lack of character. As badly as New York wanted to dump their notorious first baseman, the Highlanders passed on this fire sale.

Or was it? The *New York Times* reported that Boston had thrown in a pick of one of its catchers to sweeten the deal, and that Chance turned it down, looking instead for a first baseman of equal value to Chase in return, a ridiculous proposition. If the Highlanders turned down an enormously influential and positive team leader like Bill Carrigan, then their management consisted of fools. Rough Carrigan even up would have been a steal for New York if it could get rid of a loser like Chase, a bad apple if there ever was one.

The Sox, of course, had dodged a bullet. Chase would have infected the team, not just its young players, but also Wood and Speaker, two players later implicated by Dutch Leonard in dumping a game against Detroit while they played for Cleveland. Part-owner McRoy and Jake Stahl had their fingerprints all over the proposed deal, and quite possibly Jimmy McAleer nixed it in the end.

It did reveal that Stahl had serious doubts about playing in 1913. Indeed, he only came to bat twice all year, a development that McAleer began to regard as alarming as he figured the club had forked out big money for a player-manager, not a lame manager donning support hose. And Chase came with an $8,000 yearly salary, not counting the money he earned each year dumping games. Wiser folk must have re-thought the proposed deal in light of the amount of money committed to one position in the field, if nothing else.

Stahl could have reversed the decline in his relationship with McAleer by steering his club to a string of wins, but his concerns about his pitchers continued to deepen. Buck O'Brien, he of the spit ball and 20 wins the previous season, had completely lost it. More alarmingly, ace Joe Wood injured his thumb in April, requiring a recommended two weeks off, and he unwisely returned before he had fully healed. And the team did not have a true first baseman.

With Jake Stahl increasingly immobilized and the team mired in malaise, Bill Carrigan led the team to a critical mass in a game against Cleveland on May 7. All day the teams had endeavored to draw blood and rip flesh of their opposition, with Carrigan acting as a lord of misbehavior. More hockey power forward than baseball catcher, Carrigan rather roughly blocked Cleveland's Jack Graney at home plate, which caused Joe Jackson to slide home later with his spikes tearing right into Carrigan's shin pads.

A Cleveland ballplayer retaliated, later knocking down Janvrin at second, while Olson of the Indians elbowed Sox pitcher Rube Foster trying to cover first base. After the game, won by the Naps (nicknamed after star Napoleon Lajoie), 4–1, the teams walked to their dressing rooms, whereupon Boston's Nunamaker began jawing with Olson between the dugout and the clubhouse.

Nap Lajoie started arguing with everyone, while Carrigan, "finding that he couldn't succeed as a peacemaker, decided to take a hand in the mix-up."

Fists began flying, with Nunamaker making certain that Olson lost his two front teeth and Tris Speaker, never one to back down, getting spiked. Punches were thrown mainly at each other's heads until Manager Birmingham of the Naps and several of the Red Sox players restored order. It did little good as Boston continued to lose, and no donnybrooks could mask the decline in team production by the end of May: the club was hitting .256 while their team season batting average was .280. Their pitchers held opponents to a .256 average in '12, while this year other clubs teed off at a .280 clip.

The club continued to sink into a malaise. The *Sporting Life*, in analyzing the American League pennant race to date, acidly editorialized that the Sox had "made a miserable showing and give[s] no indication of recovery from the poor start or of the survival of the effects of Manager Stahl's enforced absence from the team ... their prospect of pennant retention will soon reach the vanishing point." The Sox had a nice run in late June before they gave up all of that ground in early July. In the meantime, all they did to try to rectify matters was to sell the useless Buck O'Brien to the Chicago White Sox.

Nothing was going right for Jake Stahl. He had a growth on his legs that begged for removal, and one night on the sleeper car of his train a thief broke in and absconded with $200 as well as his World Series' gold fob and diamond pin. To this day, it is not known if the thief was a Yankee fan or owner Jimmy McAleer, a man increasingly taking a dim view of the team's fortunes and Stahl's inability to reverse them in the right direction.

On July 15, McAleer denied that he meant to dump Stahl in mid-season, but his endorsement of his manager possessed a distinct "kiss of death" texture to it, intimating to a *Boston Post* beat writer that after the '13 campaign, "I may decide to keep him and I may decide not to." This jibed with the perception members of the press had, which it was "pretty generally understood" that Stahl was not coming back the next year, whether he knew it or not. Stahl knew it now and after learning about the lack of trust in him, he demanded a meeting the next day with Jimmy Mac. The situation harked back to 1906, with McAleer playing the John I. Taylor role and Jake Stahl understudying for another player-manger who did not play much, Jimmy Collins.

On July 16, the situation hit the fan. Fed up with constant rumors concerning his status with the team, Jake Stahl paid a visit to the Chicago hotel room of Jimmy McAleer and matters quickly escalated to the point of no return. The accounts of what happened differ a bit, and certainly Stahl and McAleer spun their best stories for the press, but in essence Stahl met with the same fate that Deacon McGuire did five years earlier when he wanted to clear the air.

McAleer told Stahl that he wanted a full-time player-manager and that with Jake's injuries, if he was not going to play the next year then why return?

McAleer may have let it slip that he did not think much of his skipper's managing style, particularly since the player-manager did not intend to serve as a first baseman in the future. Salary too became an issue. Stahl was being paid for running the team and playing a high level of ball at first base, and now it appeared that unless rectified, the club had an overpaid manager and an abyss at the first sack.

Jimmy McAleer was too good a baseball man to permit matters to degenerate to this level, and he deserves much blame for dumping Stahl in mid-season in his home in Chicago with all of his friends and family nearby, some of whom were Red Sox minority stockholders. A simple "You're doing a great job, Jake, and we understand there have been a lot of injuries this year" would have sufficed. But that is not what he did. He fired Jake Stahl, stating that "as a playing manager Stahl was a success, but as a bench manager, he didn't look so good."

For his part, Stahl always needed baseball less than the sport needed him. Being at home, he naturally believed that his life would be much simpler if he worked for a lot of money at his father-in-law's bank and did not have to worry about Smoky Joe Wood's arm or McAleer's criticism of him. As a result, he took another sabbatical from baseball. Stahl bit back, and his father-in-law bit back harder, accusing McAleer of picking on a cripple and venting, "Stahl looked anything but amiable. There was a dangerous glitter in his eyes."

Ban Johnson hit the roof when he heard the news. He naturally sided with Stahl and his fellow Chicagoans, firing off the following statement:

I deeply regret that Mr. McAleer acted so hastily. There was no reason for relieving Stahl of the management of the Boston team at this time, and he was entitled to every consideration the Boston club and the American League could give him.

Stahl won the World Championship for the American League last Fall, yet in spite of that fact he was released by Mr. McAleer in mid-season, and right in his home city, Chicago....

I feel that the American League may be sharply criticized for Mr. McAleer's hasty and ill-advised action, and if I had been in Chicago yesterday Stahl would not have been let out in such a fashion....

Jimmy McAleer had just made Ban Johnson's shit list.

The *Boston Globe* took a fairly calm view of things, mainly because John I. Taylor still owned 50 percent of the team and he had reared his ugly head to support McAleer for cutting off Stahl's. Plus, Tim Murnane liked his fellow Hibernian McAleer, so he let his friend off relatively easy.

Naturally, rumors swirled. Stahl had sat with his father-in-law and Tris Speaker, absorbing the news, and McAleer had opened a back channel with the Tigers' owner for an even-up swap of Speaker for Cobb. Cobb wanted out of Detroit and he liked Carrigan and Wagner, while Speaker did not care for these two teammates much, particularly since Wagner had been named team captain instead of him. While McAleer seemed prepared to assume Cobb's higher salary, some $3,000 more per year, the Tigers' ownership also apparently wanted the Sox to sweeten the deal with a cash payment to them of $5,000.

The proposed transaction ideally would have provided a change of scenery to two disgruntled stars, presuming, of course, Speaker intended to publicly support Stahl and promote mutiny against Carrigan, but this did not come to pass. Wisely, Speaker stayed out of the matter, telling everyone who would quote him that he enjoyed playing in Boston, thus effectively killing the deal.

McAleer named Bill Carrigan the new manager, but reports leaked out that the club had offered the manager's job first to Fielder Jones, the former manager of the White Sox, for an annual salary of $25,000. Murnane of the *Globe* vehemently denied this, but the story has a ring of truth about it, particularly since McAleer anticipated a public relations fiasco potentially developing around his sacking of a defending World Series champion manager.

Jimmy McAleer as a player. They made them tough in those days, as evidenced by McAleer fielding the ball with bare hands. But as McAleer would one day learn, no one came any tougher than American League President Ban Johnson. Library of Congress.

Rough did not want the job, at least not under the circumstances that McAleer offered it to him, emphasizing years later that "I was anything but elated. I liked Stahl very well, all the players did, and I thought he had done a fine job." He also must have sensed that the club had lost some key pieces in its overwhelming pennant run of the previous year, and that the situation might not reverse itself overnight given the current ownership, which had incurred Ban Johnson's wrath.

Others saw the power struggle in terms of a seventeenth century-style religious war between the Catholic McAleer and the Protestant Stahl, with the earlier sale of Bucky O'Brien sticking in McAleer's craw until the team's record gave him cover to dump Stahl. With John I. Taylor's involvement in the matter, it took on Byzantine overtones, and one suspects that Taylor wanted Bob Unglaub to assume the manager's role and have one more chance to make good in Boston.

McAleer and Johnson commenced a cold war while Rough Carrigan did what he was put on the planet to do—take over the Boston Red Sox and ultimately guide them to more than one World Series title. After all, they did not call him "Rough" for nothing. Trying to prevent the Sox from plunging into another public relations morass, he threatened to quit right away unless McAleer promised never to come into the clubhouse again and never to chew out a player. McAleer also had to promise that he would go to the manager only to iron out any issues troubling ownership about a particular player. McAleer agreed.

McAleer may have fired Stahl, but no one pushed Rough Carrigan around. With his team solidly behind him, Rough prohibited anyone from floating in and out of the team's dressing rooms, save the players. Once, when McAleer and scout Duke Farrell sat around a table playing pinochle, they saw their manager and some of his players come in, and they wordlessly took their game and themselves out of the room. There was a new sheriff in town.

He commanded respect, sometimes through sheer physical intimidation of opponents and teammates alike. Historian Fred Lieb recalled the following incident related to him by umpire Billy Evans:

> Carrigan was in an argument with one of the team's top stars. "You're no better than anyone else on this club," Bill roared. "When I issue an order for morning practice at ten, you're supposed to be here just like anyone else. I don't care how well you are playing. The fact that you won three or four games last week doesn't mean a thing to me. There is going to be discipline on this club, and I'm the guy to enforce it."
>
> Conversation grew more heated; soon Billy heard sounds of scuffling; then everything became quiet.
>
> Curious as to what happened, Evans asked one of the players to let him know confidentially what the rumpus had been about. "Nothing much," replied the player. "Bill just grabbed one of the boys who wouldn't listen to reason and shook him up a bit. He'll behave from now on."

This incident may have involved Tris Speaker. Not liking his star center fielder's attitude, Carrigan famously called him into his office after a game and started hollering at him, eliciting a like response from Tris. A fistfight broke out and it did not finish until Carrigan had defeated Speaker, who thereafter gave him little overt trouble. Then again, with Rough Carrigan, he may have used this mode of corrective behavior modification on others as well. For all of his toughness, though, Rough handled the technical aspects of the position well, quietly rebuilding his pitching staff around Lefty Ray Collins and some of the younger hurlers.

Memorably, Walter Johnson and Joe Wood had faced each other the year before in one of the all-time great displays of pitching. But when the Big Train steamed into Fenway on August 28, 1913, with Wood hurt through much of the season, Johnson stood unchallenged as the finest in the land. He had not lost a game in almost three months, winning fourteen straight decisions before this latest series in Boston. Facing Johnson would be the pride of Vermont, Ray Collins, backed by a team that so far had managed to lose one more game than it had won.

The changing of the guard. Bankers and successful Sox managers together shortly before Jimmy McAleer overplayed his hand and fired Jake Stahl (right), allowing Rough Carrigan to take the helm of the Boston Red Sox. Library of Congress.

No fanfare or hype preceded the game, and even though Collins had continued to perform well while so many of his mates had disappointed, few fans expected much from him. It is a shame this game has gone largely forgotten in Sox history because in some ways, this match exceeded the previous game of the century from the year before. It lasted 11 innings, with Big Train Johnson having only given up one hit in the first ten frames, to Steve Yerkes in the second.

Collins had not mastered the Senators, but he had sprayed seven hits with no runs crossing the plate, although three opposing batsmen had gotten as far as third base. In the eleventh, the pesky Yerkes came to bat and hit a single to center field. As Senators center fielder Clyde Milan ran over to cut off the ball, it skipped through his legs, and covering outfielder Danny Moeller dove for it but could not retrieve it. Racing around the bases, Yerkes reached third base before Moeller picked himself up and ran down the ball.

Heinie Wagner then sharply hit the ball to shortstop George McBride and Yerkes raced home, only to discover that McBride had whipped the ball to the plate well ahead of him. Sensing that he had no chance of scoring, Yerkes waltzed about until Wagner had run to second base before giving up the chase. With two outs, Johnson had to face player manager Bill Carrigan. Johnson should have been relieved at this point, but that is not how things worked. He threw a pitch that Carrigan got just enough bat on to split the Senators' center and left fielders as Wagner scored the winning run standing up.

At that point the crowd exploded, but so stunned by the turn of events was Rough that he stood on first base and did not relinquish it until he saw the umpire officially call Wagner safe at home, at which point he joined his joyous teammates. The game itself meant little, permitting the Sox to even their record, but it did show that while the team was going nowhere, inside of many beat the hearts of champions that day.

Maybe next year, or the year after that.

18
Papists and Protestants

A recurring theme in early Boston baseball is the often contentious relations between the Catholic and Protestant ballplayers. To alleviate this issue,
Jimmy Collins in large part recruited Catholic players like himself, perhaps
figuring uniformity might reduce tensions. In heavily Irish Catholic Boston,
the cherry picking along religious lines made sense also, as the club immediately set out to compete less with its fellow American League competitors and
more with its cross-town Boston Beaneater rivals.

Collins had chafed under the ownership of the Triumvirs, and although
he said little by nature, he had to have noticed the less-than-friendly remarks
made about his fellows by some of his Protestant teammates.

The tensions actually predated Collins coming to the team. At the end of
the 1893 season, one in which the Beaneaters ran away with the pennant, Hugh
Duffy and Tommy Tucker celebrated by drinking well into the night and apparently into the morning of the next game, at which time manager Frank Selee
benched the uncoordinated and inebriated Tucker.

That set off Duffy, who came after Selee while yelling and screaming.
Pitcher Happy Jack Stivetts interjected himself into the proceedings, and the
combatants almost began hitting each other over the heads with the baseball
bats they all clasped. Cooler heads prevailed, but the incident had ugly religious overtones. Although he missed that game due to injury, Tommy
McCarthy the next year got up from his table at dinner, calmly strode up to
Stivetts and punched him in the jaw, leaving just as sanguinely as he arrived.

Selee, a minister's son, essentially co-opted the issue later by naming Duffy
the team captain and disposing of the increasingly slow and heavy McCarthy
as soon early as he could. Nevertheless, Collins joined the team as Mac left,
and he learned to keep his mouth shut.

When it came time for him to form his team, Collins recruited fellow
Irishman Buck Freeman and German Catholic Chick Stahl. Freddy Parent, a
Catholic French Canadian, fit in with this scheme, as did other Catholics who
later joined the team, such as Bill Dinneen and Patsy Dougherty.

Ecumenism had its pull over Collins when he had the opportunity to land
Cy Young on his club. While Cy liked his liquor, he did not outwardly dislike
Catholics and his unflappable nature helped ease any tensions that might have

otherwise existed. Catcher Lou Criger also, probably cared less about someone's religion than about his personality.

In 1902, though, Collins signed catcher Jack Warner, and supposedly his
anti–Catholic feelings doomed his tenure with the team. He was gone before
1903, jumping back to John McGraw's New York Giants, where he presumably moderated his anti–Catholic views; otherwise, McGraw would have decked
him and laid him out.

Over time, Collins chose his players less for their religious affiliation and
more for their potential to help the team, particularly as the club's fortunes
sunk under the weight not of religion, but of the player's girth. By 1905, Collins'
club was an equal opportunity fat farm while the American League got younger
and faster around them.

It was this need to revitalize the team that led to the signings of Tris
Speaker from Texas and Smoky Joe Wood of Kansas City. Supposedly, Speaker
once belonged to the Ku Klux Klan, and traditionally he and Wood held little
tolerance for Papist teammates. Famously, Duffy Lewis and Tris Speaker hated
each other, and only grudging mutual respect kept Rough Carrigan and Speaker
from pummeling one another.

Again, much too much and much too little can be made of the Red Sox
holy wars. Lewis and Speaker would not have gotten along even if they belonged
to the same church. Speaker was not the easiest person to get along with at this
stage of his life, nor the most tolerant. This would change, as Speaker served
as a mentor to Larry Doby when he broke the color barrier in Cleveland decades
later, but this development did nothing to help Duffy Lewis.

Lewis famously fought Speaker after Tris knocked the hat off of his head
in public. A rural Texan, Speaker most likely did not understand Lewis' desire
to tramp about in loud clothing, although Tris was certainly a dapper enough
man. Again, personalities trumped religion with a healthy nod to the differences between growing up in Texas as opposed to California, even one hundred years ago.

Encouragingly, Catholic Harry Hooper was very close friends not only
with Protestant Larry Gardner, but also with Wood and Speaker. The move to
Winthrop, a town northwest of Boston in lieu of Roxbury's Putnam Hotel, has
been proffered as proof positive of the nativist sentiments of Speaker and
Wood. And yet, Larry Gardner and Harry Hooper also moved there, and everyone seemed to get along.

The religious differences that rended the Red Sox at various flash points
in their early history often had to do with individual personality clashes
between teammates at its essence. Once one player of one faith disliked a teammate from another persuasion, catcalls concerning the perceived beliefs or lack
thereof of the other fellow probably were made, exacerbating largely preexist-
ing tensions.

Religious differences also may have contributed to the formation of cliques

Perhaps the only Irish Catholic in Boston tougher than Rough Carrigan, Boston's Cardinal O'Connell is third from the right of the people marching. These vibrant and defiant displays of O'Connell would have been foreign to Red Sox like Speaker or Wood, but they played quite well to other Bostonians who had finally made it, the Catholics of Boston, Massachusetts. Library of Congress.

in which a shared faith may have helped players establish something they had in common with a limited group of teammates. Rough Carrigan, for one, probably did associate more with fellow Irish Catholics, but he held the respect of so many on his team that the issue largely did not come up. Stout and Johnson have referred to contemporary accounts, delineating the Protestant players ("Masons") and the Catholic ("Knights," named after the Knights of Columbus).

The issue was largely kept under wraps at the time because Protestant players did not wish to incur the wrath of their largely Irish Catholic fan base, so at least outwardly peace was maintained.

Some players like Speaker had an aversion to Catholicism not only because they lived in rural areas with only their own demographic profile, but also because they had grown up believing that the church itself was evil. When they came north to Boston, they may have fallen back on their prejudice when they saw dogma that confounded them.

For example, everybody loved Chick Stahl, and yet because he committed suicide, this very Catholic young man from a large observant family had his funeral and burial not on consecrated grounds, but performed by members of his fraternal organization. In his despair, he had committed a mortal sin (they called them cardinal sins back then) by ending his own life and had died without final absolution.

Similarly, Babe Ruth made a very public display of his Catholicism after he left the Xaverian Brothers orphanage despite the fact he had been baptized Lutheran, assuming he had been baptized at all. And yet few cavorted more with prostitutes and cheated on his wife more than the Babe, particularly during his Red Sox days.

Catholic players, on the other side, might point to Speaker as a holy hypocrite for his association, either openly or by sympathy, with the Ku Klux Klan, one of the worst organizations in American history. And what of the Protestant players who derided the Catholic faith but did not attend church services in their own branch of Protestanism?

The Boston Americans/Red Sox did not lose pennants because of Holy Wars in the dressing room that potentially might explode at any time. And with the possible exception of Jack Warner jumping back to the New York Giants, it apparently did not become such a critical issue that a player had to leave town before the fans tarred and feathered him.

It also must be remembered that the developing rivalry between the Red Sox and the New York Highlanders, now known as the Yankees, tended to band teammates together against the Evil Empire, and no matter what one's private religious views were, there was general consensus concerning who the Evil Empire was.

19
Jack Dunn Sells Out

Sometime around 1890, Joseph J. Lannin moved from his boyhood home in Quebec, Canada, to Boston, where he procured his first job there as a bell-boy at the historic Parker House Hotel. By December 1, 1913, he had bought out the shares of Bob McRoy, Jimmy McAleer and some Chicagoans, for $200,000, becoming one-half owner of the Boston Red Sox with forgotten but not gone John I. Taylor.

Of course, Ban Johnson engineered the whole affair, with McRoy and Jake Stahl (the latter back in Chicago as a very prosperous banker) professing no knowledge of the *coup d'etat*. McRoy feebly attempted to hold onto his share of the team as an investment, but he quickly disappeared, to the obvious glee of the Royal Rooters, who never forgave him for selling their tickets out from under them in the 1912 World Series. McAleer took the whole matter more stoically, understanding full well that he had incurred Johnson's wrath by firing Stahl, an act that he knew would not go unpunished.

Lannin accumulated his wealth through his shrewd investments in real estate, both in Boston and New York, and he had procured a piece of the ownership of the Boston Braves by the time he plotted the takeover of the Red Sox. He either intuited that Ban Johnson wanted a peaceful term of Red Sox ownership or received advance marching orders to that effect, because he visibly reached out to half-owner John I. Taylor, restoring that odd presence to the team. Talk even circulated of John I.'s possible return to the presidency of the team, a development Lannin quietly silenced while he quickly demonstrated his devotion to nepotism by lining the club's offices with relatives.

Traditionally, changes in Boston ownership heralded the announcement of the appointment of a new manager, but this time Rough Carrigan retained his post while McAleer and McRoy accepted their checks and disappeared. Lannin may have been afraid of him or Ban Johnson may have vouched for Rough, but in any event he stayed on and strengthened his position, going so far as to establish an off-season training regimen in Maine, known as Camp Carrigan.

Camp Carrigan permitted its founder to exert positive influence over players with potential but unimpressive results to date in their career. Clyde Engle, Forrest Cady and Olaf Henriksen attended, taking long and arduous hikes in the Maine wilderness. When it snowed, the players donned snow shoes to navigate the hills and rocks. For them, it was mostly a way to stay in their manager's good graces and enjoy a free holiday.

Strangely, while Carrigan worked his charges relentlessly at his camp, in spring training in Hot Springs he scuttled many of Jake Stahl's marches in favor of his players gradually molding themselves into shape during the preseason games, figuring that one could overdo a good thing. Also, he probably played to the press, particularly those pundits who may have wondered if Jake Stahl overworked his wonderful champions of '12 into also-rans.

During the winter, while Rough Carrigan saved his job, he reluctantly replaced old friend Heinie Wagner at short with slick-fielding Everett Scott from Indiana. Wagner had not hit well the year before and had slowed down in the field too much to permit him to clog up such an important position. Drawing lessons from the 1904 Red Sox, who grew old collectively overnight, the club anointed the successor at short quite publicly in late January. Scott subsequently developed into one of the greatest fielding shortstops in Red Sox history, while Wagner did not play for the team at all in 1914 and intermittently thereafter.

Looming as a far more threatening development than the competition at shortstop was the advent of the Federal League, the first challenge to organized major league ball since the American League formed in 1901. The American League had rapidly raided the National League, forcing the two sides into labor peace within two years, but the American and National league magnates of 1914 knew they had to outbid the new circuit for the services of the players in order to deprive the upstarts of credible and attractive rosters. As Lannin articulated to Murnane from the *Globe*, "The best way to treat the Federal League is to allow them to load up on big salaries with ordinary players."

Lannin made at least one exception to this plan once he discovered the Federals had all but signed utility man Clyde Engle. Engle had set up an appointment with officials from the new organization in New York in early February, a development that someone tipped Lannin to. A "hands on" man if there ever was one, the new Sox owner raced down to New York and intercepted Engle as he alighted from the train. He then ushered his utility man away from his appointment and taxied him over to the Biltmore Hotel, where after administering to Engle the gentle arts of persuasion, he retained the player's services.

Tris Speaker and Ray Collins exploited fully the unsettled state of labor relations by alienating Lannin from as much of his net worth as possible. Only in situations where management deemed a player expendable or overrated, for example with Ed Moseley, did the club pass on his services and permit him to jump leagues. The Federal League subsisted largely on rejects from the established National and American league clubs, with a star here and there, but little else to attract fans. But to put the upstart league down and

Another changing of the guard for the Boston Americans. From left to right, Paul Lannin, Dorothy Lannin, Ban Johnson, Mrs. J.J. Lannin and new owner J.J. Lannin. Library of Congress.

keep it down, the established league magnates had to vastly outspend the new arrivals.

But when Boston wanted to keep a player, management renounced him and lavished him with money. Center fielder Tris Speaker had voyaged overseas on an all-star junket during the off-season, and like Engle, had an appointment to meet with management figures from the Federals. Lannin again sped to New York to talk contract with Speaker as soon as he departed the boat.

This time the Federals got there first. Murnane arrived at the scene and described Speaker's meeting, where the Federals offered Tris "a three-year contract calling for $15,000 per year, with a bonus of $15,000, which was spread on the table in the form of $1,000 bills, and Tris found it a difficult matter to get out of the room, even after promising he would return."

Once freed, Speaker met with Lannin and John I. Taylor, and by the end of the evening had signed a two-year contract with Boston for $18,000 per year, making him the highest paid ballplayer in baseball. Lannin acted as if he was happy, but he had just readjusted his team's salary structure to accommodate one player, a development that reverberated within the walls not only of Fenway Park, but throughout the American and National leagues. Like Ronald Reagan during the final days of the Cold War, Lannin meant to drive the Federal League to extinction by outspending it, but that did not ingratiate the individual ballplayer like Speaker to him.

In a related case, in mid–February, Carrigan traveled to Burlington, Vermont, to meet with Ray Collins, buying him lunch and talking with him for a couple of hours until he thought he had the player signed. Collins, however, bristled and went into spring training still uncommitted, searching for that top dollar from Lannin. Collins enjoyed holding out for more money, and while he won ball games, he got away with it, but he did not build up a reservoir of goodwill and sympathy in the hearts of his employers.

Collins knew the Sox needed him, particularly since some of the other star pitchers of '12 continued to show signs of having truncated careers. He had also learned that Joe Wood had undergone an appendectomy and needed several weeks to recuperate, so he utilized this knowledge to renege on his agreement. Finding themselves over a barrel, Sox management signed Collins to a lucrative contract.

Noticing the way Lannin reacted when the Federal League came after Engle, Speaker and Collins, some of Boston's lesser talents openly began to flirt with Federal League agents lurking around Hot Springs, most notably the notoriously greedy Dutch Leonard and Steve Yerkes. Having kept tabs, Carrigan called a team meeting and gave everyone 48 hours to decide if they wanted to play for the Red Sox. Knowing Rough, he may have punctuated his point with a flying fist or two. The Federal's agent let it be known that the league wanted "stars, not ordinary ballplayers," so the Sox manager kept his teammates within the fold.

To fill the breach left by Wood, the club brought seven new hurlers to camp, and just prior to Opening Day, Tim Murnane opined that "the four men that Manager Carrigan will retain are Johnson from Syracuse, Zeiser from Lowell, Kelly from Seattle and Coumbe, a young left-hander from the New York State League. Garlow, the Indian, also will be retained as it is the proper thing to have a full-blooded Indian with every first-class major league."

Youthful promise aside, the Red Sox opened their season on April 14 with their ace, lefty Ray Collins, recently wooed away from the Federal League. Feeling festive, Lannin festooned the entire park "with red, white and blue bunting and flags." Harkening to the club's glorious beginning, one of the umpires was none other than Big Bill Dinneen, who had successfully made the transition from arguing the calls to making them.

Nothing demonstrated the changes taking place in Boston and at Fenway more than the presence of Mayor James Michael Curley, who threw out the first ball. The model for Mayor Skeffington in the novel *The Last Hurrah*, Curley in the course of his career ruled as the city's mayor on four separate occasions and served two prison sentences, capturing the public's imagination to such an extent that to this day, his statues grace an area just off Quincy Market in downtown Boston.

His presence marked another important turning point in Red Sox history—the continued diminution of influence of the Royal Rooters. Although Curley hailed from Roxbury like many of the Rooters, he was the sworn political enemy of their benefactor, Honey Fitz, and he shared the stage with no one.

The game itself encapsulated many of the problems the team experienced through the first half to the 1914 campaign: poor hitting and not quite enough pitching. While Collins pitched well and gave up no earned runs, he faced Washington's Walter Johnson, who shut out the Sox. Johnson scored this team's first run by running into Rough Carrigan at the plate. Somehow when the dust cleared, the catcher and the ball had separated as Johnson returned to his dugout with the only run he needed that day.

Parenthetically, Carrigan did not commit the same mistake that Jake Stahl did, that of cutting shortstop Everett Scott out of spring training. Despite having an effete sounding name, Scott established in his time the record for consecutive games played, a tribute to his toughness and dedication. He also fielded his key position with unusual alacrity, drawing a comparison to later Cardinals great Marty Marion by Fred Lieb due to his "remarkably high fielding average for his position."

Bill James has augmented this observation, citing the fact that Scott possessed "the highest plus factor in fielding average of any shortstop in history. He led American League shortstops in fielding percentage eight consecutive years, 1916 to 1923." Scott hit like Freddy Parent—once Parent lost his batting swing—but his peerless fielding made him an unfairly forgotten key to the great teams Carrigan fielded over the next five years.

Early in the season, though, the Red Sox needed hitting a lot more than fielding. The team collectively slumped, marring some impressive pitching performances from the young arms brought in to the Hub.

By the first week of May, the Boston batters had bottomed out, "boasting" a team average of .188, with pitcher Rankin Johnson leading the club in that category. One week later, the *Boston Herald* ominously predicted that "[u]nless there is improvement in two or three directions something will drop." Facing the cliff, Carrigan shook up the batting order, dropping Clyde Engle to seventh, leading off with Hooper and Yerkes, and, for the first time, placing Tris Speaker in the cleanup spot. The Sox responded to the shifts, but more importantly, the pitching began to carry the team.

On May 11, the rough manager was forced to pitch two rookies, Coumbe and Zeiser, and after losing to New York could have used some Alka Seltzer. One of Coumbe's pitches sailed "several yards" over catcher Carrigan's head. Management began to lose confidence in Coumbe, a premature judgment but one he fortified with nervous performances such as this one.

Newcomer Adam "Rankin" Johnson, despite possessing ordinary stuff, in his first major league start out dueled Washington's Walter Johnson in a head-to-head matchup on April 23. Although it was not Woods-Johnson II, it did flatter the team with the hope that their Johnson knew something about pitching too.

At this time, Dutch Leonard and Rube Foster jumped into the breech. Although he never could regain his all-world form of 1912, Smoky Joe Wood returned to the staff, first as a reliever and then as a starter, going the full nine innings in a late May victory. Within one month, Boston climbed from seventh place to fourth, behind Philadelphia, Washington and Detroit, and Carrigan's job was once again, at least temporarily, safe.

Precipitating Jake Stahl's departure the year before (at least if one believes Jimmy McAleer) was Stahl's intention to either not play first base in the future or to limit his time at the position. True or not, his firing left a hole at first, and in '14 the team still had not adequately addressed the issue, using Clyde Engle and Hank Janvrin there to no one's satisfaction. Carrigan had eyed Del Gainer of the Tigers during spring training, but Detroit had not wanted to part with him, perhaps believing that a decent rookie season in part-time duty warranted another look.

The *Globe* dubbed him one of the "unluckiest" men in baseball due to his propensity to injury, thanks originally to Colby Jack Coombs breaking his wrist with a fastball. Detroit tried to pass him through waivers once the season began when George Burns became the starter, but Boston blocked the move until a cash deal could be agreed upon and Gainer became a member of the Sox.

Meanwhile, the Federal League continued to tempt Red Sox players to jump their contracts, setting their sights on Rube Foster and Rankin Johnson in late June, a development which prompted owner Lannin to comment, "It's a clear case of the Federals trying to turn the head of the players, and they are picking out those who will listen...." Covertly, Lannin and Carrigan most likely leaned on the players pretty hard not to accept the overtures of the Federals' agents, although Foster and Johnson probably at least met with them, an act of disloyalty in itself.

Although the Sox had saved Carrigan's job in May with some steady improvement, by July 19 they had reached a state of equilibrium at forty-three wins and forty losses, adequate for a tie for fourth place. Wood's arm ached again and Rube Foster had injured his knee.

These pratfalls fell hard upon the collision in right-center field between Harry Hooper and Tris Speaker during the first game of a double-header with the White Sox.

Chicago's Blackburne rifled a shot that Speaker "plunged for" while Hooper with equal velocity ran right into his teammate, causing the ball to roll out of Speaker's glove. The center fielder reached for the ball residing, about a yard away, and vainly threw it into the infield, Blackburne scoring. Thereafter, Hooper and Speaker lay on the ground for "several minutes" and then gamely resumed play. Hooper had to come out of the game later, and in an unrelated incident, Duffy Lewis hurt his right ringer. After the collision, Boston stood in sixth place, but as the cross-town Braves had begun to demonstrate, in 1914 in Boston, rapid advancement in the standings was magically possible.

More than a magician, the Sox needed a reliable first baseman. Lannin and Carrigan had by then lost their lust for Gainer. They reinserted Janvrin

Fashion plate Duffy Lewis in more subdued Red Sox gear. By the time this photograph was taken, Tris Speaker knew better than to try to knock the hat off of Duffy's pate. Library of Congress.

into the lineup until in the midst of stasis, the club worked out another cash deal for a first sacker, this time Dick Hoblitzel of the Cincinnati Reds. "Hobby," like Del Gainer, hailed from West Virginia, but unlike his fellow Mountaineer, had a fairly lucky career in the National League, batting .308 one year and having some other pretty good seasons at the plate until early in the current campaign.

By the time the Reds unloaded him, Hobby dragged down the club with his .210 average and bad attitude, primarily directed against his manager. He must have liked Carrigan's management style, however, because he sped off to a .319 clip for the remainder of the year. And although his performances dropped in each of the four following seasons, he played on two World Series champions for the Red Sox.

Amusingly, he came to the team with a collection of eighteen bats of all shapes and sizes and different degrees of oiling and honing. He refused to donate any to fans or to old teammates, taking his bag of tricks with him to the Hub. Trained as a dentist, he missed his true calling by coming to the club too late to save the poor fellow whose teeth Hobe Ferris kicked in a few years earlier, but he seemed to take to playing in Boston, not an easy place to perform with all of the crowd's enthusiasm, even back then.

An often overlooked player, his presence on the team contributed to a surge, more attributable to some fine pitching perhaps, but Hobby solidified a position that had been riddled with inconsistency since Jimmy McAleer began to lose favor with Jake Stahl. The Sox did not have a great first baseman, but they now had enough of one to challenge for baseball championships again. Bill Carrigan always maintained that obtaining Hoblitzel's services was one of the best moves he made during his tenure as manager.

Not only did the Sox have a firm starter, they carried four first basemen on the roster, a luxury in the days preceding 25-man rosters, although even if they had the additional spots, the move made little sense. Attrition took care of some of the problems that centered on too many infielders, as Steve Yerkes continued to listen to the siren song of the Federal League. While it is unclear if the Sox fired him before he jumped, Yerkes left the team in late August.

Yerkes had not hit well for the Sox in 1914, batting a measly .218, but he had performed well defensively in the past and had distinguished himself when needed in the 1912 World Series. His departure probably had more to do with his own desire to leave, particularly since the Red Sox only replaced him by shifting Hal Janvrin from first to second, which was not a perfect solution offensively or defensively. It did reduce the logjam at first base, however.

The glut of first basemen narrowed even more with the firing of Clyde Engle about a month later. Engle's prospects were initially much more uncertain, as he scurried for work with a "hotel team," but he too found his home in the Federal League, with the Buffalo club. Engle had supplanted Harry Lord in the affections of John I. Taylor back in 1910, causing the team untold hardship as a result. He had performed well in spurts as a sub, but he needed to leave when the Sox became serious about making a run for the 1914 pennant.

With the exception of Ray Collins, the phenomenal young Boston pitchers who dominated league hitters less than two years before had seen their careers die at an early age. Bucky O'Brien fooled no one, his one-year wonder of a career had involved a sellout to the whims of a spitball.

But what of Hugh Bedient, who had clinched the World Series for Boston only to drift eventually to the Federal League and then out of organized baseball? Or Joe Wood, who mastered Walter Johnson only to see it all fall apart for him as the Big Train only seemed to gain strength? To Wood's incalculable credit, every pitch he threw agonized him. Still, he fashioned a 10–3 record for the year, but clearly his days as an ace had ended.

Not every word in the Hub was discouraging, though, as Rube Foster continued to grow as a pitcher. Until Cleveland scored against him in the fifth inning of a game in late May, he had gone 41 straight innings without giving up a run. He ended the season with a 14–8 record and an miniscule 1.70 ERA, which meant he gave up almost a run and a half a game less in '14 than he had the previous year.

Seeing his club suffer, Joe Lannin had little time for sentimentality, and Jack Dunn, the legendary owner of the International League-leading Baltimore

Orioles, had little money. So on July 9, 1914, the day after Speaker and Hooper had their famous collision, Dunn dumped left-handed pitcher Babe Ruth, righty Ernie Shore and catcher Ben Egan on the Red Sox, reportedly for a huge sum of money thought to exceed $25,000. Rather than endure one of the John I. Taylor-type of endless rebuilding ventures, Lannin threw money at the problem, and with Ruth and Shore, his aim was true.

Ruth was always the prize. The Red Sox had attempted to obtain him in packages before, but had balked. The other two players, Twombley and Derrick, disappeared, but Ruth remained, and fortunately for them so did Jack Dunn's fire sale. On July 9, the club pulled the trigger on the deal.

An enormous talent like Ruth could hardly escape notice—even an untrained eye perceived the greatness—but for more pressing reasons, the Sox needed Shore immediately. Although the *Globe* described Shore as "slightly more than six feet tall," his encyclopedic entry lists him at 6'4" and 220 pounds, a large man even if he lived in the twenty-first century. He had pitched quite ineffectively in a one-inning stint (more accurately a stunt) in 1912 with John McGraw's Giants, surrendering ten runs in the lone frame.

Shore returned to his native North Carolina and enrolled at Guilford College, his professional baseball career seemingly stalled until Jack Dunn came down with a line of bull and persuaded Shore to get back in the mound. Even though he joined the Orioles late in '14, he notched a 7–3 record. Four years older than Ruth, the right-handed Shore got the nod over Ruth in Carrigan's estimation.

Within the month the Sox sent catcher Ben Egan along with pitchers Rankin Johnson and Fritz Coumbe to Cleveland for left-hander Vean Gregg. The deal resembled the idiotic trades of John I. Taylor when he ran roughshod over the franchise, with past performance trumping any other consideration. Gregg had won at least twenty games the previous three seasons and his record stood at 9–3 when Boston obtained him, but his earned run average had shot up, and he was shot.

In Cleveland, Lannin and his counterpart, Charles Somers, had broached the subject, with the Sox trying desperately to force Bedient into the deal. Somers did not bite, although he did ask Lannin to a gentlemanly dinner to discuss the matter further. Finally, in Lannin's hotel room, the eventual deal was consummated, and the *Globe* considered the Sox the better for the deal. The newspaper was wrong, as Gregg was washed up, but Fritz Coumbe pitched well in spots for the Indians, even winning thirteen games as late as 1918.

The acquisition of Gregg did accomplish one major purpose in that it accentuated the team's devotion to left-handed hurlers, as Gregg's failures continued to mount in new circumstances. Dumping Coumbe did not kill the club because its left-handed pitching needs were in the process of being more than met with the infusion of such young talent as Babe Ruth. Before long, the Red

Sox had four southpaws on their roster—Ruth, Gregg, Collins and Leonard—
not a healthy mix in Fenway Park, even in the Deadball Era.

Shore made an instant hit in Boston, providing balance in the staff as a
righty and permitting most of Boston fandom to mistakenly believe that he,
not Ruth, constituted the future of the franchise. Shore's effectiveness aided
Boston's climb through the ranks as the team moved into second place in the
standings by July 22, with only Philadelphia in front of the Sox.

Ruth was more of a project, a huge talent, but then again so was Eddie
Cicotte during his largely frustrating career with Boston. But Ruth had more talent, and he had one of the greatest Red Sox managers ever to mentor him through his extended adolescence.

The emerging excellent Red Sox pitching staff consisting of, from left to right, Rube Foster, Carl Mays, Ernie Shore, Babe Ruth and Dutch Leonard. Library of Congress.

In turn, Babe loved Rough Carrigan, his first and favorite major league manager. Rough knew Ruth had come from a tough upbringing, had chafed under the strict discipline of the Xaverian Brothers at the orphanage in Baltimore, and wanted to cut loose. Realizing this, Carrigan deliberately roomed with Ruth, giving him the opportunity to watch over the impressionable rookie. Carrigan had to do the same with Dutch Leonard, but with Ruth aboard, he found it impossible to hold the hands of both prodigals. He therefore enlisted Heinie Wagner to serve as coach and baby-sitter over one of the wild men.

Improbably, the Boston Braves, in last place in the National League on July 4, had rallied, running their way up the standings with manager George Stallings, shortstop Rabbit Maranville and pitchers Lefty Tyler and one-year wonder Bill James (26–7 for the year). Lannin graciously offered the Braves the use of Fenway Park for the remainder of the season, but he may have privately seethed at the success of the team he once owned in part while his Red Sox made progress, but not as quickly. Perhaps to help keep the Red Sox in the headlines, he continued to troll for talent.

Lannin kept the pipeline alive in mid–September by purchasing another promising prospect, pitcher Carl Mays, along with outfielder Guy Tutwiler from the Providence Grays. It was not much of a purchase since Lannin had gained control of the Providence club a month and a half earlier, a shrewd move as teams edged closer to establishing formal ties between the major league franchise and its minor league affiliates.

Known later primarily as the pitcher who threw the ball that killed Ray Chapman, the only death in a big league game, Mays paid almost immediate big dividends for the Sox, winning 18, 22 and 21 games, respectively, from 1916–1918. If Dutch Leonard got on peoples' nerves frequently, Carl Mays was simply an unlikable cuss, a pitcher opposing batsmen and teammates alike despised.

But he could pitch. Kept out of the Baseball Hall of Fame in part because he was dishonest and unpopular, Mays' acquisition all but completed the transformation of the Red Sox staff from the young burnouts of 1912 to the next generation of Boston hurlers who soon would carry their teammates to their greatest glories in the twentieth century.

Philadelphia still held a commanding double-digit game lead over the Red Sox in early September, but it appeared that the gap might narrow, particularly since, with the possible exception of the Braves, the Sox were the hottest team in the major leagues. Unfortunately, as Boston began to gain on the A's, Dutch Leonard broke a bone in his right wrist "as a result of a little 'fooling' with Joe Wood on the Boston bench."

With his right arm in splints, Leonard watched as a spectator the Braves regain first place in the National League as Bill James defeated the New York Giants on September 8. Meanwhile, his own team narrowed the A's lead in the American League race to single digits, not an insurmountable deficit, but a task made that much more difficult with the absence of its ace lefty.

Another development that greatly aided the future prospects of the club came more subtly, as Connie Mack planned to implode his team for the first time, the second occasion coming years later when he virtually gave away talented ballplayers like Lefty Grove, Jimmy Foxx and Doc Cramer to a young Tom Yawkey during another incarnation of the Red Sox. In late 1914, the Boston Red Sox had become the greatest team in baseball, a fact borne out over the ensuing campaigns.

A savvy man in many ways, Mack chose to stake his claim in Philly, where the Phillies always had the heart of most fans, instead of sticking close to his boyhood home and competing directly against the Boston Beaneaters, a club primed to lose Bostonians of all walks of life to the Sox. That the Athletics remained in Philadelphia for more than a half-century is a tribute to the will of Connie Mack, but even in the decades preceding free agency, he found it tough to thrive financially even with powerhouses. In 1914, he had just enough fuel to edge Boston out of a pennant.

The sands of competitiveness in the American League were poised to shift, with Boston overtaking the A's and New York waiting to assume the mantel of the winningest franchise in baseball history. But first, the Yankees had to get past the Red Sox and Bill Carrigan.

Rough had seen it all, from the final breakdown of Chick Stahl through the craziness of John I. Taylor and the eventful 1912 World Series. He had always stood steadfast, ready to throw a punch or calm down a pitcher, and he had always bided his time and watched. All this despite being the greatest Red Sox of them all, the keystone of an often troubled franchise, but one fully capable of regenerating and rewarding its devoted fans to world championships.

The great Chick Stahl had died and Cy and Criger and Collins and Lord and even fellow stalwart Heinie Wagner had left. Buck O'Brien and Smoky Joe Wood and Big Bill Dinneen had faded and still the Sox had a chance, because each spring when the thaw began up north in Maine, the redoubtable Bill Carrigan came down for another year and guided the Sox to as many wins as he might will for his team.

President Lannin saw this too, concluding 1914 not with recriminations, but by awarding the work of Bill Carrigan by signing him for two additional years as the Red Sox skipper. Waxed Lannin, "I know that the Boston public will be well satisfied that we will have the goods to offer at Fenway Park." They had the owner, the manager and the personnel (they have always had the fans) to compete on an elevated plane, and over the next four years they won three world championships, the most sustained level of excellence in Red Sox history before a man named Terry Francona took over the legacy of the great Rough Carrigan.

Epilogue

Tiny Hugh Duffy, in his third year as the manager of the Red Sox, surveyed his 1922 team as it worked out in Hot Springs for spring training. So much had changed since he helped found and form the original Boston Americans of 1901. Tommy McCarthy, his best friend and fellow Heavenly Twin, died the year before, and most of the ballplayers he had either been teammates with or adversary to had also passed on or retired from baseball.

But there stood the diminutive Duffy, still having fun instructing young men how to play ball even though the team had another disastrous owner, Harry Frazee, sort of a John I. Taylor type without the money. Like a loyal deckhand, Duffy had to helplessly watch as Frazee dumped one star Sox player after another, usually to the rival New York Yankees, for nothing approaching fair value in return. Duffy also had to pretend as he spoke to the press that he liked each deal and thought that maybe Boston had gotten the better of it.

It was like looking into the vast reaches of the desert. It must have seemed so long since Duffy had accumulated true talent, like Jimmy Collins and Chick Stahl and Freddy Parent, for a club he would not manage for nearly two decades. He remained optimistic, with little factual evidence for that emotion on his roster. By the beginning of the next season, Frazee would fire him and hire Frank Chance as his next sacrificial lamb while the talent continued to flow directly from Boston to New York on a one way train.

Duffy floated around the team in 1923, no one quite sure what his duties entailed, and then he returned full-time the next year as a scout, instructor and occasional coach for the Red Sox for the next three decades of his life. He died in the Brighton section of Boston at age eighty-seven, with Ted Williams a frequent visitor during Duffy's last sickness.

He loved Ted like a grandson, spending hours talking hitting with him. What those conversations must have been like, with Duffy owning with the highest season batting average of all-time (.440) and fielding the questions of his eager student, the last person to ever hit .400 in a season. But Sir Hugh's final days and final decades were not wasted, because after years of moveable owners, Tom Yawkey took over ownership in 1933, and he loved to spend.

Suddenly, the exodus of talent out of New England ceased as Yawkey aggressively went after stars from the poorer clubs like Connie Mack's Philadel-

No one loved the Boston Red Sox more than Hugh Duffy (pictured to the right of B.F. Shibe) and few did more to honor it as a sacred trust for the fans of New England and the world. If Red Sox Nation had a founder, his name was Duffy. Library of Congress.

phia Athletics, from whom he obtained Lefty Grove, Jimmy Foxx and Doc Cramer. If he needed a shortstop, Yawkey went to Washington and got Joe Cronin, one of the game's last player-managers. It was worthwhile to dream again, and if the team needed a bit of luck, well then Jimmy Foxx rubbed little Hugh Duffy's head and the team started winning again.

Duffy missed out on one dream. In April 1945, he tried out Jackie Robinson and two other African American athletes and urged Yawkey to sign Robinson. Yawkey yielded to Jim Crow, and the Sox seemed to miss out on dominance because they were always a player or two short. Hugh Duffy wanted Jackie Robinson on his team for the same reason he lined up Jimmy Collins and Chick Stahl and Freddy Parent and Hobe Ferris, and that is because he wanted to see his Boston Americans win. Thanks in large part to Hugh Duffy, the Red Sox won enough to become the preeminent team in the world of sport.

Chapter Sources

Chapter 1

The Boston Globe, 1892: July 12; 1893: August 14; 1904: May 8; 1908: April 29; 1913: January 13.

Frederick G. Lieb, *The Boston Red Sox* (New York: G.P. Putnam Son's, reprint, Carbondale: Southern Illinois University Press, 2003), 10.

Peter J. Nash, *Boston's Royal Rooters* (Charleston, SC: Arcadia, 2005).

George Santayana, *The Last Puritan* (New York: Charles Scribner's Sons, 1937), 21.

Chapter 2

http://www.baseballhalloffame.org/news/ article. Collins' acuity with the bunt.

Boston Globe, 1901: March 2, 5, 6, 10. 29, April 2, May 8–9, June 11, 16, 20–21, July 16, September 6, 8–10, 14, 18–19; 1921: March 21.

Boston Herald, 1901: May 9; 1921: March 25.

Boston Post, 1905: April 22.

Lieb, *The Boston Red Sox*, 17.

Richard Lindberg, *Who's on 3rd? The Chicago White Sox Story* (South Bend, IN: Icarus Press, 1983), 25.

John J. McGraw, *My Thirty Years in Baseball* (Lincoln: University of Nebraska Press, 1995), 218.

National Baseball Hall of Fame, Jimmy Collins file, Chick Stahl file, and Cy Young file, reviewed March 7, 2008.

Sporting Life, 1901: January 26, February 9, April 6, 13, May 18, July 13.

Chapter 3

Boston Globe, 1902: April 26–27, 29, May 2, 7, 11, 30, June 23, 25, July 2–3, 5, 17, 19–29, September 16, October 5.

Boston Post, 1902: September 16.

Lieb, *The Boston Red Sox*, 29.

Sporting Life, 1902: April-12 (for a fuller view of the Boston American uniforms that year, see http://exhibits.baseballhalloffame. org/dressedtothenines, with graphics courtesy of Mark Okkonen), May 10, June 7, 14, September 20, October 4, 11.

Sporting News, 1902: January 11, February 15, March 1, April 19, October 4.

Glenn Stout and Richard A. Johnson, *Red Sox Century* (Boston/New York, Houghton Mifflin, 2000, 2004), 22.

Chapter 4

Boston Globe, 1903: March 15, 23, April 21, 28, May 8, 10, June 7, 15, 21, 28–29, August 6–9, 11–12.

Boston Herald, 1903: September 29; 1905, April 22.

Boston Post, 1903: August 6–9, 11–12.

National Baseball Hall of Fame, Jake Stahl file, reviewed March 7, 2008. The description of Stahl during his fraternity days came from university archivist Maynard Brichford on December 2, 1986; Lou Criger file, Bill Dinneen file, Tom Hughes file, reviewed June 20, 2008.

Sporting Life, 1903: March 21, 28, April-11, 18, May 9, 16; 1908: July 18; 1911: September 2.

Chapter 5

Boston Globe, 1885: June 11; 1903: October 1–2, 12.

Boston Herald, 1903: October 1–2, 9, 12.

Boston Morning Journal, 1903: October 2–4, 7–8, 11, 14.

Boston Post, 1903: October 2–4, 8–9.

Frederick G. Lieb, *The Pittsburgh Pirates* (New York: G.P. Putnam's Sons, 1948). National Baseball Hall of Fame, Fred Parent file, reviewed March 7, 2008; Lou Criger file, reviewed June 20, 2008.
Pittsburgh Post, 1903.
Pittsburgh Press, 1903.
Pittsburgh Times, 1903: October 1–2, 9–10, 12, 14.
Sporting Life, 1903: October 17
Stout and Johnson, *Red Sox Century*, 39–41.

Chapter 6

Boston Globe, 1903: December 19, 28; 1904: March 27, April 19, June 14, 18, 20, 26, July 1, 10, August 18, October 8–9, 10–11.
Boston Herald, 1904: May 6, 12, June 19–20, October 8–9, 11.
Boston Daily Record, 1943: January 12.
Boston Journal, 1904: June 20.
Boston Post, 1904: April 19, May 6, 12, October 8–11.
Lieb, *The Boston Red Sox*, 56.
http://mlb.mlb.com/mlb/history/rare_feats/index.jsp?feature=perfect_game.
National Baseball Hall of Fame, Bill Carrigan file and Lou Criger file, reviewed June 20, 2008.
New York Times, 1904: October 8, 11; 1931: November 7.
Sporting Life, 1904: July 2, 9.
Stout and Johnson, *Red Sox Century*, 57.

Chapter 7

Boston Globe, 1904: December 11, 13, 31; 1905: January 29, March 4, 21, April 15, 22, May 29, 31, August 1, 23, 26–28, October 10–11, 15, December 29, 31; 1906: January 4, 10.
Boston Post, 1905: April 22.
Sporting Life, 1905: May 27, June 3, September 2, 23; 1906: September 8.

Chapter 8

Boston Globe, 1906: May 18–20, 26–27, June 8–9, July 7, August 17–18, 29–30, September 2, 12–13.
Boston Herald, 1906: May 2–3, 21–23, June 24, September 12.
Boston Post, 1906: April 12, May 1–3, 5–8, 17–18.

National Baseball Hall of Fame, Fred Parent file, reviewed March 7, 2008. The Ferris incident was related to Bill Fleishman in a Sanford, Maine, paper.
Sporting Life, 1906: April 7, 14, 28, May 19, 26, June 2, 30, July 7, 14, 28, August 4, September 8.

Chapter 9

Boston Globe, 1906: July 4, November 11, 14, 15, December 5; 1907: March 26, 27, 28, 29; 1908: November 18–19. The Tim Murnane quote is from an article he wrote for the *Globe* in 1898.
http://www.britannica.com/eb/article-9056716/Ockhams-razor.
Chris Christensen, "Chick Stahl: A Baseball Suicide." *Elysian Fields Quarterly*, 20.2 (2003): 20–32.
City of Boston Death Records Division.
www.thedeadballera.com: Chick Stahl's obituary.
Fort Wayne Journal-Gazette, 1907: March 29, 30.
Donald Hubbard, *The Heavenly Twins of Boston Baseball: A Dual Biography of Hugh Duffy and Tommy McCarthy* (Jefferson, NC: McFarland, 2008).
David Jones, ed., *Deadball Stars of the American League* (Dulles, VA: Potomac, 2006), 418–421.
Visit to Old Calvary cemetery, December 26, 2007.

Chapter 10

Boston Globe, 1907: March 30, April 2–3, 6, 12–13, 17, 25, 27, May 2, 18, June 8–10, 14, 20, July 29, September 10, August 5, October 11, 13, November 7, 17, December 23, 27; 1912: June 24.
Boston Herald, 1907: May 1–2, June 8.
Lieb, *The Boston Red Sox*, 77.
Sporting Life, 1907: April 13, 20, May 4, 11, June 15, 22, September 7.

Chapter 11

Boston Globe, 1907: December 19; 1908: January 2, 26, February 9, March 16, April 2, 8–9, 12–13, 15, 21, June 1, 19, 23, 25–27, July 1, 11, 26, August 18, 29, September 13.
Boston Herald, 1908: July 11, 26, August 25, 29.

Frank Douskey, "Smoky Joe Wood's Last Interview," *The National Pastime*, 27 (2007): 69, 72.

National Baseball Hall of Fame, Joe Wood file, reviewed June 20, 2008.

Sporting Life, 1908: March 21, May 9, June 13, July 18.

Stout and Johnson, *Red Sox Century*, 80.

Chapter 12

Boston Globe, 1908: October 8, 20, November 12, 17, December 10; 1909: February 17–19, 22, June 19, July 16, 26, 28, October 9–11, 13–15.

Boston Herald, 1909: February 18.

Boston Evening Record, 1909: February 17–18.

Boston Post, 1909: February 18, September 11.

Lieb, *The Boston Red Sox*, 81–82.

National Baseball Hall of Fame, Charley Hall file and Joe Wood file, reviewed June 20, 2008.

New York Times, 1909: October 10, 14.

Sporting Life, 1908: December 26; 1909: May 1, 22, July 3, 10, 17, 24.

Stout and Johnson, *Red Sox Century*, 70.

Paul J. Zingg, *Harry Hooper: An American Baseball Life* (Urbana/Chicago: University of Illinois Press, 1993), 59.

Chapter 13

Boston Post, 1910: August 6, 8, 10, 13.

Boston Evening Record, 1910: August 6, 12–13.

Boston Globe, 1910: May 11, July 24, 31, October 11; 1913: January 26.

Douskey, "Smoky Joe Wood's Last Interview," 72.

Lieb, *The Boston Red Sox*, 85, 87.

National Baseball Hall of Fame, Larry Gardner file, reviewed March 7, 2008; Duffy Lewis file and Harry Lord file, reviewed June 20, 2008.

Sporting Life, 1910: April 9, 23, May 7, July 16.

Chapter 14

Boston Globe, 1911: January 8, 15, February 9, 19–21, 23 28, May 10, 21, July 8, August 18, September 3, 10, 13, 17, October 8,

10, December 11; 1912: January 24, October 17.

Lieb, *The Boston Red Sox*, 89, 91–92.

Morning Oregonian, 1914: October 2, 3, 5, 8, November 5, 6, 7.

San Jose Morning Herald, 1914: October 2, November 7; 1918: December 14.

Sporting Life, 1911: March 18, May 20, July 8, September 2, 9.

Chapter 15

Boston Globe, 1912: January 24, April 10, 12–14, 21, June 26–27, July 10, 19–20, September 3, 6–7, 15–16, 21, 23, 26.

National Baseball Hall of Fame, Hugh Bedient file, Duffy Lewis file, Joe Wood file, reviewed June 20, 2008.

Dan Shaughnessy, *One Strike Away: The Story of the 1986 Red Sox* (New York: Beaufort, 1987), 25.

Sporting Life, 1912: March 23, 30, July 6, 13, 20.

Chapter 16

Boston Globe, 1912: October 11, 15–17.

Peter Golenbock, *Fenway: An Unexpurgated History of the Boston Red Sox* (New York: G.P. Putnam's Sons, 1992, reprinted North Attleboro, MA: Covered Bridge Press, 1999), 38 (reprint edition). The quote is from Fred Lieb.

New York Times, 1912: October 7, 9–12, 16–17.

Chapter 17

Boston Daily Record, 1943: January 18.

Boston Globe, 1913: February 25, March 6, 13, 16, 23, April 8, 10–11, 23, 28–29, May 8, July 15–18, August 28.

Boston Post, 1913: July 15–16, 18.

Lieb, *The Boston Red Sox*, 115–116.

National Baseball Hall of Fame, Bill Carrigan file and Hubert "Dutch" Leonard file, reviewed June 20, 2008.

New York Times, 1913: April 30.

Sporting Life, 1913: April 26, May 17, July 19, 26, September 6.

Chapter 18

Stout and Johnson, *Red Sox Century*, 57.

Chapter 19

The Boston Daily Record: 1943: January 18.

Boston Globe, 1913: December 1–3, 9; 1914: January 31, February 13–14, March 7, April 9, 12 , 15, May 25, 27, July 9–10, 17, 19, 29, 31, September 9, 15, October 2.

Boston Herald, 1914: May 4, 11, 13, 31.

Bill James, *The New Bill James Historical Baseball Abstract* (New York: Free Press, 2001) p. 647.

Lieb, *The Boston Red Sox,* 117–118.

National Baseball Hall of Fame, Bill Carrigan file and Dick Hoblitzel file, reviewed June 20, 2008.

Sporting Life, 1914: March 21, June 27, July 18, August 8, September 5, 19.

Bibliography

Books

Browning, Reed. *Cy Young: A Baseball Life* (Amherst: University of Massachusetts Press, 2000).

Golenbock, Peter. *Fenway: An Unexpurgated History of the Boston Red Sox* (New York: G.P. Putnam's Sons, 1992; reprint, North Attleboro, MA: Covered Bridge Press, 1999).

Hubbard, Donald. *The Heavenly Twins of Boston Baseball: A Dual Biography of Hugh Duffy and Tommy McCarthy* (Jefferson, NC: McFarland, 2008).

James, Bill. *The New Bill James Historical Baseball Abstract* (New York: Free Press, 2001).

_____. *The Politics of Glory: How Baseball's Hall of Fame Really Works* (New York: Macmillan, 1994).

Jones, David, ed. *Deadball Stars of the American League* (Dulles, VA: Potomac, 2006), 418–421.

Lieb, Frederick G. *The Boston Red Sox* (New York: G.P. Putnam's Sons, 1947; reprint, Carbondale: Southern Illinois University Press, 2003).

Lindberg, Richard. *Who's on 3rd? The Chicago White Sox Story* (South Bend, IN: Icarus Press, 1983).

McGraw, John J. *My Thirty Years in Baseball* (Lincoln: University of Nebraska Press, 1995), 218.

Nash, Peter J. *Boston's Royal Rooters* (Charleston, SC: Arcadia Publishing, 2005).

Ritter, Lawrence S. *The Glory of Their Times* (New York: Macmillan, 1966; reprint, New York: Random House, 1985).

Ryan, Bob. *When Boston Won the World Series* (Philadelphia: Running Press Publishers, 2002).

Santayana, George. *The Last Puritan* (New York: Charles Scribner's Sons, 1937).

Shaughnessy, Dan. *One Strike Away: The Story of the 1986 Red Sox* (New York: Beaufort, 1987).

Stout, Glenn, and Richard A. Johnson. *Red Sox Century* (Boston/New York: Houghton Mifflin, 2000).

Zingg, Paul J. *Harry Hooper: An American Baseball Life* (Urbana/Chicago: University of Illinois Press, 1993).

Articles

Christensen, Chris. "Chick Stahl: A Baseball Suicide." *Elysian Fields Quarterly*, 20.2 (2003): 20–32.

Douskey, Franz. "Smoky Joe Wood's Last Interview." *The National Pastime*, 27, (2007): 69.

Periodicals

Boston Daily Record
Boston Globe
Boston Herald
Boston Morning Journal
Boston Post
Boston Record
Fort Wayne Journal-Gazette
Morning Oregonian
New York Times
Philadelphia Inquirer
Pittsburgh Post
Pittsburgh Press
Pittsburgh Times

San Jose Morning Herald
Sporting Life
Sporting News

Internet Articles

http://www.britannica.com/eb/article-9056716/Ockhams-razor.

http://mlb.mlb.com/mlb/history/rare_fe
ats/index.jsp?feature=perfect_game.
http://www.baseballhalloffame.org/news/
article.jsp?ymd=20070215&content_id
=300&vkey=hof_news.
http://thedeadballera.com: Chick Stahl's
obituary.

Index